EMPIRE
BOOKS

Brendan Murphy

THE BUTCHER
OF LYON

The Story of Infamous Nazi
KLAUS BARBIE

EMPIRE BOOKS
NEW YORK

For my parents
and for Barbara Van Nice,
whose love for words was
exceeded only by her concern for the truth

Acknowledgments

Researching the story of Klaus Barbie was made possible through the cooperation of numerous people in Europe, South America and the United States. Listing all those who provided help and advice is not possible, but the author would especially like to thank the following individuals.

In Europe: Raymond Aubrac, Dr. David Barnouw, Anne Marie Bauer, Mario Blardone, Jean-Jacques Bloch, Robert Bloch, Gérard Chauvy, René Aimé Chorier, Dr. Frédéric Dugoujon, Maurice Emain, Julien Favet, Jean-Claude Gallo, André Gamet, Michel Goldberg, Georgette Gomes, Alexander Halaunbrenner, Itta Halaunbrenner, Konrad Jacobs, Rabbi Jacob Kaplan, Dr. Sylvie Karlin, Beate Klarsfeld, Serge Klarsfeld, Simone Lagrange, Lise Lesèvre, Esther Majerowicz, Andre Manuel, René Nodot, Reinar Nolden, René Picod, Christian Pineau, Christian Riss, Lea Rosen, Marcel Ruby, Alain de la Servette, Gabrielle Tardy, Jacques Vergès, Philippe Viannay, Rabbi Richard Wertenschlag, Simon Wisenthal.

In South America: Sandra Aliaga, Ruth Bermudez, Fernando Bueno, Ted Cordova-Claure, Marcos Domic, Freddy Espinoza, Merry Flores, Eudoro Galindo, Jacques Leclerc, Peter McFarren, Simon Reyes, Gustavo Sanchez, Geri Smith, Andres Soliz, Carlos Soria, Gustavo Stier, Ximena Vargas, Gaston Velasco, Tracy Wilkinson, Alberto Zuazo and all those, who for reasons inherent in Bolivian politics, could not be named.

In the United States: Gene Bramel, Earl Browning, Erhard Dabringhaus, Dominique d'Ermo, Eugene Kolb, William Larned, John Loftus, William Ratliffe, Allan A. Ryan, Jr.

I would like to acknowledge the invaluable assistance of my

colleagues Ben Barber and Rich Piellisch, who carried out research and interviews in the U.S. for this book.

I would also like to express my gratitude to the following institutions and agencies for their assistance, particularly the Centre de Documentation Juive Contemporaine (Center for Contemporary Jewish Documentation) in Paris, whose library staff was always most helpful, as well as the Archives de France, Paris; Berlin Document Center, Berlin; the Bundesarchiv, Koblenz, West Germany; the Bolivian Ministry of Information, La Paz; the Institut d'Histoire du Temps Present, Paris; the Netherlands State Institute for War Documentation, Amsterdam; the Staatliches Friedrich-Willhelm-Gymnasium, Trier; the U.S. Department of the Army, Office of the Chief of Military History; the U.S. Department of Justice, Office of Special Investigations.

Special thanks also to Sara Valverde and the rest of her household in La Paz for their great kindness and hospitality, without which I would have found it far more difficult to work in an environment that was entirely new to me.

In addition, I would also like to thank Katherine Berger and others on the staff of the Centre de Formation des Journalistes in Paris for their assistance and encouragement. Similarly, my friends at the Paris bureau of the Associated Press were most helpful with their suggestions and support.

I wish to thank the staff of Empire Books in New York, including Belle Ballantyne, Laurence Zuckerman, Nancy Hahnfeldt, and particularly my editor and publisher, Martin L. Gross, for his advice and encouragement.

Brendan Murphy
Paris, France

September 1983

Contents

PREFACE

"THE BANALITY OF EVIL" WAS HOW PHILOSOPHER HANNAH Arendt described the grotesque ease with which Adolf Eichmann planned and carried out the systematic murder of six million humans.

"He merely, to put the matter colloquially, never realized what he was doing," Arendt concluded. "That such remoteness from reality and such thoughtlessness can wreak more havoc than all the evil instincts taken together which, perhaps, are inherent in man—that was, in fact, the lesson one could learn in Jerusalem."

The trial of another prominent Nazi war criminal is now approaching, but no such lesson of *banality* can be drawn from the life of Klaus Barbie, the so-called "Butcher of Lyon."

If Eichmann was the detached bureaucrat expediting millions to gas chambers and crematoria in Eastern Europe, Barbie was the very opposite. He was closer in nature to the reality of the Nazi ethos: a brutal man of evil intent.

Barbie was a middle-level Gestapo commander in a particularly sensitive post, charged not only with destroying the French Resistance but with overseeing the war on the Jews in his region. He participated personally in the death and deportation of thousands of Jews and Resistance fighters. Nothing was banal about the gruesome work in which he was obsessively engaged. He was one of those who pulled the trigger and spilled blood.

Lessons other than "the banality of evil" must be drawn from the wartime career and postwar survival of Hauptsturmführer Barbie. He was not only able to commit the crimes for which he was twice condemned to death by French military tribunals, but he was able to avoid punishment for almost forty years afterwards. His survival required the complicity of virtually everyone with whom he came into contact.

The career of Klaus Barbie suggests an operating principle which we might call "the utility of evil." It was to enable him to rise within the Third Reich, make him devastatingly effective against the Resistance in Lyon, and consistently protect him from justice in the years after. Barbie, in a vacuum, would have been nothing. With the complicity of others—first the French collaborators, then the American CIC, then the Bolivian military dictators—he became the prototype of unchastened criminality. Barbie learned that by making himself useful to those in power he could ensure his survival.

Barbie was a highly successful Gestapo agent because in wartime France he managed to obtain the complicity of Frenchmen, either through ideological sympathy with the Nazi cause or by offering money, power and other blandishments. Within the larger war, a civil conflict was raging in France and Barbie turned it to his own advantage.

The Reich collapsed, but Barbie continued. No longer a master, he became a hired intelligence hand, offering the skills he had learned in the SS and developed in Lyon. Barbie knew that there would always be a secure position for a man such as himself, even under a government that stated its priorities in moral terms. Europe was threatened by communism, and in the silent struggle of postwar intelligence, only expediency seemed to matter. Barbie's past membership in the Gestapo was overlooked by his new employers, the American Counter Intelligence Corps, who used Barbie—as they were used by him.

In Bolivia, where right-wing militarism had roots, Barbie once again turned his talents to the use of others. Barbie cultivated the worst instincts of the dictatorships that succeeded one another during his thirty-two years in the Andean country. It was only the political accident of a major shift in Bolivian government that finally delivered Barbie to French justice.

Had he been judged at the war's end and executed, as were many of his French collaborators, Barbie would have been a mere footnote in the histories of the French Resistance and the Holocaust. But surviving through four decades, this ex-Gestapo captain has acquired an extraordinary dimension. He has become a living symbol of Nazism.

Edmund Burke has often been quoted on his admonition to society that if good men do nothing evil will triumph. Barbie's life not only confirms this, but leads to the sobering conclusion that there are many who are willing, even anxious, to be the employers and accomplices of those who understand the utility of evil.

THE RETURN

To THE FLIGHT ATTENDANTS ABOARD THE LLOYD AERO BO-liviano shuttle between La Paz and the provincial capital of Cocha-bamba, it was clear that the old man with white hair and a Tyrolean hat was someone of importance. A frequent traveler on that route, he was invariably the first passenger cleared for board-ing the worn Boeing 727s of the Bolivian national airline.

He always took the same seat on the right-hand window of the front row and rarely spoke to the flight crew. But Bolivians are quick to distinguish the nuances that bespeak authority. Some of the Cochabambinos who glanced at the elderly gentleman might have recognized him as the same person who was unfailingly saluted by military guards at the entry to the Bolivian Army's Seventh Division headquarters in downtown Cochabamba, the same white-haired man who often took coffee with the police *jefe* in the Café Restaurant Continental on the Plaza Principal.

In the political capital of La Paz, he was an even more familiar figure, strolling mornings on the Prado, the city's main boulevard, past the scores of shoeshine boys, newspaper vendors and bowler-hatted, copper-cheeked *campesino* women in bright shawls hawking cigarettes from wooden stands in the shadow of the great steel-and-glass commercial banking houses. Short and thickening around the middle, the old man was regularly accompanied on his rounds by a much younger and taller associate, a contrasting figure with black hair slicked back from Latin features obscured by dark glasses, dressed in tailored suits that failed to disguise the deformed hump between his shoulderblades.

Klaus Altmann Hansen, the older man, and his bodyguard, Alvaro de Castro, usually completed their walk at the top of the Avenida Mariscal Santa Cruz, the beginning segment of the Prado. That street and the Avenida General Camacho converge at a public square dominated by a statue commemorating Bolivia's failed War of the Pacific in which the country had lost its Pacific coastline to Chile. Where the two streets meet stands the Club de La Paz.

The two men would enter the cafe on the ground floor, sometimes after Altmann stopped at a stand to have his shoes shined by Lucio. Inside the cafe, they would take their accustomed places at a table against the wall farthest from the door, at which Altmann drank black coffee or tea, read the newspapers and chatted with his acquaintances. The Confiteria Club de La Paz was, in a way, his office. Altmann was in the business of knowing people, and this was a place where his contacts could be freshened and maintained.

The official seat of political power in La Paz was the Plaza Murillo, several blocks up the hill from the Avenida General Camacho, on which were located the presidential Palacio Quemado and the Palacio Legislativo. But the Confiteria Club was an unofficial center of power. Around its aged hardwood tables gathered the city's brokers of influence: the politicians who intrigued; the businessmen who made deals; the journalists who listened.

A cynic had once labeled it *el valle de los caidos*, "the valley of the fallen," since the cafe also served as a retreat for those who had been temporarily displaced in Bolivia's perpetual political shuffle and were impatiently awaiting their return up the hill to the Plaza Murillo. "This is where it all happens in La Paz," says a Bolivian journalist in the Confiteria Club, identifying two men just entering as the country's foremost labor leader and an influential member of the Bolivian Senate.

Altmann knew and was known by those who regularly frequented the cafe, but he usually held himself somewhat in reserve,
limiting his contact to a polite nod or a few pleasantries. This was
true even with members of the La Paz German colony, from which
he seemed estranged. "Altmann never frequented the spots where
the German community assembled," recalls one German who has
spent nine years in the Andean country. "In fact, he avoided
involvement with most of the Germans."

There were also the inevitable journalists—American, German,
French—who headed directly for Altmann's table. He sometimes
agreed to speak with them, but most often he politely declined. To
the foreign journalists he was not Altmann, but Barbie, Klaus
Barbie, ex-Nazi and SS Hauptsturmführer, a war criminal twice
sentenced to death by French military tribunals for having ordered
or participated in over 4,000 murders and nearly 8,000 deportations of Resistance members and Jews while Gestapo chief in the
city of Lyon during World War II. The journalists had another
name for him, one that inevitably found its way into international
headlines: The Butcher of Lyon.

Altmann, or Barbie, or Altmann-Barbie, as the Bolivian newspapers referred to him, had been telling journalists the same thing
for the past ten years. *"La guerra es la guerra,"* he insisted. *War is
war.* He conceded that he had been stationed in Lyon during the
war, but he insisted that he was a soldier then, battling the French
Resistance for his Führer. Yes, he had captured Jean Moulin, the
leader of the French Resistance, but he denied beating Moulin to
death in 1943. In any case, Moulin had been his enemy in war.

His response to charges that he had murdered and deported
thousands of Jews was similarly unvarying. *"Nada tuve que ver con
los judios."* *I had nothing to do with the Jews.* Altmann-Barbie was
utterly unrepentant about his Nazi past. "What is there to regret?"
he once said. "In a war, everyone kills. In a war, there is neither
good nor evil. I am a convinced Nazi. I admire the Nazi discipline. I
am proud to have been a commanding officer of the best military
outfit in the Third Reich, and if I had to be born a thousand times
again, I would be a thousand times what I have been. For the sake
of Germany and Bolivia."

Many Bolivians, including the military governments that held power in Bolivia for most of the thirty years Altmann spent there, readily endorsed this point of view. A decade before, in 1972, Beate Klarsfeld, a German woman married to a French Jewish lawyer, had torn away the Altmann identity under which Barbie had received Bolivian citizenship in 1957. The French government subsequently demanded his extradition and the two years that followed were a test of the strength of Altmann-Barbie's political contacts in Bolivia.

For several years prior to that Barbie-Altmann had been the general manager of landlocked Bolivia's maritime shipping line, Transmaritima Boliviana, a position that allowed him to cement his relations with the Bolivian generals and the presidents. "He used his connections throughout the world to supply arms to just about everybody here," says a French diplomat stationed in La Paz. A Bolivian official who was involved in audits of Barbie's Transmaritima firm concurs. "Altmann had tremendous power," he says. "Anytime you called his attention to something, he'd show up with a couple of generals or admirals, or he could call on them to call you."

President Hugo Banzer Suarez, a friend and protector of Klaus Barbie, was in power in La Paz in 1972 when Nazi-hunter Klarsfeld initiated her campaign for the extradition of Barbie. She came to La Paz twice that year, but her efforts did little more than inconvenience Altmann-Barbie, who merely hired more bodyguards. At one stage of the legal battle, Barbie even arranged for his own incarceration in the prison on the Plaza San Pedro in La Paz, hoping to thwart any assassination attempt or to avoid the fate of Nazi Adolf Eichmann, who was kidnapped from Argentina by Israeli commandos in 1960 and executed in Jerusalem.

The French extradition request was disposed of late in 1973 by the Bolivian Supreme Court, which ruled that Klaus Altmann Hansen, whom they acknowledged was the same person as Klaus Barbie, was a Bolivian citizen and could not be extradited. No treaty providing for this contingency had been signed by France and Bolivia, they pointed out. Moreover, the court ruled, the crimes of which he was accused had taken place too many years in the past to be prosecuted.

There was now little in Altmann's appearance to suggest the former Gestapo officer who virtually controlled Lyon, the third largest city of France, during World War II. His advanced stage of balding gave prominence to his heavy eyebrows and blue-gray eyes surrounded by wrinkles. What remained of his silver hair was combed back behind his ears and fell over his collar. He might easily have passed for an elderly German in semi-retirement, a pleasant, reserved character with many casual acquaintances but few close friends. Altmann dressed more informally than most of the clients of the Club de La Paz, where a neatly pressed suit and a tie were marks of the Bolivian business and ruling class. The old German's tastes inclined toward turtleneck sweaters under sports jackets, topped with a Tyrolean-style hat. His business suits were plain, worn over a white shirt and dark tie, and like most men of his class in La Paz, Altmann had his shoes shined at least once a day. At a few pesos this was an inexpensive luxury on the dusty streets of the Bolivian capital.

Altmann was deeply attached to his family and was greatly affected when his only son, Klaus Georg Altmann, was killed at the age of 34 in May 1981 while practicing for a hang-gliding competition at a park not far from the Altmanns' residence in Cochabamba. His daughter, Ute Altmann Messner, was married and living in Austria. The old man devoted considerable attention to the two small children left by his son, who lived with their French mother in Santa Cruz, some 400 miles from La Paz. He was an ideal husband: Friends described the relationship between Altmann and his wife, Regina, as very close, even though she had suffered periods of mental illness. In 1980, when she developed intestinal cancer and required treatment at the German Clinic in La Paz, the Altmanns transferred their main residence from Cochabamba, where they had lived since 1974, to the capital.

Altmann's house in Cochabamba, built in the mid-1970s, was protectively surrounded by a high fence and a black steel gate and had an estimated worth of $100,000. Its modern exterior lines suggested affluence, but it was situated on a small lot and furnished with simple Bavarian-style wood pieces. The Altmann home was not outstanding by comparison with the great haciendas in the center of Cochabamba, where the upper classes lived behind high stucco walls amid manicured lawns, palm trees and jacarandas. The Altmanns lived comfortably, but without ostentation.

Apart from his family and the ever-present Alvaro de Castro, Altmann did not have many close relations, and did not move in any clearly defined Bolivian social circle. His friends were mainly members of the prominent German colony in La Paz, people like Gerardo Kyllman, founder of the highly successful Hansa import-export house whose modern office building looms over the Avenida Mariscal Santa Cruz. Another was Fritz Hermann, a conservative businessman whose fortune built the Edificio Hermann, a large office building also on the Prado. Some Bolivians felt there was prestige in associating with Altmann; they discounted the stories of his past and current activities. "That's all been exaggerated," says a prominent La Paz attorney, producing a snapshot of himself and a smiling Altmann on an outing to nearby Lake Titicaca.

But there were inconsistencies in this picture of a benign, grandfatherly figure in semiretirement. Practiced in handling firearms, Barbie-Altmann regularly shot with a .22 pistol or a rifle at the Polygon firing range in La Paz, and went skeet shooting at the La Paz Fish and Game Club. He was not known to carry a gun, but most people assumed that his constant companion of ten years, Alvaro de Castro, was armed. Intensely loyal to Barbie, de Castro, with his hard features, discouraged any hostile advances on his employer, and was sometimes joined by other bodyguards on watches outside Altmann's La Paz apartment.

Barbie could also call on the services of two distinguished La Paz lawyers, the senior of whom was Constantino Carrion, a figure of long-standing influence in Bolivian political and judicial circles. For years an advisor to the Bolivian Foreign Ministry, Carrion was a former superior court judge, senator and cabinet minister. All this amounted to an excess of personal protection for a supposedly harmless old German businessman enjoying a quiet Bolivian retirement. But for an aging war criminal living in fear of retribution or kidnapping, it was a bare minimum. Altmann had a past, one that had never stopped following him.

Altmann downplayed his role in Bolivian military and political affairs, but he occasionally betrayed a certain pride in his access to power. "When the government needs help or an opinion, they call me," he told a German reporter. "I have a very good reputation."

In reality, Barbie was much more deeply entrenched in Bolivian politics than he admitted. Since the late 1960s, Altmann had played the role of *asesor*, or advisor, in arms and intelligence matters to a series of Bolivian rulers, beginning with General René Barrientos Ortuño. This role continued through the regimes of General Alfredo Ovando Candia, General Hugo Banzer Suarez and General Luis Garcia Meza. The generals came and went, but Altmann-Barbie remained, adept at survival in the bloody arena of Bolivian politics.

Aware that high visibility means high vulnerability, Altmann rarely permitted his role to be publicly confirmed. But his influence with the Bolivian military was dramatically displayed one day in August 1981, when two *New York Times* correspondents attempted to interview Barbie at his Cochabamba home. Peter McFarren, a free-lance writer and photographer working with *Times* staffer Marisabel Schumacher, had obtained the address of the Altmann house, and together they stood outside the heavy metal gate barring the driveway, persistently ringing the doorbell. Although Altmann's Volkswagen was parked just inside the gate and McFarren pressed the buzzer dozens of times, there was no answer.

Suddenly there came a response, but from an unexpected quarter. A jeep and a van carrying Bolivian soldiers and paramilitaries armed with machine guns drew up behind the two journalists. An officer got out and placed them under arrest. McFarren and Schumacher were locked in the back of the unmarked, windowless Ford van and brought to the army's Seventh Division headquarters in the center of town. The reporter later learned that the Seventh Division, the largest military garrison in the country, was commanded at the time by a Colonel Guido Vildoso, reportedly a close friend of Altmann's. The soldiers had obviously come at the request of the German.

The two journalists were interrogated for hours and threatened with torture if they would not reveal how they had obtained Altmann's address. McFarren recalls the trying incident. "One guy threatened to kill us," says McFarren. "He said, '*Te vamos a matar.*' Then they separated us and took me to a small, dark room. One whole wall was covered with intelligence material, lists of student groups and political parties."

McFarren, a dual national born in Bolivia to American missionary parents and fluent in Spanish, gave his interrogators some useless information but withheld the names of his sources. He also suggested to the major in charge that he and Schumacher were expected back in La Paz that evening; there could be serious consequences if two *New York Times* correspondents were mistreated. The officer finally released them, while inadvertently corroborating their suspicions. "The next time, you should be more careful," he told McFarren. "If you want an interview with Klaus Barbie, call us here and we'll arrange it."

Barbie's relations with the Bolivian military were based on his role as an intelligence expert in a nation perpetually torn between rival left and right factions. He was well qualified for the role. Not only had he been a Gestapo counterinsurgency specialist during World War II, but he had also worked for the U.S. government in occupied Germany after the war as an American counterintelligence informant assigned to penetrate communist groups in Bavaria. It was natural that Altmann, the ex-Nazi, would be consulted by the fascist elements within the Bolivian armed forces.

But Bolivia's left-wing and liberal opposition saw Barbie as a corrupting influence, someone who nurtured the worst tendencies of the nation's authoritarian forces. "It's a classic case," Gustavo Sanchez, subminister of the interior in the leftist government that assumed power in Bolivia in 1982, commented when interviewed in his office on Avenida Arce. "A man sentenced to death by tribunals as a murderer in the Second World War serves the U.S. as an agent. Then the same person comes here to educate generations of military to create criminals in this country, to bring death to Bolivia."

In 1980, Altmann-Barbie was at the summit of his influence as General Luis Garcia Meza assumed the presidency through the 188th military coup Bolivia had experienced since it achieved independence from Spain in the early 19th century. Altmann's main sponsor in the Garcia Meza government was Colonel Luis Arce Gomez, who had been director of Bolivian Army intelligence prior to the coup, and who became minister of the interior in the new government, retaining command of the country's security forces. Arce made the relationship between the government and the German *asesor* clear when he later graciously introduced Altmann to reporters at a ceremony at army headquarters in La Paz as "my great friend, Don Klaus."

During the Garcia Meza regime, Altmann-Barbie was a regular visitor to the Seventh Division headquarters in Cochabamba, traveling frequently between that town, La Paz, and Santa Cruz, the country's third largest city. Don Klaus's job was the coordination of paramilitary groups in Bolivia's eastern region with the central security forces at army headquarters and the Ministry of the Interior in La Paz. "He had direct control, as an advisor," says a former Interior ministry official in the regime of Hugo Banzer Suarez. "He was on top of everything political in Cochabamba, Santa Cruz and La Paz. In fact, in all of Bolivia."

"Once Barbie was tied in with Arce Gomez, who then started to organize the paramilitary groups, the brain of this organization was no longer Arce Gomez but Barbie," says Interior subminister Gustavo Sanchez, a brooding, impenetrable man. "This is why Barbie held such an important role in the Garcia coup."

According to Sanchez, Barbie was given an office in the Ministry of the Interior and carried identification as an honorary lieutenant colonel in the Bolivian Army, with a photograph showing him in uniform. But he was still careful to avoid publicity of his Bolivian political role. "Barbie always stayed in the shadows," says Sanchez. "The people who stay in the shadows are more important than those who are up front."

Ω

Finally, on October 10, 1982, the last vestiges of Bolivian military power were swept aside when socialist Hernan Siles Zuazo assumed the presidency. The abuses of the Garcia Meza regime had so discredited military rule and ravaged the Bolivian economy that there were two subsequent changes of regime within a year. The new president, General Guido Vildoso, the last of Barbie's protectors, was forced to convene the Bolivian Congress, which called Siles out of Peruvian exile to take over the office he had won in a 1979 election, but which had been denied him by the military. One of Siles's first announcements was that he intended to expel Nazi Altmann-Barbie from the country. The Bolivian president made it clear that an extradition request from the West German government filed the previous May would find support within his administration.

Altmann was not seen in public for weeks after the Siles inauguration, giving rise to conjecture that he had fled the country. At the request of the West Germans, Brazil issued orders for his arrest should he turn up at a border crossing, but soon after, despite the obvious threat hanging over him, Barbie surfaced again in La Paz. Announced one La Paz newspaper in October: "Altmann Will Be the Next," a warning that he had been targeted for arrest.

The pressures on Altmann-Barbie were not only political. When the socialist-communist coalition of Siles's Union Democratico Popular took power that October it found the state's treasury empty and the country's external debt at the $4 billion level. The Siles administration instructed the federal auditing agency, the Contraloria, to press for collection of debts owed the government, and one of the first dossiers considered was Barbie's.

The case, a carry-over from his days as manager of Transmaritima Boliviana, had been in the Contraloria files since November 1981, when the state mining corporation COMIBOL had charged that Altmann still owed it $10,000. He had accepted the money in the early 1970s for the transport of minerals, but Transmaritima had never undertaken the shipment. The debt had been forgotten under the military regimes, but the Contraloria now decided that COMIBOL's claim was legitimate; at the end of 1982, Altmann-Barbie was ordered to pay the $10,000 debt.

By mid-January 1983, according to Jaime Urcullo, the *sub-contralor* who rendered judgment in the case, Altmann had failed to make payment on the debt. On January 25, 1983, Urcullo issued a *mandamiento de apremio*—an arrest warrant—that was posted publicly on the ground floor of the Contraloria building a few blocks away from the Plaza Murillo. La Paz has a population of 800,000, but in the transmission of interesting news it is a small town, and within a short time Altmann learned of the arrest order and went to the Contraloria to look into the matter.

Barbie was acting against the counsel of Constantino Carrion, his attorney since the 1972 extradition proceedings, who had advised Barbie to leave the country, suggesting that Paraguay, where the right-wing dictator General Alfredo Stroessner was in firm control, would be much safer territory for the ex-Nazi. At 86, Carrion was ailing, but a lifetime of experience in Bolivian politics told him the balance had shifted heavily against Altmann over the past few months. But Altmann ignored his warnings and remained not only in Bolivia, but circulated in plain sight on the streets of La Paz.

Altmann had come back to La Paz in late 1982 to hospitalize his wife in the German Clinic, where she died of cancer on December 10. Some 30 Bolivians and Germans stood in the German Cemetery of La Paz and watched as a grieved Altmann scattered a bouquet of flowers over the coffin. The old Nazi was inconsolable at the passing of his spouse of over 40 years; the loss came only a year after his son's death. "He seemed to have aged ten years overnight," says journalist McFarren, who met him on the street in La Paz a few weeks later.

During the last weeks of his wife's illness Altmann developed a friendship with Bolivian journalist Merry Flores, an impressionable woman who reported for the Catholic newspaper *Presencia*. Flores was chiefly motivated by journalistic curiosity, but she also found herself intrigued by Barbie's charismatic personality and strong beliefs. "He was a fascinating man because he had ideas that were firm, unequivocal," recalls Flores. "He thought Latin America could be the only opposition to communism. I didn't see him as a cynical man. He was very educated, very polite, very correct. Finally, he wasn't an arrogant man. He was kind, likeable. I think he was a victim of circumstances. He was trapped by his past, and every government used him."

The Altmann that Flores met was no longer the arrogant Nazi of World War II, or even the advisor to presidents securely anchored to the Bolivian military. He was a sick old man with a nerve disorder in one leg that gave him a slight limp. "I saw him suffer," says Flores. "The death of his wife affected his mind. He told me, 'Nothing matters anymore.' He seemed hopeless." Altmann seemed unaware of, or uninterested in, the threat emanating from the Siles government. "I don't think Siles Zuazo will throw me out," Altmann said to Flores. "He gave me my Bolivian citizenship. He is my friend."

This combination of resignation and overconfidence seemed to impair Barbie's judgment. On the afternoon of January 25, 1983, the same day his arrest warrant had been posted, Altmann climbed to the second floor of the Contraloria to the *seccion coactivo* and demanded to see his file. He became involved in an argument with a junior clerk over the exchange rate between pesos and dollars.

But things had already gone too far, Urcullo says. "Our *policia coactivo* knew Altmann and knew that an arrest warrant had been issued. So they put him under arrest and took him to the Panoptico jail on the Plaza San Pedro." Urcullo, a reserved bureaucrat with a studious manner, expressed his dismay at the international reaction that followed his administrative procedure. "It drew the attention of the world press," he says, "but it was a very routine matter."

Ω

Despite Urcullo's disclaimer that the arrest was "routine," within twenty-four hours Bolivian Interior Minister Mario Roncal had informed the French and the German governments that Altmann would be deported.

But where? And how? The most logical destination was West Germany. The extradition request filed the preceeding May by that government was before the Supreme Court in Sucre, Bolivia's constitutional capital to the south of La Paz, but it had raised a number of problems. The Germans expressed a willingness to send a Lufthansa jet to take Altmann out of the country, but hesitated to assume responsibility for him in the event that legal complications arose. Their jet would have to stop along the way for refueling, and the possibility that landing in another country would short-circuit extradition procedures troubled officials in Bonn. A member of the West German diplomatic corps in La Paz summed up the ambivalent German position: "You have made a decision to expel him. We prefer the legal extradition. But if you decide to expel him, it is your responsibility."

In Paris, the government of President François Mitterrand was not interested in waiting for the decision of the Bolivian Supreme Court; France had unsuccessfully taken that route before with Barbie. As one French diplomat in La Paz observes, the extradition was not assured despite the favorable disposition of the new Socialist government in Bolivia. "The government had changed, but the conservative opposition still had the majority in the Supreme Court," he says. "Extradition was practically ruled out. The court has eleven members, and Siles needed seven votes. But he didn't have them." France began to press for the simple expulsion of Barbie to France or Germany, fearing either his escape or a court judgment in his favor. "The main thing," French diplomats told the La Paz government, "is that he stand trial for his war crimes."

The prospect of Barbie's being deported to Germany for trial raised the question of his nationality, for after carrying a Bolivian passport for more than twenty years he may no longer have qualified as a German citizen. If Barbie were not a German citizen, then the courts of the Federal Republic might not have jurisdiction. If he were a German citizen, the German constitution forbade his extradition to any other country.

The Germans were, some believed, less than enthusiastic about taking Barbie, particularly in 1983. West Germany had just that month marked the 50th anniversary of Hitler's accession to power as Reichschancellor, and the Bonn government was not eager to see a highly sensational war crimes trial revive the guilt and trauma of the Nazi era. "It wouldn't be very pleasant for them to judge a German 40 years after the fact," said one La Paz diplomat.

By contrast, the French were anxious to take Barbie into custody. Mitterrand's government was aware of the public relations benefits of such a move. Economic problems had eroded support for France's Socialist Party and municipal elections were coming up in March. Barbie's return would be an act of justice—with significant political dividends.

It has even been alleged by one of Altmann-Barbie's attorneys that the French government made a cash payment to certain Bolivian officials to ensure Barbie's transfer to France. One source in the Siles administration believes that money changed hands, estimating the amount at $1.4 million. He adds that "the president [of Bolivia] probably doesn't know" about the bribe.

Five days after Altmann-Barbie's arrest, following numerous discussions among Bolivian Interior Minister Roncal, French Ambassador Raymond Césaire and West German Ambassador Dr. Hellmut Hoff, a decision was reached: Barbie would go to France. It remained only for the French to make the necessary arrangements.

Ω

On the evening of February 4, 1983, a heavy rain was falling on the tarmac of the Basa Aerea, the military airfield adjacent to La Paz's El Alto Airport, as a van and several accompanying vehicles pulled up in front of a hangar. Armed soldiers bristled with attentiveness as the van's passenger stepped out, his wrists joined with handcuffs. A deep chill suffused the air of the Bolivian altiplano, and someone draped a military parka over Klaus Barbie's shoulders. An agent of the Ministry of the Interior removed his handcuffs, while Sanchez, the impassive subminister, personally oversaw the operation.

Barbie showed little concern, making casual small-talk as though he were not worried about being deported. The debt for which he had been jailed had been paid the day before, when Carrion had delivered 1,454,000 pesos, the Bolivian currency equivalent of $10,000, to COMIBOL. Earlier that day another 756,000 pesos in interest and penalties had been deposited with the Contraloria.

But the payment had made no difference, for ever since January 26, 1983, the Siles government had been developing its case against Altmann-Barbie. It finally decreed that the German had obtained his citizenship in 1957 under fraudulent pretenses and that he had interfered in Bolivia's internal politics as the organizer of paramilitary groups. By executive pronouncement, without the benefit of formal extradition orders, he was to be expelled from the country.

A Hercules C-130 air transport stood ready on the runway as Barbie was driven out to the foot of the ramp leading up to the aircraft's passenger hatch. Aboard the plane, the pilot and crew nervously awaited their passenger, casting anxious glances out into the darkness as though a Nazi rescue commando might suddenly materialize. But there was only night and rain as they took their seats in the cockpit and prepared for the departure.

A three-man Bolivian television unit, headed by its director, Carlos Soria, was also boarding. Soria noticed that Barbie was smiling sardonically as he climbed the steps to the plane, seemingly disdainful of the proceedings. Subminister Sanchez gave last minute instructions to his agents, who would stay aboard with Barbie, then the hatch slammed shut. At 10:30 P.M., as the Hercules began rolling toward a runway in the international section of the airport, the passengers, who also included a doctor, looked for places to sit. There were no passenger seats in the cavernous interior, but they found canvas tarpaulins and arranged a makeshift place for the old Nazi.

As the plane passed the El Alto civilian terminal, the passengers saw bursts of light flashing from that direction, the last efforts of the numerous photographers and journalists who had been diverted to the terminal by an official decoy operation. The transport sped down the runway and then lifted. Klaus Barbie had left Bolivian soil.

Not until a half hour after takeoff did Barbie exhibit any concern about his future. By then his facade of insouciance had vanished. Soria asked him if he could conduct an interview, but Barbie demurred, asking first for confirmation of where they were bound. "Am I going to West Germany, or where are we going?" he asked, bundled in the large anorak, the hood up over his balding head to ward off the cold.

Barbie's thoughts were already on the ground in Europe. He worried out loud: "How am I going to live?" he asked. He thought for a moment, then said, "How much does a razor cost now in Germany?" The strain of the past ten days was beginning to show. Soria and Barbie chatted casually, Soria angling for an interview, Barbie talking about his grandchildren, lamenting that his son was dead and that the youngsters were orphans.

When Barbie finally agreed to be interviewed, he became vehement in his criticism of the method used to expel him from Bolivia, claiming that his right as a Bolivian citizen had been abused.

Soria spoke to Barbie for 30 minutes, until the doctor interrupted to give the prisoner a brief check-up. When Barbie complained of thirst, someone located a Coca-Cola, which he used to wash down a tranquilizer supplied by the doctor. Soria interviewed him for another half hour, after which Barbie dozed off. Seven hours after takeoff, the aircraft nosed into a long descent and touched down.

Barbie was tense as the plane taxied in rain to a halt on the unidentified runway. The Bolivian police led Barbie to the doorway, from where they could hear men's voices out in the darkness. They were speaking French.

The prisoner knew instantly what this meant. *"Mi vida esta perdida,"* he told Soria. *My life is lost.*

Barbie, flanked by the two Bolivian policemen, walked down the ramp into the semi-circle of French authorities, then stepped onto the runway at Cayenne, in the Overseas Department of Guiana, French national territory, where he was arrested in the name of the French Republic.

Barbie was then driven in a van to a hangar at the edge of the airfield and listened as a French official read a two-page indictment prepared by a judge in Lyon, the southern French city where Barbie had persecuted thousands. Later the two Bolivian policemen were to argue about whether Barbie had broken down and wept as he heard the charges read; one said he had, the other claimed they were not tears, only raindrops. In either case, the Klaus Barbie who walked out of the hangar in Cayenne was a defeated man. "That ironic smile, that sarcastic attitude was gone," says Soria. "You could see at the first glance that he was destroyed."

A French DC-8, one of a fleet used by Mitterrand on official trips, stood on the runway, ready for immediate takeoff. The plane had deposited the French president in Morocco before being dispatched to Cayenne to pick up Barbie, who, again shackled in handcuffs, was brought aboard and settled into a seat near the back. The French guards took no chances: Policemen sat on either side of him, while another two took seats directly in front and behind Barbie as the jet took off and headed northeast, for Lyon, France.

Barbie slept through most of the nine-hour trip from Cayenne to the Orange military airfield 110 miles south of Lyon. It was night again as the plane landed and a squad of French soldiers took up a position around the jet. The lone prisoner stepped onto metropolitan French territory, where he was transferred to a helicopter near the runway. The Bolivian television crew were again permitted to follow, though a military officer cautioned them against shooting any film.

As the Puma helicopter lifted from the Orange field and moved toward Lyon, Soria observed that Barbie, wetting his lips constantly, had progressed a further stage in his collapse. But another humiliation awaited him: A French police officer held Barbie in check with a leash attached to his handcuffs during the 45-minute flight to the Corbas military airfield outside Lyon. At 9:45 P.M. his guards led him from the helicopter to a police van, part of a convoy of fourteen vehicles that left the base on the final segment of Barbie's voyage.

With blue lights flashing, the motorcade entered Lyon from the east along the Boulevard des Etats-Unis and the Avenue Berthelot, turning right onto the Boulevard des Tchécoslovaques. The curtains were tightly drawn on the windows of his van; Barbie saw nothing of the city he had once controlled. The convoy pulled into the compound of Fort Montluc, the nineteenth-century military facility where Barbie imprisoned his Resistance and Jewish victims, and came to a halt in front of a large gateway over which was etched *"Prison Militaire."* To the right of the gate was a stone plaque: "Here suffered under the German occupation ten thousand prisoners, victims of the Nazis and their accomplices. Seven thousand died."

The van containing Barbie passed through the gate, which closed behind it. Outside the large prison building in the center of the compound, the French authorities opened the door of the vehicle to release the former Gestapo chief. His hands freed of the cuffs, still carrying the jacket given to him in La Paz and surrounded by guards and officials, Barbie walked through the door of Montluc prison. It was 39 years after he had fled Lyon ahead of advancing Allied forces, leaving behind him the bitter traces of the thousands of tortures, deportations and killings he had ordered.

The Butcher of Lyon had returned.

THE ECOLE DE SANTE

T HE WAR CAME TO LYON ON THE AFTERNOON OF ARMI-stice Day, November 11, 1942, as Wehrmacht and SS troops entered the city in strength, shocking the thousands of Lyonnais who were in the midst of observing the victory of their last war with the Germans. "It was startling," recalls Marcel Ruby, historian and a former member of the Lyon Resistance. "We were celebrating the victory on the day the Germans invaded us."

This was not the first time the Germans had conquered Lyon. The initial German occupation of the city had taken place more than two years before, in June 1940, after the Nazi Blitzkrieg overwhelmed Holland, Belgium, Luxembourg and France in just over five weeks. By the time the Germans arrived in southeastern France, Lyon had been declared an open city, and it was taken with barely a shot. What remained of the French Army had already retreated to the south, leaving the Germans the unquestioned masters of Lyon.

After securing such key points as the Gare de Perrache and the smaller Gare des Brotteaux to the east, the city's numerous bridges and all the major intersections and squares, the Germans set out to convince the city's inhabitants that they had nothing to fear from the Third Reich. As in the rest of France, Nazi propaganda portrayed the Aryan warlords as the protectors of a population shamefully abandoned by its leaders and defenders.

Each morning a German military band goose-stepped around the Place Bellecour in the heart of the city and moved on to the Place des Terreaux in front of the city hall for an encore. But few Lyonnais were charmed by the strains of Prussian marches, and the concerts were abandoned after a week. Then, in keeping with the terms of the Armistice signed on June 22, 1940, the Nazi troops withdrew from Lyon and the rest of the newly declared "Free Zone" in the southeastern part of France. The first occupation of Lyon had lasted only eighteen days.

The November 1942 reoccupation by the Germans came as a direct consequence of the successful Allied amphibious landing in North Africa on November 8, 1942. Three days later, an irate Adolf Hitler sent his army marching across the Demarcation Line that had, since June 1940, separated the Nazi-occupied north and Atlantic coastal regions from the ostensibly free part of France.

Hitler had now effectively abandoned the convenient fiction of Vichy France, that portion of the country which had remained nominally French, controlled by the government of Philippe Pétain and Pierre Laval from the southern resort town that gave it its name. The Vichy government was to remain in place almost until the end of the war in France, but the German seizure of the Unoccupied Zone demonstrated the impotence of the French wartime government. Except for a small piece of territory administered by the Italians and a northern region that in 1940 had been tacked onto the Nazi-held Belgian territories, France was now entirely under the iron rule of the Militarbefehlshaber in Frankreich, the German occupation authority based in Paris.

Strains of German military music once again sounded in the Place Bellecour, but this time the Germans found that while Lyon was a conquered city, it had not been mastered. Two days after the arrival of the German forces, a Wehrmacht vehicle parked in the Rue Stella was bombed. On November 28 a German enlisted man was wounded by pistol fire in a 6:00 P.M. ambush at the intersection of Rue Victor Hugo and the Rue François-Dauphin, just blocks away from SS headquarters in the Hotel Terminus.

The first German soldier to die in Lyon at the hands of the French Resistance, Karl Sommerschuh, was killed on January 12, 1943. On January 25 a grenade was lobbed at a German detachment passing along the Avenue Condorcet, in another of the bold attacks through which the Resistance was posing a direct challenge to Nazi rule. The war was no longer being conducted solely on Nazi terms.

Ω

Jackboots clicked with urgency on the marble floors of the ornate salons and dining rooms of the Hotel Terminus in those closing days of 1942. The hotel was the headquarters for the Kommandantur der Sicherheitspolizei, the central office of the SS in Lyon. From the outside the Terminus was a square granite box with a mansard roof, but inside its reception rooms were richly appointed with finely carved wood paneling, mirrored columns and frescos depicting idyllic scenes from Parisian and Provençal life.

Obersturmführer Klaus Barbie had little time to contemplate the luxurious interior as he hurried through the hotel lobby to meetings in those first weeks of the German occupation. It was no small commission that Barbie, just 29 years old, held when he arrived in Lyon in the days immediately following the November 11 takeover. The young SS lieutenant's assignment was to head the Gestapo in the Lyon area, a jurisdiction covering the city and the countryside within a a hundred mile radius. He was to seek out and destroy the principal networks of the burgeoning French Resistance.

All available intelligence told Barbie that Lyon was rapidly becoming the capital city of the French Resistance and the nerve center of a web of opposition touching every major city of southeastern France. Barbie could visualize the Resistance links in a complete circuit of the compass: Mâcon and Dijon to the north; Grenoble and the Jura Mountains, a stronghold of the *maquis* guerrilla fighters, to the east; Nice, Marseille and Montpellier on the Mediterranean coast to the south; St. Etienne and Clermont-

Ferrand to the west. There also was evidence that the insurgents were in contact with other centers of anti-Nazi activity in Paris, London, Switzerland and Portugal.

Across the Rhône River from the Hotel Terminus and the Gare de Perrache, in offices established in the Ecole de Santé Militaire, a former French Army medical school, Barbie pored over the files of the Donar Mission, his German intelligence predecessors in Lyon. Led by his current commander, Sturmbannführer Rolf Müller, the Donar Mission was composed of agents from the Gestapo and the Abwehr, the intelligence branch of the German Army, who had worked in the Lyon area clandestinely during the pre-occupation days. Under the cover of the German Armistice Commission based in the Hotel Terminus, Müller and his associates had monitored Resistance radio transmissions in the region. Several French agents, most of whom had been parachuted in or recruited locally by the British, were arrested by the Germans after their transmission sites were pinpointed by trucks carrying electronic homing gear.

Now that the Gestapo could operate openly in Lyon, Barbie was charged with assembling a commando group that could penetrate and destroy the Lyon-based networks of the Resistance. His Einsatzkommando would be the chief operational wing, the striking force of the Lyon SS. Its actions were to be coordinated by Barbie's section of the SS, formally the Geheime Staatspolizei but otherwise known and feared as the Gestapo. Its mission was the elimination of political enemies of the Third Reich, particularly the Resistance fighters whom the Nazis preferred to refer to as "terrorists," along with communists, socialists, Jews and Freemasons.

It was a challenging assignment, but Barbie came to it well prepared. During his seven years in the SS he had moved through a variety of posts as he rose in rank. He had helped organize one of the first large-scale deportations of Jews in Holland and, just before his posting to Lyon, Barbie had been involved in an important counterintelligence operation on the Swiss border. He spoke French almost as fluently as a native and the previous June he had completed a special counterinsurgency course in Berlin.

Barbie did not look like the prototypical Aryan of Nazi myth. On meeting him, people noticed that he was relatively short—only five feet, seven inches. His features were blunt and coarse: His wavy black hair was combed back from a heavy brow, and he had the broad nose of a Westphalian peasant. Only his sharp blue eyes gave evidence of any Nordic heritage.

One German Army officer later recalled his first impressions of the Gestapo chief. "He was a little bit smaller than I was, about one meter sixty-seven to one meter sixty eight, with black hair. He spoke High German and spoke French just as well." He was immediately struck by Barbie's "presumptuous and even arrogant attitude," a swaggering demeanor that was disrespectful of German officers outside the SS.

"We soldiers had been disagreeably surprised to note that he hadn't even recognized the obligation to honor our commander with a salute," the officer remembers. "His belt was always askew and leaning to the side where he had attached his pistol holster. He carried a 9 mm American pistol. He was gloved and seemed like a man who didn't know fear. He moved around without any protection and obviously was totally unafraid of being killed by the partisans."

Some in Lyon had given Barbie the nickname "Gorilla Ears," a reference to the peculiarly simian shape of his ears. But the insult was never said to his face. It was something the baggage handlers at the Gare de Perrache could nervously laugh about as they watched the young German step out of the Hotel Terminus, accompanied by his Alsatian dog, and head up through the Place Carnot and past the monument to the French Republic for a stroll in the center of Lyon.

But there was nothing humorous about Obersturmführer Klaus Barbie. He smiled easily, but not in a way that put people at ease. It was more a statement of arrogance, of his certainty that he was in absolute control. It was a smile that his victims would remember years after their physical suffering was over.

Ω

Barbie's headquarters was in the Ecole de Santé Militaire, a building well-suited for the work of the Gestapo. The heavy, grimy structure of grayish brown stone was on Avenue Berthelot, a boulevard running directly east from the Rhône River in a direct line with the Gare de Perrache and the Hotel Terminus. The four sides of the Ecole de Santé enclosed a courtyard in which prisoners could be loaded and unloaded from trucks out of sight of passersby on the street outside. It had deep basements and thick walls, though not stout enough to prevent nearby residents from hearing anguished cries in the night.

The Ecole de Santé was the Gestapo interrogation center, the focus of Barbie's work of intimidation, torture and murder, the principal instruments of his campaign to break the will of French Resistance prisoners and use them to find the leaders of the insurgency. As he had learned in his counterinsurgency training in Germany, he had only to decapitate the Resistance to destroy it.

Death at the Ecole de Santé was meted out at the caprice of Barbie, who personally killed prisoners when they were of no further use. One survivor of the Lyon Gestapo chief's brutality was Mario Blardone, a Frenchman of Italian extraction who had enlisted in the Resistance at 19 and was captured by Barbie two years later. Blardone, who is now retired in the village of Saint-Geoire-en-Valdaine in the countryside east of Lyon, was witness to Barbie's murderous techniques. One day while Blardone was in the basement, handcuffed to a chair in one of three large cells where prisoners awaited interrogation, he heard footsteps and looked up to the top of the staircase where a prisoner, bloodied from the questioning, began to descend the steps between two armed SS guards. Then he saw another figure appear at the top of the stairs: Klaus Barbie. Blardone assumed he had come to select his next subject for interrogation.

There were eight steps on the short staircase and Barbie stopped on the top one. The prisoner had gone down two or three steps when Barbie took out his revolver and leveled it at a spot just below the skull of the man beneath him. He pulled the trigger. The report echoed through the cavernous basement as the prisoner sprawled forward to land on the cement floor, dead. Barbie casually holstered his gun and returned to his office on the second floor.

The Nazis called it a *Nackenschuss*, a bullet in the back of the neck, a simple and efficient execution. For Barbie it was a way of demonstrating to those awaiting their turn in the basement that he was not bluffing. Each time thereafter, whenever Blardone descended those same steps with Barbie behind him, he waited for the impact of the deadly bullet in his neck. "When you've seen something like that three times," Blardone says "and you know Barbie is behind you, you think, 'That's it, it's all over.' "

Blardone had been arrested at a time when the conflict between the Nazis and the Resistance had erupted into open warfare on city streets and in remote mountain regions, particularly in the Lyon region. He was captured by the Germans, along with three other Resistance members, while traveling by car from Lyon to the city of Lons-le-Saunier, 80 miles to the northeast in the Jura Mountains, where they had been sent to pick up instructions for a mission. Blardone was carrying a .765 caliber revolver of Spanish make, with eight bullets in the cylinder and another in the chamber, three more rounds than in a standard French small arm.

The road to Lons was blocked by a German checkpoint, but Blardone had passed it on numerous other occasions without difficulty. His forged credentials had always stood up under inspection, and there seemed to be no reason why this day should be different. As the car slowed to a halt for the document check, Blardone and his men reviewed their story, but they were never given a chance to use it. The German police, machine pistols in hand, ordered them out of the car. They were immediately handcuffed and searched; Blardone watched helplessly as the police confiscated his Spanish revolver.

Who had betrayed him? Blardone asked himself. It was obvious they had walked into a trap set by the Gestapo. Betrayal had become commonplace in wartime France, where nearly every clandestine Resistance network was infiltrated by French and German agents. Within minutes Blardone and the others were on their way to the Gestapo headquarters at Lons, from which they were soon transferred to Lyon, the capital city of the Rhône *département*, and brought to Barbie's Ecole de Santé.

Blardone was taken to the second floor and into an office where he faced Obersturmführer Klaus Barbie for the first time. Barbie greeted him politely, offered him a chair and began to question him calmly. The Gestapo chief was well-groomed, dressed in a civilian suit with a clean white shirt and a tie. He might have been a minor German bureaucrat settling a few troublesome questions in a dossier.

Barbie studied the arrest documents, then began to review the case with Blardone. Did Blardone realize that he had been arrested in possession of arms? Blardone knew there was no point in denying it, though this was an offense punishable by death under occupation law. He decided to appeal to whatever sense of military honor Barbie might have, and admitted his guilt on the charge of carrying arms. Yes, he told Barbie, he was in command of the mission and accepted full responsibility for the consequences.

"I am a French officer in the Secret Army of Charles de Gaulle," the 21-year-old Resistance fighter told Barbie in a surge of bravado. "I am the commander and I demand that you treat me as such."

"We don't recognize de Gaulle's clandestine army," Barbie scoffed. "You don't come under the Geneva military conventions. That has nothing to do with you. You're not an officer. To me you're a bandit, a terrorist, nothing more."

Blardone was dismissed, led down the stairs to the courtyard, loaded into a truck and brought to Fort Montluc prison two kilometers away from the Ecole. The next morning he was returned to the Ecole and subjected to interrogation in the room adjoining Barbie's office. While Barbie stood off to the side his two German assistants beat Blardone, varying their instruments: first fists, then clubs, whips, and boots. "You're going to talk," they assured Blardone between blows. As they struck him, they demanded the names of other Resistance members, showing Blardone books filled with photographs of suspects. He recognized some of the faces, but said nothing.

By degrees they increased the level of brutality, selecting their tools with precision. They hoisted Blardone from a pulley set in the window frame, using a rope attached to his hands cuffed behind his back. But after six days, the ordeal no longer affected Blardone, who had been beaten beyond pain.

Ω

Blardone, who was now learning the cost of resisting the Nazi occupiers, had enlisted in the Resistance in September 1942 when a former French air corps officer, André Demogue, came to the Blardone home near Lyon to talk to his father about helping to oppose the Germans. "It was just friendly conversation at the time," recalls Blardone. "They didn't have the means to do anything, but they were looking for people they could count on."

Young Mario joined Combat, the Resistance network headed by former French Army Captain Henri Frenay, and was given the job of distributing the underground newspaper *Combat*, from which the armed movement took its name. Blardone was soon moved into more hazardous work and developed close ties with Albert Chambonnet, regional commander of the Secret Army, a paramilitary organization formed in September 1942 just as Blardone was joining the Resistance.

One of Blardone's first assignments was to gather intelligence by seeming to join the enemy. Pretending sympathy for the Vichy "National Revolution," Mario presented himself for conscription in the Chantiers de Jeunesse, a youth organization run by the collaborationist Vichy government. After three weeks of observing the training program, Blardone left camp and was subsequently convicted of desertion, in absentia, by a Vichy court. Blardone was now an outlaw of the New France.

A small but resilient young man, Blardone was sent into the Jura Mountains northeast of Lyon where the *maquis* were fighting. Under the tutelage of Henri Romans-Petit, he was taught weapons handling, sabotage and security techniques. Once trained, Blardone was detached to the direct service of Chambonnet, known at the time only by his *nom de guerre*, Didier. Blardone had become part of the security service of the Secret Army and was assigned the job of protecting Resistance leaders at clandestine meetings.

Meetings were sometimes held in apartments and office buildings in Lyon, but these sites were usually shunned as too easily compromised by hostile or curious neighbors. Instead, the Resistance made use of the Saône and Rhône rivers, which converge at Lyon and whose banks and bridges provided more secure locations for rendezvous, with clear visibility of approaching threats and multiple avenues of escape.

The Resistance meetings were also held in Lyon cafes, while Blardone and his security colleagues loitered outside, their weapons concealed but ready in case of a Gestapo raid. One meeting place was the Café du Commerce, on the long avenue east of the Rhône called the Cours Gambetta. The Café Jurassien and the

Café de la Marine, both on the Rhône's Quai Gailleton, were also prominent rendezvous points for Lyon's *résistants*. In case of emergency—a raid by Barbie's men or the Vichy police—Blardone was one of those who were to ensure that the Resistance leaders made their escape. It was a suicide mission in which only a few shots could be fired before the Resistance soldiers were gunned down. Fortunately for Blardone, he never had to make such a stand, but others did and paid the price.

Security units such as Blardone's were called Groupes Francs, a reference to the Franc Tireurs, a volunteer militia group that sprang up in France during the Franco-Prussian war of 1870, when the country was also invaded by Germans. The Groupes Francs carried out the deadliest work of the Resistance, including killing those who betrayed or threatened the security of the Resistance networks. Scheduled for assassination were French informers and members of French fascist political groups linked with Vichy and the Nazis—collaborationists considered as dangerous to the Resistance as Obersturmführer Barbie himself.

One day Blardone was called to a meeting with a superior officer of the Secret Army at a cafe in Lyon. The Resistance leader pushed three small photographs across the table to Blardone and pointed to one in particular. "See this man? If you run across him and the situation is right, kill him." Blardone recognized him immediately. It was a photograph of Francis André, the man called "Gueule Tordue," or "Twisted Mug," whose deformed jaw and reputation for cruelty made him Lyon's most prominent and feared collaborator.

André was the Lyon leader of a French fascist paramilitary organization, the Parti Populaire Français, the PPF, which had become so closely associated with Barbie's unit that the Lyonnais referred to it as "la Gestapo Française." Long active in extreme-right French politics, André had even volunteered in 1941 to fight for the Germans on the Russian front. Some of his PPF troops were as politically motivated as André, but most were criminals, recruited from the streets and even from French prisons, who saw collaboration with the Germans as an opportunity to commit violence and rob with impunity.

Before his meeting with Barbie on his first day in Gestapo

headquarters, Blardone was shoved into an office where, staring at him across a battered desk, sat Gueule Tordue. Blardone was shocked, but he had had the presence of mind to chew André's photograph to a pulp soon after his arrest. André would never know he had been Blardone's target. To Blardone's relief, André showed little interest in him other than to ask the guard about the arrest. "He's not one of ours," André said. "Take him down to the chief of the German service."

Ω

Blardone's ordeal of torture in the Ecole de Santé went on for eighteen days, but he kept his silence, and survived. "What I kept thinking was, 'If I talk, it's finished for me,'" he says today. Blardone used the technique of showing more pain than he actually felt, impressing upon his torturers how well they were doing their job. "I think everyone who was tortured had to simulate, play out the role, play the part of the torture victim." In the circumstances, it was an easy role to assume.

Another survival technique, Blardone explains, was to simulate fainting. Knowing how and when to faint was useful, especially as Blardone approached the limits of his endurance, at which point he would abruptly fold up and drop to the floor. To test whether he was truly unconscious, the Gestapo men would kick him in the ribs and Blardone had to stoically accept the pain without flinching. If Barbie saw signs of consciousness return, he would order the SS men to bring him around and resume the torture.

But there was a drawback to this strategem: It meant that Blardone had to lie in the corner of the room, or in the corridor, while others were being tortured, without showing any reaction. At times this was worse than being interrogated himself, particularly when women prisoners were being questioned. "You suffered twice as much when a woman was being tortured," Blardone says. "They burned them on the breast with cigarettes. They did that to the men, too. I was burned with cigarette ends. With the women it had to be even more painful."

Blardone never saw women tortured with their clothes on. When the session began, Barbie immediately ordered them to strip, part of his technique of humiliation. This apparently added to the enjoyment of the torturers. "With Barbie, it was a pleasure, as it was for the others," Blardone recalls with anger. "It was a pleasure for them to say, 'Take your clothes off.' "

Barbie had a French secretary, Simone, with whom he would toy between and even during interrogations, embracing and kissing her in front of the prisoners. But her presence did not spare the women some of the most degrading humiliations imaginable, Blardone observed. Barbie kept two dogs in the Ecole de Santé, German shepherds which the Gestapo employed during interrogation sessions to intimidate and even attack prisoners. One was a vicious guard dog that snarled and hurled itself at prisoners, restrained only by the handler's leash. Blardone recalls seeing a naked female prisoner backed into a corner, cowering before the lunging, snapping animal. The dog, when given more leash, suddenly dug its teeth into the uncovered limbs of the terrified woman.

The second dog was trained for an even more revolting task. One day as Blardone lay in the corridor, he saw the animal brought into a room where Barbie and three SS men had been beating a stripped woman prisoner. Barbie was not finished with the "interrogation." At his command, the soldiers forced the woman onto her hands and knees. She did not realize what was happening until the dog was placed in a position to sexually mount her.

"The dog was obviously trained for this act," Blardone says. "The three SS men were holding the woman down while she screamed and wept. We were off to the side and couldn't see everything, but we knew what was happening. I'll never forget that day. They were laughing, with Barbie to one side laughing with them. He was there, directing everything."

This was not the urbane SS officer who had debated the niceties of international military conventions with Blardone during his first interrogation. "I saw him in different moods," Blardone said. "I knew him as a mild man, sensitive, who offered me a drink, food, cigarettes. But there were also times when he was savage, and would strike me across the face with his whip."

While Blardone was enduring these tortures he did not know that his principal tormenter was named Klaus Barbie. "He was the Gestapo chief, that was all I knew," says Blardone today. "You could tell he was in charge. Even in civilian clothes he was saluted by everyone as he climbed the stairs and walked down the corridors."

Barbie instilled fear in his own Gestapo staff as well, Blardone observes. "He had two German SS men who tortured the prisoners, the same two who tortured me. At times he shouted at them, and you could feel that he was so ferocious that even the SS people were afraid."

Ω

Barbie was a brutal, dogged policeman, but some of those who survived were not impressed by him as an interrogator. Although they admit that he had an uncanny knowledge of the Resistance movement, they feel that he could sometimes be outwitted by a clever prisoner. "He constantly repeated the same questions: Where are the arms caches? Where is the money? Where is so-and-so?" says Raymond Aubrac, a former Lyon Resistance leader captured by the Gestapo. "He didn't strike me as a very intelligent interrogator, or very coherent."

Blardone came away with the same impression. "He was very incoherent as an interrogator. He didn't have the skills of a man who knows how to conduct an investigation. He went about it in a brutal way, what I'd call incoherent. But he had an idea in his head, a theory. For him, the men in the Resistance were terrorists, bandits. If they weren't bandits, they were communists. If they weren't communists, they were Jews. That was all he could think about.

"For him, it was Jews and communists. There were only two things that mattered, you could tell right away. Really, it was something that was an obsession with him. As soon as he ran across a Jew, he went for him. He would become furious, totally furious."

One Resistance leader who survived by outwitting Barbie was Christian Pineau, who was to become a cabinet minister in several French postwar governments. A trade union official in 1940, Pineau had formed a Resistance network called Libération Nord in Paris, but he went underground after the Gestapo arrived at his home in January 1942.

That February Pineau made his first trip to London to ask de Gaulle to issue a manifesto for the developing Resistance. The imperious French general agreed and charged Pineau with the task of creating an intelligence network inside occupied France. Pineau divided his organization into two separate sections and personally headed the southern division, code-named "Phalanx." By bicycle and train he traveled regularly between the Occupied and Unoccupied zones, posing as a worker going to his job on the other side. Phalanx proved to be highly productive, largely because Pineau had an agent in Vichy close to Prime Minister Laval who provided him with the minutes of the weekly cabinet meetings.

Pineau was arrested in Lyon in May 1943 just after his Resistance group had helped a British officer escape from France, and he was brought to Barbie's headquarters for questioning. Today, in his Paris apartment in a middle-class neighborhood on the Left Bank, Pineau, a charming, animated man in his late seventies, described his eleven-hour grilling by Barbie. "He gave me the impression that the Gestapo used a wholesale method," says Pineau. "They arrested people and tried to intimidate them right away. When that worked, it worked, and when it didn't work, depending on the case, they either tortured them or didn't torture them. The person who was tortured was the person who said nothing. You had to invent a story; that was indispensable. You had to drag out the conversation."

Pineau was one of the few Resistance members interrogated by Barbie who was neither beaten nor tortured, mainly because he had a cover story prepared when he was arrested and maintained it even under repeated questioning. "It was a game of cat-and-mouse between Barbie and me. I was the mouse. Barbie started by saying, 'M. Grimaux'—that was the name I was using at the time—'I know that you are Francis, the head of the network,' " Pineau recounts. "I told him, 'I don't know what you are talking about.' He answered, 'The proof is that I know all about you.' Then he did what no policeman should ever do: He told me everything he already knew. By deduction, I then knew everything that he didn't know. And so I began to construct a story."

Pineau told Barbie that his job was to seek information on French food supplies. It was an area of his intelligence work that he deliberately chose to reveal since it did not concern German military matters and was less likely to lead him to a firing squad. But it was Barbie who had given Pineau his lead. By telling Pineau what he knew about his network, Barbie had allowed him to weave his concocted story into what the Gestapo chief already knew, giving it the ring of truth. "I made up a whole story with characters and all," says Pineau.

In spinning his deception, Pineau described two imaginary confederates to Barbie using as models two movie stars of the era. The movie models gave Pineau a clear image of his imaginary characters, making it less likely he would be tripped up on subsequent interrogations. He planned well; he was forced to repeat his story several times during an all-day interrogation, but never contradicted himself. "I always described the same personalities to Barbie. In fact, they ended up by really existing in my imagination.

"Finally," Pineau concludes, "at ten o'clock at night, Barbie said to me, 'I'm going to finish with one question: Do you like the Germans?' I thought for a fraction of a second, and I told myself that if I say I like the Germans, he'll take me for a liar, and he won't believe anything I've said. So I said, 'I don't like them, because I don't like anyone who occupies my country.' Barbie turned to his associates and said to them in German, 'This isn't the one we're looking for. He's an imbecile.' "

Pineau couldn't have been more pleased; his strategy had worked. He was still in the hands of the Gestapo, but his true identity remained a secret. After the questioning, he was brought to Montluc prison and locked up.

Ω

In retrospect, many are surprised that a person with Barbie's low rank—he was only a Gestapo lieutenant—could wield such enormous power in occupied Lyon. But to observers of the Nazi system, it was quite in character. "Do you know how the Nazi system of repression worked? They gave great powers to people who weren't very high up," Raymond Aubrac explains. "There were at least three or four generals in Lyon who appeared in public, whose names were in the newspapers and on the circulars. But everyone knew that the real power was held by the SS, the Nazi party, not by the military. And Barbie was SS and the head of the Lyon Gestapo section."

The internal relations of the SS commandant's office in Lyon also created opportunities for Barbie to exert maximum personal power. There were several levels of administrative authority above Barbie in Lyon. At the top of the Lyon SS hierarchy was the KdS, the Kommandeur der Sicherheitspolizei. Initially held by a Sturmbannführer Rolf Müller, this post was filled in the spring of 1943 by Obersturmbannführer Werner Knab. Knab's adjutant was Hauptsturmführer Heinz Hollert.

Knab, an ambitious and ill-tempered man, had been sent to Lyon after serving on the Norwegian and Russian fronts. He had been accused of cowardice in Norway, but was given an opportunity to redeem himself in Kiev, on the Eastern Front. A cultured officer isolated from his Lyon SS corps, Knab had particularly hostile relations with Hollert, a former carpenter who was his second-in-command. Hollert had commanded the Lyon SS before Knab arrived, and despite Knab's objections, had stayed on. A member of the Nazi party since 1933, Hollert had used his connections in Berlin to keep his relatively comfortable post in Lyon.

It was an ideal situation for the ambitious young Barbie. While Knab and Hollert pursued their rivalries, Barbie created his own fiefdom, drawing on the other SS sections, or "Amts," as he needed them. Though the Gestapo was the heart of the SS, it was formally known as Amt IV of the Reichssicherheitshauptamt, or RSHA. The RSHA, the Central Security Department of the Reich, was the main administrative arm of the Reichsführer SS, Heinrich Himmler. The Gestapo was only one of seven RSHA Amts, but it was the section that went to the heart of the SS mission: terrorizing all opponents of the Reich.

Amt I was administrative, handling the finances and logistics of the Lyon SS. The second Amt handled liaison with the French police and courts; it was led by a glacial, solitary Obersturmführer named Schaureck, a former functionary in the German judicial system. Amt III gathered economic intelligence, monitoring production in Lyon's industries. Amt IV, the Gestapo, was headed by Barbie. Amt V, also known as the Kriminalpolizei, dealt with black market activities and common law violations committed by Wehrmacht troops.

Taken together, the Gestapo and the Kriminalpolizei formed the Sicherheitspolizei, or Security Police. Amt VI, the Sicherheitsdienst, exercised power similar to that of Barbie's Gestapo. It was the intelligence service of the SS and ran its own agents. Barbie was to work closely with its first chief, Obersturmführer August Moritz, until Moritz was replaced in April 1944 after a feud with Knab. There was no Amt VII in Lyon; this "ideological research" section was located higher up, in Paris and Berlin.

Within this structure Barbie was formally under Knab and Hollert, but as the testimony of numerous survivors of the SS in the Rhône-Alpes region indicates, he usually operated in an autonomous manner. His assignment as leader of the Einsatzkommando, combined with his position as chief of Section IV, the Gestapo, gave him powers that in real terms equaled those of Knab and Hollert. Nothing indicates that Barbie was ever restrained by either of these superior officers. In fact, all available evidence shows that he was a law unto himself, holding the power of life and death. "The real chief in Lyon was Barbie, there's no doubt about it," says Resistance historian Marcel Ruby. "It was Barbie who exemplified and led the Lyon Gestapo throughout the occupation."

While the chain of SS command in Lyon led from Barbie up through Hollert and Knab, documents and cables issued by Barbie's Section IV during the war suggest that he was in certain ways directly accountable to the Paris head office of the SS. That headquarters was controlled by the Hoherer SS-und Polizeiführer Carl Albrecht Oberg, the supreme secret police commander in France, who reported directly to Himmler in Berlin. Immediately below him was the head of the Security Police in France, SS-Obersturmführer Helmut Knochen. Under these two men came a broader group of officers responsible for specific areas of police work. One of these officers, Hauptsturmführer Theodor Dannecker, had been dispatched to Paris by Adolf Eichmann's Berlin office for Jewish matters to handle the deportation of French Jews. Another recruit from Eichmann's office was Kurt Lischka, an Obersturmbannführer who worked closely with the Gestapo and was also involved in Jewish matters. The SS hierarchy was complicated, but for an ambitious young officer like Barbie, who understood the organizational levers of power, it could be very effective.

Ω

Author and *résistant* Albert Camus called Lyon "that big,

somber city of conspiracy," while others have referred to it as "the capital of the Resistance." By any description, Lyon, the third largest city of France, was the stage of a subterranean battle, the logical center for French resistance against the Germans.

The city was the hub of the French rail system's southeastern network, and each day scores of trains left the Gare de Perrache and other stations bound for Paris to the north, Grenoble and Switzerland to the east, Marseille in the south and Toulouse in the southwest. This last was a stepping stone to neutral Portugal, itself a way station to London and the French forces led by Charles de Gaulle.

In peacetime, Lyon had been a rather conservative, stolid city whose dominant rhythm was one of productivity, and which was was known worldwide for its fabrics and metal products. Silk and steel had raised the stately, pastel-colored mansions that lined the quais of the Saône and Rhône, and made Lyon the dominant economic force of southeast France.

Two rivers define the outline of Lyon. The Saône, flowing from the north, and the Rhône, streaming in from the northeast, set a parallel course about a half-mile apart to form the *presqu'île*, or peninsula, that is the heart of Lyon. On it are located the Hôtel de Ville, or city hall, the Gendarmerie, the central post office, the Grand Théâtre, the stock exchange, the Hôtel-Dieu hospital, and the Gare de Perrache. There are also the great squares, the stages of Lyon's public life: the Place des Terreaux, with its ornate fountain in front of the Hôtel de Ville; the Place Carnot by the Gare de Perrache; and, above all, the Place Bellecour.

From the Place Bellecour one obtains a sweeping perspective of Lyon. High above it, west on a bluff across the Saône, looms the four-towered Basilica of Notre Dame de Fourvière. Just to its right is the *tour métallique*, a scale reproduction of the Eiffel Tower built in 1893, four years after the original. The southern third of the immense Place Bellecour, 300 meters long and 210 meters wide, is covered with trees, fountains, benches and pavilions. The northern portion is broken only by an equestrian statue of Louis XIV. At the east and west ends of the Place Bellecour stand two monumental buildings, their facades modeled after those at Versailles, the Sun King's summer palace.

Though provincial in style, the Lyonnais of the late thirties were intellectually active. Sixty bookstores catered to their reading tastes, and they could choose between more than a half-dozen newspapers published locally in addition to the major Paris dailies. The city's metropolitan population of over 800,000 was more than moderately religious. Forty-six Catholic publications originated in Lyon, and His Eminence Pierre Cardinal Gerlier held a prominence equal to that of Lyon Mayor Edouard Herriot, a former president of the French Chamber of Deputies.

Given this rather bourgeois profile, Lyon might have seemed an improbable city for clandestine activities, but in other ways it was eminently suited to the growth of an underground movement. The city's secret, mystic side predated even the sixteenth century, when the astrologer Nostradamus carried out his arcane studies there. Even in the mid-twentieth century, there remained a tradition of spiritual esoterism, and its style of architecture still seems to reflect this hidden aspect. Thousands of passageways lead off the busy city streets through silent courtyards from one thoroughfare to another. The older neighborhoods are laced with elaborate sets of covered passageways called *traboules*, some of them labyrinths that can be negotiated with ease only by those who have lived in Lyon for generations.

The war heightened this secretive aspect of Lyon's physiognomy. Even before the Germans arrived, the population had been swelled by refugees from the German occupation of the north as well as by the victims of Nazi persecution in other countries. Among these were tens of thousands of Jews. Many found that in Lyon the hunted could obtain false identity papers that would enable them to survive, even lead an almost normal life. This was equally true of the political outlaws sought by the Nazis and by Vichy: the communists, the socialists, and those whose loyalties lay with Charles de Gaulle in London rather than with "le Maréchal" in Vichy, who had adopted a policy of collaboration with the Germans.

Initially the Resistance was slower to develop in the southern zone than in the Paris region, where the French quickly learned the brutal realities of German occupation. But the fact that Lyon, like Marseille, Grenoble, Clermont-Ferrand and other southern cities, lay in unoccupied territory until late 1942 enabled the Resistance to grow there in a relatively sheltered environment. Its members were sometimes subject to arrest by the Vichy police, who were trying to repress the Resistance, but this was far preferable to being taken by the Gestapo.

The difference in harshness between the two zones was apparent in the punishment meted out to the *résistants* to Nazi rule. Fifty members of the Combat resistance network who were arrested and tried in Vichy courts in October 1942 received prison sentences ranging from three months to ten years. In the Occupied Zone, a similar proceeding under German authority resulted in death sentences for sixteen Resistance members, who were executed by ax. Six women spared this penalty were deported to a concentration camp, from which only two returned.

Ω

By the time Barbie arrived in Lyon, the Resistance had advanced to a point where it represented a serious threat to the Germans. The movement in Lyon began soon after the debacle of May 1940, when the despair of defeat became epidemic, and the disembodied voice of a tall French tank commander, General Charles de Gaulle, who had escaped to Britain after the fall of France, represented the only hope. Seated in a BBC radio studio in London, de Gaulle addressed his countrymen across the Channel and reassured them. "Come what may," he said, "the flame of French Resistance must not go out and will not go out."

Lise Lesèvre and her husband, Georges, were among the first *résistants* to take courage from de Gaulle's words. The two local university teachers were stupified by the rapid advance of the German troops through France. Each morning during the offensive, Georges Lesèvre studied his Michelin map of the region in which the battle was taking place and, based on radio reports, marked the fighting fronts. Like others who had not heard of the Blitzkrieg, Georges assumed a front would be established and the war would proceed slowly, much as it had in 1914. But by early evening his map had become useless as the front moved deeper into French territory, more rapidly than anyone could keep up with it. France, ostensibly the greatest military power in Europe, was crushed in just five weeks' time. "The armistice just fell on our heads," recalls Mme. Lesèvre, today a widow living quietly in Paris. "We were anesthetized by that affair. No one expected such a *débacle.*"

But the Lesèvres did not fall into the despair that paralyzed most of their countrymen. Instead they reacted to the sight of Hitler and Marshal Pétain cordially shaking hands at post armistice talks by forming a group of *résistants* at their university. "We said 'No!' " Mme. Lesèvre remembers. "We said 'No!' to what was happening, to what was going to happen. At first, we talked with people, trying to turn their opinions against Vichy and its policy of collaboration with the Nazis. Then we made tracts. I spent 24 hours at the typewriter using lots of carbon paper. We had received a tract from students in Paris, so we reproduced it and put it in letter boxes. We told people to fight, to resist by every means."

The Resistance gained momentum, Lesèvre says, when the Germans reoccupied Lyon. "There was a greater movement of revolt then," she says. "The population became more aware of the work of the Resistance." But the pressures upon the *résistants* also mounted as the Gestapo became a constant threat. "It was very violent. They were the masters. At that point it started getting very difficult."

Raymond Aubrac's path to resistance was different than the Lesèvres', but his motivation was the same. Originally named Raymond Samuel, he took the name of his fiancée and future Resistance comrade, Lucie Aubrac, as a *nom de guerre.* Aubrac was Jewish and risked persecution but he was also a member of the French army and had escaped from a German prisoner-of-war camp with his fiancée's help. While visiting Raymond in the POW camp, Lucie passed him pills that stimulated a high fever, permitting him to be transferred to the hospital. From there he made his way over the camp wall where Lucie was waiting in a car. The couple moved to Lyon, safely inside the Unoccupied Zone, and set to work. This was not the only time Lucie would help Raymond escape from incarceration.

In Lyon, their first challenge was to fight the pervasive defeatism that had beset France after the German victory. Insistent German propaganda was matched by a parallel campaign mounted by fascist Vichy, which together strongly influenced the despondent population. "At the beginning this country was like someone who has been hit on the head," says Aubrac, who today heads a Paris economic development consulting firm. "The most anyone could do was to place a few question marks in front of the propaganda messages—the double propaganda, Vichy's and the Germans'. You tried to act a little, sometimes in a childish way, with graffiti on the walls, denouncing collaboration, denouncing Pétain, denouncing the Germans, warning people."

Aubrac, who was a civil engineer at the outset of the war and continued to use that profession as a cover for his Resistance activities, tapped his pipe into an ashtray as he measured his words. "In the beginning it was very limited. You talked with your friends, you tried to understand what was going on. A large part of the Resistance's activity was to discuss, to analyze, to try to understand, to try to influence people. What was missing the most in this country at the beginning of the occupation was hope. The country was truly desperate. So the people in the Resistance had at least one thing in common: they tried to create a little bit of hope."

In that first period, Aubrac relates, he traveled widely throughout the Unoccupied Zone organizing support for the Libération network of which he later was to become chief military officer. Most people in France were not yet ready to oppose Vichy, even if they hated the Germans, a view which defeated a plan he put into action on November 11, 1942, the day the Germans reassumed control over the southern zone.

Aubrac hoped to convince an army officer stationed at Bourg-en-Bresse to transfer military arms caches from the Armistice Army to the budding Resistance. "I took a truck and I went to get the arms," Aubrac recalls. "In one pocket I had false German police paper, and in the other I had false French police papers. I was stopped four times—three times by the French and once by the Germans. When I was stopped by the French, I showed them the German papers; when I was stopped by the Germans, I showed them the French papers. It worked."

At Bourg, however, his plan fell through. The officer in charge not only refused to turn over the weapons, but threatened to arrest Aubrac. Still, as Aubrac stresses, the officer did not follow through on his threat; there was at least tacit, if not active, support for the

Resistance at that point.

Aubrac was arrested by the Vichy authorities in March 1943, but he was again freed through the intervention of Lucie. Mlle. Aubrac approached the Vichy prosecutor and threatened Resistance reprisals if her husband was not freed—a threat backed up by a coded message broadcast by the BBC. Aubrac was released by Vichy in early May.

By early 1943, Aubrac and his associates were becoming aware of the existence of Obersturmführer Klaus Barbie. "We called him 'Barbier' at the time," says Aubrac. "We knew that he was at the head of the Lyon Gestapo, that he was in charge of the repression. He had the reputation of being brutal, of being a hard-core Nazi."

Ω

People such as the Lesèvres and the Aubracs had found their way into the three main Resistance networks based in the Lyon region. The largest was Combat, the child of Henri Frenay, a former captain in the French Army who was taken prisoner during the German offensive and later escaped from a POW camp to rejoin the 110,000-man Armistice Army. Posted to Marseille, Frenay decided to work against the official policy of collaboration with the German occupier.

Marshal Pétain was acclaimed by the French when he came out of semiretirement at the age of 84 to lead the stricken nation after "la Débacle." But by October 1940 when he met with Hitler in the town of Montoire southwest of Paris, it had become clear that Pétain was ready to accommodate German war aims by offering French passivity and cooperation. On October 31 Pétain announced, "I enter into the way of collaboration."

While still a member of the Armistice Army, Frenay launched what then seemed like a quixotic venture: the National Resistance Movement, whose aim was to drive the Nazis from French soil. Frenay began to clandestinely circulate a bulletin of information that he culled from foreign news broadcasts. By good fortune he was transferred to Vichy and assigned to the Deuxième Bureau, the French Army's intelligence branch, which provided a rich source of information for his underground publication.

In January 1941 Frenay resigned his commission and moved to Lyon, where he launched a small underground paper called *Les*

Petites Ailes, "Small Wings," which was printed in the Lyon suburb
of Villeurbanne by a printer willing to run the risk. From initial
carbon-copy editions of 18, Frenay's newspaper leaped to a circulation of 3,000 per issue. As an evasive tactic, *Les Petites Ailes* was
first transformed into *Verité*, or "Truth," then, in May 1941, took its
permanent name: *Combat*. The newspaper began to attract both
public interest and the most forceful voices of the underground
press, including Albert Camus's. By the end of 1941, the Combat
network had developed into a true Resistance movement with
regional antennae extending through southern France, to Marseille, Montpellier, Toulouse and Limoges.

The nucleus of another major network, Libération, came together in 1940 in the city of Clermont-Ferrand to the west of Lyon.
Its driving force was Emmanuel d'Astier de la Vigerie, a former
naval ensign turned journalist. Another original member was Lucie
Aubrac, then a history scholar who had followed her University of
Strasbourg professors in their exile from the German-annexed territory of Alsace-Lorraine to Clermont. One of them was Lucie's
fiance, Raymond Aubrac, who became a member of its executive
committee, in charge of military action, then rose to second in
command of Combat. While Combat was politically to the right of
center, Libération fell more to the left, and its ranks included
numerous trade unionists. The first issue of its newspaper, *Libération*, came out in July 1941.

Franc-Tireur, the third major Lyon-based movement, was
begun by Jean-Pierre Lévy, a Strasbourg engineer who joined
forces with an already existing Lyon group called France-Liberté.
Its activities had consisted mainly of spreading anti-German, anti-
Vichy propaganda, using stickers called *papillons*, or "butterflies,"
which could be affixed in public spots as a small gesture of de-
fiance. But Lévy then decided to move Franc-Tireur in the same
direction as Combat, toward eventual armed struggle with the
Nazis through the creation of a regional network.

These organizational lines seemed well defined, but at the time
the members of the emerging Resistance movement were feeling
their way slowly and often blindly. The shift from clandestine
publications and propaganda to military actions and sabotage was
not easily made. There were isolated attacks against the Germans

and increasing sabotage, but the powerful occupying force could not be confronted directly. Small arms were of little use against Panzer tanks.

To obtain help, the Resistance established links with the outside—with the forces of Charles de Gaulle in London, whose organization first went by the name of France Libre, and later France Combattante. The British, who had not yet accepted de Gaulle as the undisputed leader of the French, created their own intelligence service, which drew heavily on the information gathered by French Resistance groups. Soon the Americans were also trying to make contact with Resistance elements inside France, working mainly through diplomatic contacts in Switzerland.

In the early days, Resistance work was above all a matter of attending to detail: distributing clandestine newspapers, obtaining false identity papers, transporting arms from one point to another. Although some were routine, these activities required careful planning and inevitably involved high risks. By late 1942, with the arrival in Lyon of the Gestapo, headed by Klaus Barbie, these risks became even greater as failure often carried fatal consequences.

"Of course, we knew it was a dangerous game," recalls Aubrac. "But we also knew we had to take risks. Because we began with nothing at all, at zero. We had to organize something, and as soon as you organize things, you have to take risks. You have to see people."

Lines of communication had to be established. It was possible, though not practical, to send agents into France through Portugal or Switzerland, but more direct means were quickly developed: airplane landings at remote airstrips in the heart of occupied territory; parachute drops of agents, arms, equipment and money. Lyon became a principal organizing point for these activities.

During the first two years of the war, the Resistance steadily gained support among at least a sizable minority of the French public as the people recognized Vichy France for what it was and took courage from the bold anti-German acts of others. In November 1942, as the Germans reoccupied the southern zone and closed in on the Mediterranean port of Toulon, French naval officers scuttled approximately a hundred warships to prevent them from falling into German hands. The "suicide of the fleet" was the first indication that substantial segments of the French military leadership had set a limit in following Vichy's policy of *la collaboration*. It was a boost in morale for those working in the underground.

Another result of the Allied landing in North Africa was that Hitler forced Vichy to dissolve the French Armistice Army. Although this force had never been of any consequence, its demobilization sent more than 100,000 trained soldiers into the civilian sector, many into the arms of the Resistance.

At the end of 1942, the disparate Resistance forces began to take on the shape of a unified movement. On November 11, as German troops were entering Lyon, *l'Armée Secrète*, the Secret Army, was officially established by order of de Gaulle and placed under the command of French Army General Charles Delestraint. On November 27, while the French fleet was settling to the bottom of Toulon harbor and the Armistice Army was being demobilized, the Secret Army's top command held its first meeting in Lyon. Present were Frenay, d'Astier and Lévy, the leaders of the three main southern networks, along with Jean Moulin, a former French departmental prefect who had established links with de Gaulle in London and who would, by the following year, become the prime target of Klaus Barbie.

Ω

As the Lyon Resistance became increasingly bold, it even mounted an attack on Barbie and the Gestapo. One day a woman came to the Ecole de Santé, presenting herself to Barbie as an informer. She told Barbie she could lead his troops to an important member of the Resistance and gave him the address in Lyon. Barbie enthusiastically drew up a plan of attack, and at 7:00 A.M. his men encircled the house. As a precaution, they had brought the woman with them. Barbie and his men were dressed in clothes similar to those worn by the *maquis* Resistance fighters: jackets with fur collars and large pockets to hold grenades, with inside pockets sizable enough to hold broken-down Sten II machine guns which the *maquis* received in Allied air drops.

Even as Barbie and his Einsatzcommando surrounded the house, he intuitively felt that something was wrong with the situation; it had been too easy. When he and his men got within 30 meters, the Resistance fighters inside the house opened fire with machine guns, pistols and grenades. The Germans and their French Vichy cohorts retreated, losing several men in the process. But they counterattacked and two hours later captured the house. Inside, dead, was one of their own agents who had been sent in to reconnoiter.

Furious, Barbie interrogated the woman, who eventually admitted she was with the Resistance and had intended to lead his unit into an ambush. "I ordered her to be executed," Barbie later recalled, "and to cover our tracks, told them to throw the body in the Rhône." The body was later found by the French police, who brought it to the Gestapo for identification.

As the tempo of the war between the Nazis and the Resistance increased, Barbie redoubled his efforts to identify the leadership, convinced that once the Resistance had lost its directors, the movement would founder. For a while Barbie believed that in Lise Lesèvre he had captured an important leader of the Resistance. It was not true, but in the process, Mme. Lesèvre was brutally victimized by Klaus Barbie.

She had been arrested by the Gestapo outside the Gare de Perrache, where she had met with a courier from Paris who handed her a newspaper with an envelope tucked inside. The envelope contained instructions for her Libération network on the use of explosives to blow up an SS barracks to the north of Lyon. The rendezvous seemed successful until the man from Paris, sitting next to Lesèvre on a station bench, whispered: "Get out of here. There's a man sitting across from us who was outside my hotel this morning." She left quickly, but several Gestapo men closed in at the station door.

The Germans searched her immediately, and seized the envelope, on which was written the name "Didier," a Resistance cover name that was to cause her untold anguish. "Didier" was the name of the liaison agent who was to receive the envelope, but it was also the *nom de guerre* of Albert Chambonnet, Rhône regional chief of the Secret Army. Lesèvre held only a relatively minor position in the Resistance, but this coincidence made her a prime Gestapo target: She was interrogated by Barbie for nineteen days and tortured during nine of them.

After her arrest Lise was brought by car to the Ecole de Santé a half mile away on the east side of the Rhône. During the short ride, she rapidly began to destroy incriminating papers. "I had certain things on me, especially some photographs someone had given me in the afternoon to make false identity cards," Lise explains today. "I chewed them, but there was no way to swallow them, since they weren't edible. I took what I had chewed in my handkerchief and then I put it in a space in the car door. But I had to be careful. I couldn't put it all there."

At the Ecole, Mme. Lesèvre was ushered into a large office and left there under guard. "On the wall there were large portraits of the top Nazis: Hitler, Göring, Goebbels," Lesèvre remembers. "But there was another that I didn't recognize, a man with a narrow face. I asked who that man was. I was trying to give the impression that I was relaxed, though I wasn't. 'That's the head of the Gestapo in France,' the soldiers told me, 'but don't expect to meet him. He only bothers with serious cases.'

"While they were talking with me I had stuffed my gloves with all that I had chewed and not been able to swallow. Then I put them on the desk, thinking that with the gloves sitting right there they wouldn't bother to look. I also had pieces in my handkerchief, which I put inside a wide leather belt I was wearing. I used it from time to time to wipe my face."

Abruptly, the door to the office swung open to admit the man with the thin face in an impressive SS uniform, obviously someone of high rank. He marched directly over to the desk where Lesèvre had laid her gloves, picked them up and shook out the contents onto the floor. Then he grabbed her handkerchief and repeated the gesture.

"You are Didier," he told Lesèvre, "head of the AS."

"AS?" she asked. "What does that mean?"

"Armée Secrète," he pronounced.

"I am highly honored," Lesèvre said, "but I think that's going to mean a lot of trouble for me."

"You're right. A bit of trouble," the thin-faced man said as he left.

The interrogation that followed lasted until 4:00 A.M., but there was no violence, only innumerable questions and numbing fatigue. Lesèvre tried to give her captors a plausible explanation that would clear her without revealing anything of importance. "I had a friend named Didier and I was at the station to give him a letter," Lesèvre told the SS, "but I didn't find him because he had to take a train for Paris tonight. That was my only contact with the Resistance."

The SS laughed at her explanation. "I was treated as though I was the head of the AS, and very badly treated," Lesèvre recalls. "I spent that night in a basement with some unfortunate people who were covered with blood. There was one woman who was pitiful. They had shown her the body of her husband who had been tortured to death. She hadn't been tortured yet, but she was later on. The next morning at 7:00 A.M. the trucks arrived with people who had been brought from Montluc to be interrogated at the Ecole de Santé. They came to get me at noon, Barbie's butchers, and that was when I first met Barbie."

The guards led her up to the second-floor office where Barbie was waiting eagerly to talk to "Didier," the head of the AS, or at least someone whom he believed could identify the Resistance leader. As she sat in the straight chair before Barbie she studied his face for a clue to his character. "He was terrifying to see," Lesèvre recalls, "because he had small eyes, like marbles, that moved constantly. They made you think of a wild animal, those eyes that went from one side to the other. He had a riding crop, and he slapped his boots with it constantly. He always had a riding crop or a club."

"You are going to talk," Barbie told her confidently as he hit her across the face with his hand.

"Who is Didier?" he demanded. When Lise remained mute, Barbie struck her again.

"Where is Didier?" Her failure to respond was followed by a flick of his whip and more blows to her face.

"You are Didier, admit it!" Barbie shouted, raining abuse upon her. Barbie pursued this line for what seemed hours to Lesèvre, as she continued to absorb pain with resolve.

Finally he stopped, disgusted. "Take her back down," he told the guards. He turned back to Lesèvre to assure her that he was far from through. "You are going to talk," Barbie warned. In the basement she saw something that wounded her more than Barbie's blows: Her husband, Georges, and her 16-year-old son, Jean-Pierre, being led handcuffed into basement cells.

Barbie changed techniques that afternoon. He attached manacles to Lesèvre's wrists and hoisted her off the floor, arms now spread wide apart. "Who is Didier?" he repeated for the hundredth time. As Barbie struck her with the rubber truncheon, she writhed in pain and struggled at her bonds. Lise could feel the tendons and ligaments in her arms straining, perhaps tearing. Breathing became difficult; before long the room had gone dark before her eyes.

She woke up on the floor, someone kicking a boot into her bruised ribs. She looked up and saw Barbie staring down at her furiously, his eyes now filled with rage. "You are going to talk!" he screamed. Lise was overwhelmed by fear, but she was sustained by the thought that she had already experienced the worst. Once more she was dragged back to the cellar and thrown into one of the holding cells. It was now evening; there would be a few hours' respite before they came for her again.

Over the next weeks, Barbie tortured Lesèvre systematically, several times beating her while she was hung by her wrists. "Once I had been hung up, Barbie asked me questions—the same ones about Didier over and over again—and when I didn't answer, he hit me," Lesèvre now recalls. "When you got hit like that, it makes you move and it stretches you. I had torn ligaments as a result, so today I can't lift my arms very high."

The interrogation was unceasing; the variety of tortures seemingly unlimited. One day Lesèvre was placed on a metal stretching table, where cuffs were put on both her wrists and ankles. Her body was pulled in both directions as Barbie repeated his incessant demand: "Who is Didier? Where is Didier?" "Barbie then hit me," Lesèvre remembers. "It was always Barbie. Sometimes he had someone relieve him, but he always took over again to finish up. It was terrible."

More than one survivor of the Ecole de Santé has described Barbie as having a sadistic nature, of taking pleasure in personally beating his prisoners. "The man used his fists as a method of interrogation," said Raymond Aubrac, who was questioned and beaten by Barbie every day for a week after his arrest in June 1943.

Aubrac's hands were cuffed behind his back as Barbie questioned him, lashing out with his fists if there was no response.

"I think it gave him pleasure," says Aubrac. "I had the impression that this man was happy to be giving out punishment, to be hitting someone. He seemed quite pleased to be in power. You could feel that he was the boss and that we were in his hands. And in fact, we were in his hands."

Barbie's usual style of interrogation was brute punishment, but he occasionally employed a more refined form of sadism, particularly with prisoners such as Lesèvre who displayed a high level of tolerance for physical torture. Sometimes a malevolent twist that played on a prisoner's strained emotions or on their loyalties was all that was needed to crack them.

In an attempt to shatter her will, Barbie had Lesèvre brought into his office, where he motioned her to a corner of the room where a number of articles were spread out on a table. Lesèvre stifled a cry: on the desk were arranged her son Jean-Pierre's imitation leather blotter and some samples of his handwriting. There were poems the boy had written, along with a sheet of paper on which, perhaps the night she had been arrested, he had written the word "mother" over and over. On the walls of the office Barbie had arranged the same pictures that hung over Jean-Pierre's desk in their home. Lesèvre turned toward Barbie in rage and looked for a handy weapon, but her anger was futile. Barbie smiled, but the threat he was making was quite clear. Still Lesèvre maintained her silence.

But she had yet to face *la baignoire*. It was a special torture designed for the most recalcitrant of his victims, a device that could cloud the most obstinate spirit with excruciating pain until an oath of silence seemed breakable and cooperation logical. *La baignoire* was just what it said, a bathtub, but it held infinite terrors. The subject was placed in the tub, hands bound or cuffed behind the back, while the feet were tied to a bar laid across the tub to which a rope or chain was attached. With one sharp pull Barbie would plunge the head of the helpless prisoner under water and keep it there as long as he judged necessary.

The experience was akin to repeatedly drowning. When one surfaced, barely conscious and gasping for air, the questions were repeated; if there were no answers, one went back down again. Some prisoners believed that the best thing to do was to violently inhale the water of the bathtub, committing suicide by drowning. But this took a strong will, or extreme desperation.

The *baignoire* almost broke Lise Lesèvre. One evening at midnight, Lesèvre was roused by the guards and led across the courtyard of the Ecole de Santé and into a large bathroom, where Barbie stood expectantly alongside the tub. He had carefully taken off his watch so as not to get it wet and laid it on a small table. Lesèvre was curtly ordered to strip naked, then her hands were cuffed behind her back and she was abruptly plunged into the frigid water. Every nerve in her body protested the cold as she realized she had not yet experienced the worst of the Ecole de Santé. She strained to keep her head above the water, her feet firmly attached to the bar running across the tub.

"Now," said Barbie. "Who is Didier?" When Lise said nothing, Barbie seized the chain attached to the bar and yanked. She went under, taken by surprise, and struggled as the Nazi guards held her head under water. Lesèvre felt she was about to drown, to suffocate, but just before lungs with were about to burst, she was pulled to the surface by her hair.

"Who is Didier?" someone was shouting in her face. She pulled air into her lungs, spitting out water, choking and coughing. The question came again: "Who is Didier?" When she did not answer she was pulled under again, with barely enough time to gulp the bit of air she knew would not be enough. She came up again, knowing that she could not endure much more. Barbie was leaning over her, shouting the same question "Who is Didier?" It was 2:00 A.M. The session in the *baignoire* had lasted two hours, but Lesèvre had lost the sense of time.

The question was repeated, and once more she went to the bottom of the tub. This time she knew she was drowning, that she would die and never again taste air coming into her lungs. Then Lise broke surface and suddenly thought she was in a beautiful chapel with bright candles flickering all about her. She could not understand until the water cleared from her eyes and she heard herself saying "Rue Tronchet" to Barbie's shouted demand for the address of Didier.

But Barbie was not satisfied; he wanted the house number. Lise immediately felt a deep surge of remorse for having given the name of the street, but then suddenly, thought of a way to minimize the damage. "Number 115 Rue Tronchet," she said. Didier lived at number 25; 115 Rue Tronchet was her own home. Barbie was now delighted; he would soon have Didier in his hands. His Gestapo aides lifted Lesèvre out of the *baignoire*, uncuffing and drying her, suddenly bestowing kind attentions. She was theirs now. The first betrayal was the hardest; each one thereafter pained less.

But Barbie suddenly realized that Lesèvre had revealed her own address, and wheeled on her angrily. "Yes," she told him. "Didier comes to my house every Wednesday morning to pick up his mail." Barbie was mollified; the story was credible and he could check its veracity the following morning. But for Lise it had bought time, twelve precious hours before Barbie would learn that she had lied to him. Until midday on Wednesday, Lesèvre would have a respite from torture. She descended to the limbo of the basement cells, where others waited their turn to mount the stone steps to Barbie's chamber of terror.

Ω

Almost two months after her arrest, Lise was condemned to death by the German military tribunal at Montluc prison. On the morning of May 11, she was startled to hear her name called for another interrogation; she had assumed that Barbie was finished with her when he tossed her into Montluc in March. When she was brought back to the Ecole de Santé, Barbie came personally to the basement to fetch her. At his sides were three of his German SS aides, who flailed at her with their clubs as she climbed the stairs. Barbie was white with anger.

Instead of taking her up the staircase to Barbie's office, the four men led her out the door into the courtyard. She was seized with dread: this was the way to the *baignoire*. But they stopped at another room furnished with a solitary chair in which Lesèvre was strapped. Barbie produced his latest torture instrument, a knout, an instrument from the Middle Ages perfected with a modern adaptation. At the end of a long handle was a leather ball studded with metal points. The cruel assembly was spring-driven and hit with constant force when released against the human body.

Barbie handcuffed Lesèvre on her stomach over the chair, naked, and began applying the knout. As Barbie worked her over, she learned what was behind this latest session. Barbie's commando had carried out an operation against the *maquis* forces in the Jura Mountains and had captured a number of the partisans who, under torture, had divulged her name. Lesèvre had often worked as a liaison agent between the Jura *maquis* and the Lyon Resistance, and Barbie was infuriated that she had withheld this information from him.

Lise regained consciousness in a bedroom with a gray carpet and a rose in a vase. Someone was playing the piano. She could not understand; had she lost her senses or had everything before been just an extended nightmare? Then she recognized the cynical smile of Barbie, now by her bedside telling her that he admired her courage, but that eventually she must give in. Everyone had a limit.

Barbie began to question her again about the *maquis*, but added a sadistic turn to his technique, calling out a long list of cover names of *maquis* officers Lesèvre had known: Jérome, Cheval, Sarrazac, and others. As he did, one of his accomplices replied: "liquidated"; or "terminated."

Even though Lise Lesèvre had been condemned to death by the military tribunal, she was spared by chance and loaded aboard a convoy of deportees that needed to be filled out. That was on May 19, 1944, as Lise, now 81 and still a woman of impressive spirit, confirms today by consulting the tattered yellow diary she kept through her interments in Ravensbruck and a labor camp near Leipzig. She found her sixteen-year-old son, Jean-Pierre, in the Montluc convoy, but he later died with many others aboard the Nazi prison ship *Cap Arcona*, which was sunk at sea. Her husband, Georges Lesèvre, died of typhus in Dachau in January 1945.

Ω

Lesèvre had suffered because Barbie believed she held the key to the identity of a Resistance leader, but many *résistants* involved in the routine tasks of the insurgency were treated as brutally. The Lyon Resistance workers carried out their chores with courage, particularly in the face of Barbie's growing reputation as a ruthless Gestapo policeman. One patriotic Frenchwoman in Lyon did what she could and paid with permanent pain and disability at Barbie's hands.

"I spent my life in trains during the war, night and day, distributing an anti-Nazi newspaper for Libération," relates Anne Marie Bauer, whose family moved south to Clermont-Ferrand from Paris after the defeat of 1940. "The trains weren't heated, so there were often temperatures of below freezing. I would arrive frozen, especially at night."

Eventually Anne Marie was assigned to a group planning parachute drops and small aircraft landings and began traveling to remote country locations to map out drop sites and potential air strips, particularly on the moors of the Corrèze *département* west of Lyon. "My brother directed the first parachute drop," she recalls. "Afterwards, there were hundreds." In Lyon she worked with the Délégation, a centralized Resistance agency that handled the logistics of parachute drops, airplane pick-ups and the assignment of radio operators to various networks.

Anne Marie Bauer was arrested by the Gestapo in July 1943 on the Place de la République in Lyon, the victim of the carelessness of another Resistance member. A friend had sent a letter to London via courier through Switzerland, foolishly putting the address of her network's office in the missive. When a French agent came to the office to spy for the Gestapo, Bauer, trying to sound out his intentions, made an appointment with him for the following day. A fellow Resistance worker followed her to the rendezvous in case she was arrested.

"I stopped to lace my shoe to see if anyone was following," Mlle. Bauer recalls, "and all of a sudden someone put his hand on me. It was the Gestapo." She was taken to the Ecole de Santé, where Klaus Barbie began to question her immediately. "At the beginning, Barbie was very friendly," Anne Marie remembers. "He showed me pictures of his children and told me that he loved them, and that he was a good father."

The cordiality did not last. "When they saw I wouldn't talk, they began to torture me, hanging me up by my hands tied behind my back. It was horribly painful. Then they put fire beneath my feet. I ended up telling them who I was and where I lived, but my friend had already had time to warn the others."

In hopes of escaping, Bauer told Barbie she had a rendezvous with a woman named Victorine in the city three days later. This was a ploy: Victorine did not exist and Bauer had no such rendezvous, but she hoped the Gestapo would try to set a trap for the fictional *résistante*—thus providing her with an opportunity for escape. But in the Place Bellecour Bauer realized she was surrounded by too many Gestapo agents to successfully break for freedom. Rather than admit she had fabricated the rendezvous, Bauer very deliberately removed her hat and put in back on again, then informed one of the Gestapao agents that she had just given a warning signal to "Victorine," alerting her to the trap. When no one appeared the Gestapo realized that they had been fooled.

"She was furious," Bauer said of the female Gestapo agent involved. "I was slapped, of course, and then they took me back and made me go down in the cellar. Barbie was there with his dog. They pushed my head against the wall. There was one man with a machine gun and another who held a revolver against the back of my neck. They said, 'Do you have any last words or is there anyone you want notified?' I gave the name of a girlfriend whose family was behind Pétain, and who ran no risk of being arrested. Then they fired a blank. They didn't kill me, but just threw me in a cell. At the time, I was sorry I didn't have a cyanide pill like the ones they gave the parachutists and I was very sorry they hadn't shot me."

Mademoiselle Bauer today lives in retirement in her small apartment near the Luxembourg Gardens in Paris, not far from the Rue Pierre Curie where she grew up in an academic family. Lying on a couch to take the strain off her neck, still feeling the effects of her wartime ordeal, she recalls that she was actually happy when she was finally deported from Montluc prison in Lyon to Ravensbruck, a concentration camp in Germany. "I was alone in Montluc, alone with the fear of being tortured again by Barbie and talking." She concedes that some of the pains in her neck, thumbs and wrists are due to age, but adds: "Most of the pains are from Barbie."

The Resistance could not have grown in the face of Gestapo and Vichy pressure without the tacit support of many French citizens who, unlike Mlle. Bauer, were not in the Resistance, but who silently aided it. "There weren't very many of us in the

Resistance, it's true, but what we did, we were able to do because we had outside help," says Lise Lesèvre. "Shopkeepers often didn't use their mailboxes, since the mailman would hand them their mail directly in the store. And they let us use their mailboxes, to drop our messages. And when the Germans learned of this, there was a heavy backlash against the shopkeepers. Also if the butchers had refused to accept our false ration tickets, we wouldn't have been able to feed the men who were in the *maquis* or who were living clandestinely in the city. There was a certain complicity by many of the people."

Raymond Aubrac relates a story of a train trip he made from Lyon to Grenoble, carrying 25 pounds of underground newspapers, when this discreet sympathy for the Resistance came to his aid. "The trains were very full at that time, since there were few trains and people had to travel a lot," Aubrac remembers. "So I settled in as I was accustomed to, with the suitcase in a compartment while I stayed in the corridor. When I got to the station at Grenoble, the suitcase was gone, stolen. But even so, I later learned that the newspapers were distributed." Aubrac believes that when the thief found what the bag contained, he abandoned it. It was then most likely found by a railroad worker who made sure the papers went into the underground distribution channels.

Lise Lesèvre recalls the case of a courageous woman imprisoned by the Germans who modestly felt she had done little to help the Resistance. She met the young peasant girl in one of the concentration camps to which Lesèvre was sent following her interrogation in Lyon. "I said, 'Why are you here? What did you do?' And she said, 'I didn't do anything.' So I said, 'That's a pity, but why were you arrested?' She said, 'The doctor in the area hid American and English pilots who parachuted into the region, and when he didn't have any room for them, he brought them to my house.' And she said she hadn't done anything!"

Ω

Barbie had made the Ecole de Santé a hated and feared edifice among those who resisted Nazi rule, but the grimy nineteenth century building was only half the closed universe of the Lyon Gestapo. The Ecole was where the paperwork was done, and as the prisoners were led handcuffed down its corridors they could see into the offices, hear the murmur of German and French voices and the clacking of typewriters that meant the SS was busily going about its work of political repression and control.

As one came up the stairs from the basement, there was even a brief glimpse of the outside world. A door was there, leading into the courtyard, and outside to the Avenue Berthelot and freedom. But an attempt to flee would have been suicidal; there was always a soldier in the doorway with a machine gun. Each evening a truck pulled into the courtyard of the Ecole, backed up to that door, and loaded the prisoners for transport to Montluc, the Gestapo prison which was the second half of Barbie's empire.

Montluc was located near the railroad tracks on the east side of Lyon, and the prisoners could catch a glimpse of the city during the five- to ten-minute drive across town before the truck was within the stone walls. Built early in the nineteenth century, Fort Montluc had largely fallen into disuse by the time the Second World War broke out, when it was occupied by just one company of soldiers. But the prison suited the needs of the Gestapo, which cared little that it had no plumbing and barely any ventilation. Comfort was not a consideration; Montluc could hold many bodies, and the security was excellent. Of the 10,000 who passed through its gates during the war, only one—a Resistance leader—escaped.

The prison was set on approximately four acres of land enclosed by a high cement wall. After entering the gate, one went straight toward the main prison, a three-story building that contained about 120 cells ranged along the back and front walls. Along the right side of this central building was another one-story "refectory," which held about 50 prisoners. Behind the main prison was a one-story building that had been a storehouse before the war, but that now housed Jewish prisoners.

Montluc was horribly overcrowded. A woman who spent months there before being deported to Ravensbruck recalls that nine women had to live in a cell measuring only six by six feet. There were no toilets or running water, only a bucket in a corner of the cell. The worst of Montluc, say several former inmates, was its infestation by lice, bedbugs, fleas, mice, cockroaches. "The vermin!" one prisoner related after the war. "At Montluc the bedbugs made the nights unendurable and all rest impossible. That ravenous horde, as soon as darkness fell, dropped in bunches from the ceilings, the crevices in the walls, and did not stream back until daybreak." The prisoners mustered the courage to joke about it since they were unable to effectively defend themselves from what they called "le parachutage."

"I cannot sleep, I am smothering for lack of air," wrote another prisoner. "The beating of my heart is irregular. I am oppressed, I have palpitations. The vermin are devouring me, my body is covered with welts. The bedbugs, the lice and the fleas are so abundant that it isn't even worth taking the trouble to kill them. You never get rid of them. The toilet buckets, the bedclothes that have been used by so many people without ever being washed, the sweat of men given neither the time nor the means to wash themselves make the air unbreathable."

The prisoners would be awakened at 7:00 A.M. Their first chore was to file outside with their toilet buckets, which they emptied into a cistern to the right of the main gate. Only in the morning could prisoners file into a small wash shed that accommodated six people at a time. There was barely enough time to wash one's face, let alone the body, and there was never sufficient time to wash clothes.

Following the morning toilet, prisoners were given 20 minutes for exercise, to walk around in the courtyard between the main building and the barracks where the Jewish prisoners were held. Prisoners were then returned to their cells, where they received their ration of food for the day: a lump of bread made from potatoes, a slice of sausage, a thin soup made from green vegetables. The diet amounted to between 800 and 1,000 calories, less than half the daily adult requirement.

Survivors recall that the living conditions of the Jewish prisoners were the worst in Montluc. Resistance organizer Christian Pineau recalls seeing the Jewish prisoners packed into a shed just inside the prison's main gate. "There were up to two or three hundred of them in there at a time," Pineau remembers. "It was very small, and I don't know how they could stand it. They seemed stupified, clinging to their children and their baggage. It was terribly sad.

"Among us there was a certain realization that we couldn't

reproach the Germans for having arrested us, we couldn't reproach them for having deported us. It was war. Whereas with the Jews, it was different. We had the impression they hadn't done anything, so it was an act of total cowardice by the SS, pure racial hatred and a crime against humanity.

"One time I saw a terrible thing. I saw a little boy of about four years come out, all alone, to go to the toilet. And I could see the guard who was accompanying him, with his finger on the trigger. And I thought, if that child is afraid and runs, the guard is going to shoot." The child made it safely back to the Jews' barracks, but the image continued to haunt Pineau.

Life in Montluc was a constant hardship, but the anguish of not knowing what was ahead was worse for many prisoners. "In the morning when you woke up you immediately felt relieved; you had one more day," says Mario Blardone, who was imprisoned there by Barbie before his deportation to Buchenwald. The German military tribunal based at Montluc handed out death sentences based on the Gestapo's "evidence," and executions were carried out in the prison courtyard by a firing squad. Other times, groups of prisoners were simply loaded onto trucks and driven away to be executed at a country roadside.

The worst time of the day was the early morning when the guards read off the *appelles*, or rollcalls. There were three kinds of *appelles*: with baggage, without baggage, and interrogation. Interrogation meant a trip to the Ecole de Santé and painful questioning at the hands of Barbie and his men. The *appelle* "with baggage" meant deportation. While no one was sure what lay at the other end of the line, it was mistakenly considered to be an improvement over Montluc. Finally there was the *appelle* "without baggage." All knew that this meant the firing squad.

The *appelle* "without baggage" usually came at four or five in the morning; hardly anyone slept through it. The condemned would file out under German guard. Several minutes later those still inside would hear the "Marseillaise", or "Le Chant du Départ," the Song of Departure, being sung in the courtyard, and raise their voices in unison. A few minutes later the rattle of a machine gun would resound through the courtyard and the prison halls, and it would be over. The next morning prisoners would lie on their bunks or their spot on the floor listening for the sound of their own names when the guard began the *appelle* "without baggage," Klaus Barbie's sentence of death.

III

THE COLLABORATORS

FROM THE OUTSET, BARBIE AND HIS EINSATZKOMMANDO
proved devastatingly effective against the French Resistance. But
the conflict between the Gestapo and the loyal French in the Lyon
region was not a simple war of competing enemy forces. There was
a third player on the scene, a Nazi ally who, in many ways, was
more dangerous to the Resistance cause than the Gestapo. It was
the French collaborator, who sometimes infiltrated Resistance
ranks to betray another Frenchman, other times denounced his
neighbors, all the while proudly professing allegiance to the new,
fascist France. Without the assistance of these Frenchmen, the
Obersturmführer would have made only marginal inroads against
the insurgents. *La collaboration* was a particularly inglorious chapter
in French history, one that made Klaus Barbie possible.

Betrayal of one Frenchman by another was Barbie's most
potent weapon in his battle against the Resistance. *"On m'a vendu,"*
was the angry complaint of many prisoners at the Ecole de Santé. *I
was sold.* Collaboration began as a deliberate national political

policy enunciated by France's wartime leaders in Vichy, but it resulted in countless individual acts of ignominy. As a policeman, Barbie understood the value of an informer; as a Nazi, he was a skillful corrupter who seized upon the unhealthy impulses within the French national soul to help carry out his missions.

Lise Lesèvre was one Resistance fighter who personally observed Klaus Barbie savor his role as suborner of the French. During the nineteen days of her torture by Barbie in the Ecole de Santé, Lesèvre was a witness to the spectacle of Frenchmen coming to sell each other. She did not observe it by chance, but because Barbie wanted her to see the eagerness with which her countrymen betrayed the Resistance fighters.

Lesèvre recalls one telling incident in which Barbie and his aides were interrogating two men being transferred from St. Paul Prison to Montluc. To save themselves from further punishment, they gave the Gestapo chief the addresses of Jews living clandestinely in the Lyon suburbs. As they were being beaten, the men promised Barbie they would lead him to other addresses they could not remember.

During the interrogation, Mme. Lesèvre had been off in a corner of the room awaiting her turn. She noticed a well-dressed man enter Barbie's office and initially concluded that he was German—until he began to speak to Barbie in perfect unaccented French. He and Barbie shook hands, then the Gestapo leader filled out a slip which he handed to the Frenchman. Barbie stared directly at Lesèvre as he announced in French, in a loud, clear voice, "The pay office is that way."

The man walked out slowly, carefully examining the pay voucher in his hands, until he stopped. "Is there something wrong, monsieur?" Barbie asked.

"Excuse me," the Frenchman answered. "But there were two of them."

La délation, the denunciation of Frenchmen fighting the Nazis or Vichy, was a common phenonemon throughout wartime France as people informed on their neighbors with extraordinary frequency, and for a variety of reasons. Some truly believed they were serving their country, but others betrayed the Resistance for profit, or for spite, in revenge for personal grievances.

There was no shortage of French informers. For Barbie, the problem was how to best handle the massive flow of information being offered by collaborators. "I used a clever method at the beginning," he was later to boast. "I ordered that the denunciations that came to us should be rigorously selected. Denunciations by Frenchmen of the Resistance activities were pouring in. My criteria excluded anonymous denunciations. The true informer had to personally provide me with facts and precise information. That way, I was able to come to know them well and induce them to collaborate with us."

The system was perfected as the war continued. At first, informers presented themselves at the Sicherheitsdienst, Amt VI of the SS, operated by Obersturmführer August Moritz, and from there, were sent to the appropriate service of the SS. But after notices were placed in newspapers by the SS promising rewards to informers, the office on the Boulevard des Belges in the northern part of Lyon was so besieged with French informers that the SS could not handle the flow. In the beginning of 1944, a special information bureau—headed by a Frenchman named André Jacquin, whose pseudonym, "Milneuf," was an alliteration of his SS serial number—was created in the Ecole de Santé to receive informers, interview them and transmit the information to the appropriate office.

One of Jacquin's underlings later described the system: "My office was just inside the Ecole de Santé, on the left, under the portico. I received an enormous number of people, up to 150 a day. I took their declarations on a typewriter, in triplicate. The informers didn't sign the depositions, but their names and addresses were mentioned in the reports."

Not all informants walked through the door of the Ecole de Santé; some were personally cultivated by members of Barbie's Gestapo staff to perform their onerous task. Simone Lagrange, then only 13, learned the dangers of trust in wartime France when her family was arrested in 1944, on June 6, the day of the Allied landing in Normandy. An SS officer, came to the door of the Kaddouche home to place Simone her mother and father under arrest. Minutes before, a neighbor, a young woman, Jeanne, had come to visit the Kaddouche family, weeping to Simone's mother,

Rachel, that her husband had been arrested by the Gestapo. During the torture, she claimed, his fingernails had been pulled out. Her parents had expressed their sympathy for the young woman, but young Simone was intuitively distrustful of the French woman. "She seemed false," says Lagrange, who later endured beatings by Barbie, suffered imprisonment at Auschwitz and survived. "I wanted to tell her to get out."

Simone's intuition soon proved correct. The doorbell rang once more, but this time Simone found the SS officer waiting. As her father came to the door, the German drew his revolver and took all three members of the Kaddouche family into custody. It was apparent that Lagrange and her parents had been betrayed. When the SS officer entered the home Jeanne rushed to him, embracing and kissing him. "I told you that you could arrest them tonight," she said jubilantly.

Lagrange, whose parents died in German death camps, later learned that Jeanne had served as a productive informer for the Lyon Gestapo. "She had become the girlfriend of an SS officer and she was paid money if she turned people in," Lagrange recalls. "She denounced her husband and her brother-in-law as well. She had no shame." After the war Jeanne was tried, convicted, and sentenced to three years in prison; but she served only three months before being freed. "It hardly cost her anything," Lagrange bitterly concludes.

Ω

French informers were of great value to Barbie and the Gestapo, but perhaps the most tragic, and effective, type of collaborator was the Resistance fighter who, under the threat or pain of torture, succumbed to Barbie and "turned." Paid informers could supply Barbie with valuable information, but the best sources of information were those already in the Resistance networks. Barbie's greatest coup was to turn a Resistance member and make a collaborator out of a patriot.

Torture was his main instrument, but as Mario Blardone learned, Barbie had other inducements as well. One day Barbie placed a sheet of paper in front of Blardone and instructed him to sign. The prisoner examined the sheet, but there was nothing written on it.

"What am I signing?" Blardone asked. "There's nothing here."

"Go ahead," Barbie urged Blardone. "Sign it. And come work for me."

The Gestapo lieutenant then placed a substantial pile of franc notes in front of him, along with a pistol and a Gestapo identification card, a passport to freedom. "Everything you need," Barbie told Blardone. "Sign and you'll be out of here working for me." Barbie then had a sandwich and a beer brought in for Blardone, and when the prisoner had finished, he offered him a cigarette and lit it.

"That was Barbie's system," said Blardone. "He had his soft side and his hard side. He told me, '*Voilà*, you sign, there's your Gestapo identification card. We put on your photo and you walk out of here a free man."

Blardone refused and continued to resist the beatings, but not every Resistance fighter had his level of endurance. Within the walls of the Ecole de Santé and Montluc, Resistance members knew that they could no longer trust each other. Barbie's torture and the hope of personal survival had destroyed their bond. "When I was arrested, there were two guys in there who had been arrested fifteen days before I was," Blardone relates. "The only order I gave them was, 'You don't know me.' And they had every interest in not knowing me. The risk you ran when you were arrested was that you had a colleague who knew about your activities and caved in. Then you were in trouble. It was because of this that we were distrustful. We didn't even talk to each other."

It was a cruel but common practice, Blardone explains, for the Gestapo to place a "turned" Resistance member in a cell with one who had not yet given his torturers any information. The informer would then engage the other prisoner in conversation, trying to elicit incriminating information. Such Nazi plants were called "sheep."

"Even in the cells at Montluc they had 'sheep,'" says Blardone. "You were automatically suspicious, even with buddies you were sure of. You didn't talk. There was suspicion among us, even among those who had been close friends in the Resistance."

Barbie usually accomplished his "turning" through torture, but if the prisoner resisted, there were other, more subtle, ways to bring *résistants* over to the German side. A French collaborator condemned to death after the war told investigators one method used by the Gestapo chief. "Barbie was incredibly effective," the collaborator testified. "Several times, he freed *résistants* even though he hadn't gotten anything out of them. It was done just to compromise them. If a man was released by the Gestapo it was usually because he had made a deal. Rejected by his friends in the underground, the guy became easy game for Barbie's recruiting. Several *résistants* were turned that way."

Barbie had succeeded in sowing distrust even within the heart of the French Resistance, and forty years later it would remain one of his most bitter legacies. The French could accept that a Nazi had tortured and murdered; it was more difficult to believe that many of their own countrymen had become traitors. "There was treason in many networks, unfortunately, and it was Frenchmen who did it," says Blardone. "If the Germans hadn't had Frenchmen to help them, they might never have captured so many important *résistants*. Now, in the history of the Resistance, that's coming out. But before, no one dared speak of it. We were so traumatized by having been betrayed by Frenchmen."

Ω

Ordinary Frenchmen participated in the collaboration, but it was the leaders of French wartime society who provided a model for traitorous political behavior. "The main person responsible for the success of the Gestapo was Marshal Pétain," says Resistance leader Raymond Aubrac. "Without the cooperation of the French authorities, the Nazis could never have exerted the control they did. The efficiency of the Gestapo was tied to its French agents—the Milice, the Vichy authorities, the police, and those Frenchmen who denounced other Frenchmen."

It has been estimated that a total of 400,000 Frenchmen were involved in the French Resistance, a liberal estimate which accounts for only two percent of the French population. Arraigned against them in all of France were only 2,200 German Gestapo agents. It would have been a totally insufficient force if the Gestapo had not been augmented by 4,000 French Gestapo members and a 10,000-strong paramilitary army of the Vichy Milice, which had another 30,000 members.

The assistance given to Germany in quashing opposition to the occupation led directly from the course that Marshal Pétain decided upon when he first met with Adolf Hitler and announced, on October 31, 1940, that "it is with honor and to maintain French unity...in the framework of a constructive activity in the new European order, that I enter today in the way of collaboration."

To Frenchmen in 1940, collaboration simply meant "cooperation" with the conqueror. If they were uneasy about the policy, their fears were lost in the enthusiasm with which France greeted the leadership of Pétain, the World War I hero of Verdun, who left semi-retirement in an attempt to resurrect France after the humiliating 1940 German assault. Immense crowds greeted Pétain as he toured the major cities of his shrunken France, now limited to the Unoccupied Zone in the south. Young girls handed him flowers as schoolchildren sang, *"Maréchal, Nous voila!"*

Pétain had launched a National Revolution aimed at restoring France to her former glory. *Patrie, Famille, Travaille,* became the slogan of the New Order, one which insisted that *la nation* had gone soft, corrupted by easy living, low moral standards, and leftist politics. A renewal, based on friendship with the Nazis, was necessary.

Pétain was the symbolic figurehead whose "patriotism" gave respectability to the Vichy policy of collaboration with the German conqueror. But Pierre Laval, whose personal politics were a strange amalgam of base opportunism and misguided pacifism, was to outdo *le Maréchal* in cooperating with the Nazis. Having decided that Germany was unopposable, Laval shocked the nation and assured his own execution after the war when on June 22, 1942, he announced in a radio broadcast: "I wish for the victory of Germany, for without it, communism will take over Europe."

In the opening days of the war, Pétain found an ally in the Catholic Church, which saw a renewed influence for itself within the structure of a New France which eschewed the secularism of the old democratic administrations. It mattered little that Pétain himself was an infrequent churchgoer and a reputed libertine; he had shown the church the appropriate deference and presented it with an opportunity to share power.

In Lyon, Pierre Cardinal Gerlier, the Primate of the Gauls and spiritual leader of France's Catholics, was one of Pétain's most enthusiastic supporters. Gerlier, who saw the National Revolution as the pathway to national salvation, even rationalized the defeat: "If we had remained victorious, we would probably have remained the prisoners of our errors. Through being secularized, France was in danger of death."

Gerlier—who would later prove surprisingly heroic in his defense of the Jews—was unequivocal in his enthusiasm for Pétain. At a reception in Lyon on November 16, 1940, he told *le Maréchal*, "France needed someone to lead her to her eternal destiny. God allowed that you be there." Then in words that would be held against him for many years, Gerlier continued, "Have you noticed, *Monsieur le Maréchal*, that the vibrant cries of the crowd...have become often mixed in two shouts: '*Vive Pétain! Vive la France!*' Two shouts? But no, because only one is required, for Pétain is France and France, today, is Pétain!"

This effort at national revival was the least destructive of Vichy's programs. Far more insidious was the search for scapegoats for the 1940 defeat, a propaganda campaign which encouraged the worst aspects of the French character; xenophobia and anti-Semitism, traits that had been partially submerged in democratic France. The left had weakened France's resolve and military force, Vichy alleged. A Fifth Column had been at work, sabotaging even before the attack, ensuring that France was incapable of defending herself. Blame was placed on the Popular Front, a coalition of left-wing parties that had held power briefly in the mid-1930s under socialist Prime Minister Léon Blum, a Jew. In this climate, anti-Semitic legislation was passed by Vichy in the autumn of 1940 and anti-Jewish abuse filled the pages of the right-wing Parisian press. That the Jews were considered to be enemies of Nazi Germany, France's invader, seemed not to matter.

Those who rejected the Armistice of June 1940, represented mainly by de Gaulle, had retreated to England, the United States and, in the case of some French communist leaders, to Moscow. France quickly became estranged from its former ally across the Channel, an attitude which turned into open hostility in July 1940 after the British Navy conducted a surprise attack on the French fleet anchored at Mers-el-Kebir in Algeria. The British wanted to prevent the fleet from falling into German hands, but over 1,200 French sailors died in the assault.

Vichy saw the French Resistance, which was linked to de Gaulle and the British, as a subversive force that challenged its legitimacy and had to be destroyed. Collaboration by French citizens with the Germans, including informing the Gestapo of Resistance activities, would be interpreted as a patriotic act, the government declared. "A certain number of people continued to believe for a long time that their duty as Frenchmen was to help the Germans," recalls Raymond Aubrac. "That was what Marshal Pétain had told them. Those who fought against the Germans or the government were called bad Frenchmen, Jews, communists and terrorists. We lived in that atmosphere and people were affected by it."

Resistance fighter Anne Marie Bauer believes that a large segment of the French population held honorable intentions but was confused by the propaganda and the ambiguous politics of wartime France. "To show you how public opinion was fooled by Vichy, I had a room in the home of a woman who was very *Pétainiste*, yet she always helped me in working for the Resistance," Mlle. Bauer relates. "When I was arrested she and her aunt said novenas for me, and she would never have turned me in. Many *Pétainistes* believed that de Gaulle was a little with Pétain. They couldn't imagine that Pétain would betray France as he did."

Ω

When Barbie arrived in Lyon in late 1942 after the reoccupation he found the area well prepared for collaboration. Vichy had already commissioned paramilitary groups to support its power base, but these Frenchmen were to serve Barbie and the Gestapo with equal loyalty. This phase of the collaboration began with a relatively innocuous organization called the Légion Française des Combattants, which, in August 1940, began recruiting war veterans to the banner of Marshal Pétain. On one level, the *légionnaires* were meant to function as a link between Pétain and the French people, but the Légion was designed to serve as a propaganda tool for Vichy as well. Members pledged: "I swear to consecrate all my force to the Country, the Family and to Work," echoing the motto of the National Revolution.

Their role was further clarified in February 1941 when Vichy gave instructions that members provide "light and assistance" to the Vichy powers "in everything that concerns the application of the principles of the National Revolution." More ominously, they were told, they should be "cadres of instruction, leadership and, if necessary, control." As the true function of the Légion as a political device became clear, resignations came pouring in. In Lyon, the Légion drew Resistance opposition and Légion offices were bombed on seven occasions between October 1942 and November 1943.

The Légion had proven to be a disaster politically, but Vichy moved forward rather than retreat. In the summer of 1942 Vichy's secretary general for the maintenance of order, Joseph Darnand, formed the Service d'Ordre Légionnaire, which advanced the Vichy paramilitary strategy one step further. The SOL had a 20-point doctrine. It was against, among other evils, "individualism, anarchy, egalitarianism, useless freedoms, international capitalism, Gaullist dissidence, bolshevism, Jewish leprosy, and pagan Freemasonry."

SOL members, who wore a khaki uniform with a black tie and a beret, were directed to strike at those perpetrating antigovernment propaganda, to repress dissent and assure the functioning of public services. It was an obvious invitation to abuse, not unlike that afforded Hitler's brown-shirted SA storm troopers in Germany in the 1930s. A more elite unit, the Groupes Mobiles de Reserve, was also constituted by Vichy. Organized along stricter military lines and armed, the Groupes Mobiles in their navy blue uniforms with a lion's head insignia on the left arm, were intended for use against public disturbances and Resistance activities.

The SOL and the Groupes Mobiles were soon to be put to use in Lyon. On July 12, 1942, an investiture ceremony was held for the newly created SOL in Lyon's Place des Terreaux. On that Sunday morning, 4,500 SOL members—2,000 of them from the Rhône department of which Lyon was the regional capital—gathered in formation on the plaza. The Vichy official who addressed them urged these new shock troops to become the "strong, supple and sure instrument" of the Vichy regime. Before a torch parade closed the ceremony, he told the people of Lyon, "We are resolved: France will rise! *Vive le Maréchal! Vive la France!*"

Two days later, these men proved their worth to Vichy. On a call from the Resistance, a crowd estimated at 30,000 turned out in the Place des Terreaux on Bastille Day. Waving banners against Hitler and Laval and in support of England, the crowd marched south through the city, passing the Place Bellecour and the Place Carnot to arrive at the Hotel Terminus, which was then the head-quarters of the German Armistice Commission, the unseen repre-sentative of the conqueror. As flowers were being laid before the Monument of the Republic in the Place Carnot, the Vichy paramili-tary troops attacked, viciously assaulting the demonstrators. Hundreds were arrested and put in the Saint Joseph prison, later to be deported by the Germans to concentration camps.

Vichy had still further plans for repression. On January 5, 1943, Pétain announced the creation of la Milice, the Militia, whose members had to be of French birth, non-Jewish and free of past membership in such societies as the Freemasons. Apparently, a criminal record was not an impediment to enlistment. The group was headed by Joseph Darnand, but the Milice was also intended to serve the personal political ambitions of Pierre Laval, who had been in eclipse between December 1940 and April 1942 but had returned to power in Vichy with German backing to assume the post of prime minister.

In Lyon, a constitutive assembly of the Milice was held on February 28, 1943, at the Palais d'Hiver, where 2,000 people looked on as Lyon's 700 Milice members were called into service. In April, a 47-year-old former naval officer named Joseph Lecussan took command of the Lyon contingent, which was to gain a reputation for brutality, lawlessness and indiscriminate assassina-tion. They established offices in several locations in Lyon, in the headquarters of the Lyon newspaper *Le Progrès*, which closed on November 11, 1942, rather than submit to German occupation press controls.

"In the beginning the Milice was raised to defend the Vichy regime against the Resistance," explains historian Marcel Ruby. "Laval thought he could use the Milice for his personal power, but it slid out of his grasp and the Milice no longer served Vichy but the Gestapo. Eventually the Milice became an army of mercenaries in the service of the Gestapo. They were paid by the Germans, they killed for the Germans. They had a lot of advantages, not only financial. They had gasoline, food, women, anything they wanted, without a problem. And they had arms, too, of course.

"Two kinds of people were recruited into the Milice," Ruby explained in his Paris apartment. "There was a small minority of men, young and from the extreme right, who really believed they had to fight bolshevism to save the western, Christian values that bolshevism was going to destroy. The rest were either those who came into the Milice because they were well paid or ate well, and so on, or just plain trash, people from the underworld, bandits, gangsters, who saw that they could operate in total security."

In July 1944 a Lyon *milicien* named Jean Reynaudon sent a letter to national director Joseph Darnand confirming their criminal effort on behalf of Vichy. "In Lozanne, Rhône, some Jews gave us 600,000 francs. This money was given to our chief, as well as some cigarettes and other merchandise. He gave us 200,000 francs for our group's expenses...At Sainte-Foy-Les-Lyon, we seized 3 million francs worth of merchandise from a Jew. We executed him in retaliation for the assassination of Philippe Henriot [Vichy's minister of information, killed in Paris on June 27, 1944]." Reynaudon concluded: "*Voilà*, chief, a glimpse of part of our activity since the creation of our team. I think we have done our duty. So why do people treat us now like the lowliest of cowards?"

Though Lecussan was the first chief of the Lyon Milice, the most notorious of its leaders would be Paul Touvier. He began his career in the service of Vichy in the spring of 1942, when he took a post as an SOL official in the region of Chambéry, a city to the east of Lyon. Twenty-seven-year-old Touvier led his Milice shock troops against Gaullist sympathizers in his area so forcefully that he was once arrested by the Vichy police for his excesses, only to be released through the intervention of higher political powers. Upon the formation of the Milice in January 1943, he became its intelligence chief for the Savoie region. By the autumn of 1943 he had become the second-in-command of the Lyon Milice.

Touvier organized a team of 30 other activists to work against the Resistance, but more particularly against the Jews. He allegedly was involved in the taking of hostages who were subsequently executed by the Germans in reprisal for the assassination of Vichy propaganda official Philippe Henriot in Paris. Like other Milice members, Touvier enriched himself by seizing the belongings of Jews in Lyon, an activity that provoked dissension between rival factions of the Lyon Milice.

According to a complaint later filed in the Lyon court, the Milice intelligence group headed by Touvier was implicated in the January 1944 assassination of Victor Basch, a Jew who was the president of the League for the Rights of Man. Basch, 80, and his wife were arrested on January 10 in the suburb of Caluire. Lecussan, who also took part in the abduction, later testified that "it was decided Basch was too old to arrest, so we decided to execute him." The Milice detachment took Basch and his wife out on an isolated country road and murdered them.

Perhaps even more violent and lawless than the Milice was the paramilitary arm of the Parti Populaire Français, founded in 1936 amid the turmoil of the Third Republic by the right-wing politician Jacques Doriot. The party salute of the PPF was the raised clenched fist, although many members preferred the Nazi salute. Before turning to the extreme right, Doriot had been a leftist. He had received training in Moscow and was one of the most prominent French communists of his time. In 1931, he became the Communist mayor of the Paris suburb of of Saint-Denis, but an ideological disagreement set the French Communist party against him, and at the party congress of 1934 he was drummed out.

From then on, Doriot was a fervent anti-communist, a dedicated fascist whose striking weapon was the PPF, a working class anti-communist group not unlike Hitler's National Socialist Party. With the rise of Vichy, Doriot began to gain in power, and in October 1940 he launched a fascist newspaper in Paris, *Le Cri du Peuple*. After the German invasion of Russia in June 1941, Doriot enlisted in the Légion des Volontaires Français, an anti-Soviet unit that was dispatched by the Germans to the Russian front. He returned to France in 1942 to recruit more Frenchmen into his Légion.

The life pattern of Francis André, the Lyon leader of the PPF, was remarkably similar to that of Doriot. Born Charles Francis André to a family of grain merchants in Lyon, his first political involvement came in 1933 when he joined the French Communist party. But André broke away from the communists and within months had gravitated to the extreme right. He joined the PPF in April 1937 and in the years between then and the war he took part in the often violent struggle between the French left and right, organizing strike-breaking activities throughout France's southeast region.

In 1939 he attempted to enlist in the French Army but was rejected, possibly because of the accident that had deformed his jaw and earned him the nickname "Gueule Tordue." Instead, André secured a position in French intelligence, the Deuxième Bureau, which he held until the war. After the defeat, André began to drift through the right-wing and fascist political milieu of Vichy.

After a stint as propaganda director for the Union National de Travail, Vichy's labor organ, André followed Doriot into the Légion des Volontaires Contre le Bolshevism in 1941. Sent to the Russian front, André rapidly became disillusioned when his unit was assigned to cover the German rear, where the French fascist troops were prey to Soviet partisan attacks. André returned to France in May 1942, and was soon back into Vichy politics, forming anti-Resistance teams drawn from PPF members. His groups were particularly aimed at the Franc Tireurs et Partisans, a French communist Resistance group separate from the Franc-Tireurs begun in Lyon by Jean-Pierre Lévy. After the war an SS officer named Ernst Floreck described the PPF operation in Lyon. According to him, André was "very brutal with prisoners. He often made arrests against formal orders. The service received numerous complaints of thefts, looting, murders."

Although the SS intelligence department was André's first Lyon contact, the PPF leader had already bypassed the local bureaucracy and made contacts with higher-ups in Paris through the PPF political bureau in Paris. It had been agreed with the highest-ranking German police official in France, Hoherer SS- und Polizeiführer Carl Albrecht Oberg, that any spoils obtained from the PPF's operations would be retained by André's party. Half would remain with André and his men, half would go to the PPF's Paris office. André preferred this arrangement to the 200,000 francs a month the Germans first offered.

In Lyon, André was soon dealing not only with SS intelligence, but with Barbie as well. It was a natural arrangement since Barbie's unit was the most active element of the SS forces in Lyon. André's private army of nearly 200 men was made up of PPF members from the Lyon region, from the *départements* of Drôme, Isère and Ardèche, and from Paris. André also worked with members of the intelligence division of the Milice, as well as a few "specialists" in Jewish affairs.

The Germans gave André permission for his PPF men to carry arms and freely operate vehicles, and in return, André made one concession to the Germans. A Gestapo officer would be present at all executions carried out by the PPF; but with time, even this formality would be bypassed.

Ω

This was the array of collaborationist forces Barbie found at his disposal by early 1943, just as he was launching his first serious strikes against the Resistance and the Jews of Lyon. Of all the groups pledged to Vichy, the Lyonnais particularly despised the Milice. "When they began to recruit the Milice, people said, 'All the hoodlums are becoming *miliciens*, and think they are someone important," says Anne Marie Bauer. "They were hated, detested because they worked for the Germans. The *miliciens* were very poorly regarded; they were Frenchmen who betrayed."

Barbie formed particularly close links with André's PPF. The relationship suited both parties; André liked the near-absolute freedom he enjoyed working within the Gestapo at the Ecole de Santé. From Barbie's vantage point, the PPF were not restrained by any formal links with Vichy and were more ruthless than most other collaborators.

These French collaborators who had joined the Nazi anti-Resistance campaign often seemed to treat their own countrymen even more viciously than the Germans. Lise Lesèvre recalls that after Barbie had given her his share of punishment in one torture session, he called in Francis André to take over. As he worked on Lesèvre, the French fascist slaked his thirst with a mixture of beer and cognac. When another French agent offered to relieve him, André brushed him aside. "You ask the questions; I'll hit."

The PPF worked so intimately with the German Gestapo that it came to be known as the "French Gestapo." But it had its own program of free-lance terror as well; in fact, the group had formed an assassination squad to carry out its condoned brutality. By then André was working with Amt VI of the SS, the Sicherheitsdienst intelligence service which had given the PPF a house on the Avenue Leclerc for its headquarters and was to preside over their reprisal executions to give them a facade of legality.

On November 13, 1943, a PPF tract was distributed in the streets of Lyon, headlined: "TERROR FOR TERROR." The text read: "Attacks are on the rise. They are assassinating in the city, raiding in the countryside, trying to starve us by burning the harvests. We say enough. Since the public authorities are powerless, a group neither subject to Germany nor bought by Anglo-American Jewish capitalism, a group of Frenchmen who want France to rise, will answer blows with blows.

"For every national assassinated, a terrorist leader will be executed," the tract concluded. It was signed, "Mouvement National Anti-Terroriste." Included was the information that the MNAT, a group formed by Francis André from PPF volunteers, had already claimed its first victim, a Dr. Jean Long, suspected of contact with Resistance elements. The PPF's intelligence branch had learned that Long was in contact with a certain Philippe, a former Socialist deputy in the French National Assembly who was in exile in London, and had decided to use Long to set an example.

At 10 P.M. on the night of October 22, PPF member Jean Gargaro and two officers went to Long's home, where the Germans demanded that Long accompany them. Instead of taking Long to the Nazi headquarters, the three men drove him out to a remote spot in the eastern suburb of Bron. They executed him there, then dumped the body, to which they had attached a note: "Terror against terror. This man paid with his life for the murder of a national."

In Gargaro, André and other such Frenchmen who collaborated with the Nazis in occupying their homeland, Barbie saw kindred spirits. "Many of the French collaborated with us in the repression; for us they were friends, colleagues," Barbie later explained. "As a general rule, the French personnel of my commando were very faithful and dedicated to Germany. We were waging a common struggle."

THE JEWS OF LYON

THE WINTER SUN WAS SETTING QUICKLY OVER THE SAÔNE River on a Friday evening in December. Shadows were gathering up the city of Lyon into another blacked-out occupation night as a few score Jews observed the arrival of their Sabbath in the Great Synagogue of Lyon on the Quai Tilsitt running along the east bank of the river. Inside the temple the moment was approaching for the Canticle of Leho Dodi, the song of welcome for the Sabbath, the recognition of the commencement of a day of rest and religious observation. Leading the prayers was Rabbi Jacob Kaplan. At his sign all turned around to symbolically greet the Sabbath, the bride of Israel, as it entered, and they intoned the words of the Leho Dodi: *"Boi chalo, boi chalo."* "Enter, bride; enter, bride."

The door swung open abruptly to admit not a beneficent spirit but a lone man carrying three grenades. He had come to kill, but he stopped in his tracks as he realized that a crowd of singing people was carefully following his every move. Hesitantly, he pulled the pins on the grenades, then hastily lobbed them onto the floor of the temple before fleeing out the door.

Kaplan saw three bursts of yellow flame leap up from the floor at the back of the temple and recoiled at the triple concussion that shook the building. "It seemed like someone was firing a machine gun," Kaplan, 88, the former Grand Rabbi of France, recalls in his Paris home. "After three explosions it stopped. We were waiting for a fourth, but it didn't come. I yelled, 'It's over!' to encourage the people. At first I thought no one was wounded, because no one cried. I said, 'Let us continue the prayer.' " Then a wave of shock swept through the congregation. At the back ten people lay wounded from the impact and shrapnel of the three grenades, but miraculously, no one was dead.

As the injured were treated and removed, those remaining quickly reconstructed what had happened. The sacrilegious interruption had been the work of the Lyon Milice, the shock troops of the Vichy government. As the service progressed inside the synagogue, the paramilitary hoodlums had burst through the iron grillwork street doors leading to an intermediary courtyard, waving their guns at the doorkeeper and holding him captive while they prepared a bloodbath for the congregants inside.

Some of the Milice stood guard at the outer entrance to prevent anyone raising an alarm while others cut the telephone lines. Then one of the Frenchmen crept forward armed with the grenades, assuming the job would come off as planned. No one was likely to notice him enter; the congregants would be facing the altar with their backs to him. He could simply toss his murderous weapons into the thick of the praying multitude without ever being seen.

But the would-be assassin was met not with the backs of unsuspecting victims, but by dozens of accusing eyes. Rabbi Kaplan, surrounded by mementoes of a lifetime of religious service in his study, recounts what he believes was an "act of providence." "Certainly he was a specialist," says Kaplan. "His intention, evidently, was to throw the grenades where there were the most people. He figured he could do it calmly, because usually people turn their backs to the door when they say their prayers."

But at just that moment the congregation was reciting the segment of the Leho Dodi in which it must suddenly turn around and face the door of the synagogue. The prayer lasts only 30 seconds, but that coincided exactly with the would-be assassin's arrival. "At the moment the assassin came in to throw the grenades, everyone in the synagogue was looking directly at him," Kaplan recalls. "And no one is afraid. It is he who is afraid to be recognized, because they can see his face. Instead of picking the best spots, he threw the grenades anywhere, just to get rid of them. If he had come a moment before or a moment after there would have been a massacre."

The way the Jews of the Quai Tilsitt congregation were spared that night was extraordinary, but given the times it was not unusual that an attempt had been made to murder them. Outside the doors of the synagogue a war was raging; all those sheltered within its walls knew that to be Jewish put one at special risk. They knew that many of their friends and relations were behind barbed wire, that others were rolling to the East packed in freezing cattle cars. They strongly suspected, although they did not yet know for certain, that annihilation awaited those who arrived at the dark terminus.

That a group of men who probably considered themselves Christian should resolve to massacre a group of defenseless Jews at prayer was totally consistent with the brutal norms of the era. The surprising thing about the attack on the Quai Tilsitt synagogue is that a synagogue was operating at all in occupied France on the date it took place: December 10, 1943.

France had been under German control for three and a half years, and both the Germans and the Vichy French had been herding the Jews of France into concentration camps for two and a half years. The first convoy of Jewish prisoners had left for Auschwitz from the Paris-suburban concentration camp of Drancy nearly two years before. Lyon had been occupied by the Germans and its Jews subject to the Gestapo's predations for over a year. Yet on a December evening at the end of 1943 the Jews of Lyon held a Sabbath service in the Great Synagogue of Lyon behind open doors.

Even the grenade attack did not close the synagogue. Not until six months later, when the Gestapo burst into a Saturday afternoon service and arrested all those in attendance, did France's highest Jewish authorities decide it was time for their remaining commu-

nity to go underground. They had endured far longer than anyone
might reasonably have expected. In the circumstance, it was evidence of immense courage, profound religious faith and—perhaps
—a strong measure of foolhardiness.

The continued operation of the Quai Tilsitt synagogue through
most of the war offered a symbol of continuity and fortitude for the
Jews of Lyon. As Rabbi Richard Wertenschlag, the current Chief
Rabbi of Lyon, points out four decades later: "There was a spiritual
resistance in the face of the enemy in which people came to pray
more than ever at the synagogue, in spite of the climate that
reigned."

But keeping the synagogue of Lyon open so late in the war also
reflected certain profound illusions particular to the Jews of France
—illusions that ultimately led to the destruction of many of them.
The functioning of the synagogue suggested that normal life could
continue despite the mortal threat facing the Jewish community.
The delusion was that Vichy officials would work to ensure that all
"patriotic" Frenchmen, Jews or Christians, could continue to live
in peace if they cooperated in the "National Revolution" that
depended on collaboration with the Germans. But behind this
comforting facade lay the reality of Jewish life in Lyon during the
occupation: a fugitive existence of paralyzing anxiety that frequently culminated in arrest, deportation and death.

Ω

It should have been clear to every Jew in Lyon that no one was
safe after the events of February 9, 1943, ten months before the
synagogue blasts erupted. That was the day Klaus Barbie's Einsatzkommando burst into the Lyon offices of the Union Générale des
Israélites de France, UGIF—the national Jewish relief organization
that served as a liason between the Jewish community and the
Vichy government—and opened the general offensive against the
Jews of Lyon.

One thought ran through Lea Rosen's mind as she climbed the
staircase of the building at 12 Rue St. Catherine in Lyon that
afternoon: Rabbi Bernard Schonberg had to be warned of the raid
the Gestapo planned to carry out the following day at his synagogue. A friend of her family, a French policeman, had told her
about the raid and she had run to the synagogue to give the

warning, only to be told that the rabbi was at the offices of UGIF, on the Rue St. Catherine. Lea was only 17 years old, but she knew the meaning of a Gestapo raid; her father was already in a concentration camp somewhere in France.

Opening the door to the UGIF's office, Lea immediately sensed that something was wrong. Three or four men in leather coats were standing in the entryway as she walked in. Beyond them a group of people stared intently at her with pained expressions on their faces. She did not realize they were trying to warn her away.

"I saw a lot of people that I didn't know and they were all gesturing at me as though to say, 'Get out, get out,' but I didn't understand," recalls Lea, who survived the war and still lives in Lyon. "They were telling me not to come in, but I didn't understand. How could I have known? Then, in German, the men told me, *'Komm hierein, komm hierein.'* When I saw that they were speaking German, I said I had the wrong floor, that I had come to look for a doctor for my mother, who was ill. But they made me come in and they closed the door."

Then she understood. As the Germans inspected her papers and noted the red-inked stamp of "Juive" across her French national identity card, she realized this was the trap she had been warned of. She stammered out the improvised excuse that she had been looking for a doctor's office in the building; she needed a physician for her mother, who was very ill. The Germans heard all this without listening to the small, frightened, red-haired girl. *"Ja, ja,"* they said as they pointed her into the office where the others were standing in a subdued crowd.

"What's going to happen to us?" she asked no one in particular in a low voice.

"This is the Gestapo," someone explained. "We're being arrested."

As the afternoon wore on Jews kept walking in the door to be met by the Gestapo, who took their wallets and purses and threw them onto a mounting pile on the floor. By 6:00 P.M., the hour at which the office normally would have closed, there were 87 Jews held prisoner on the Rue St. Catherine.

The Gestapo agents finally decided no more people would be climbing up the stairs to UGIF headquarters. They started to bring their prisoners down to the courtyard in small groups to load them onto trucks, starting with the men. An elderly man went into one corner of the room and faced the wall to murmur a prayer before he was led out the door.

Then Lea's turn came. Once again, the girl launched into her story, this time hysterical with fright as she explained that her mother was very sick. Who would take care of her if she didn't return home that night? "I told him that the next morning I would come wherever they wanted me to," Lea relates. "He told me, 'I don't understand French.' So I got up my courage and started to talk to him in German, partly because I knew a little and partly out of fear." The Gestapo officer listened to the story of the terrified young girl. "He told me that I could go now, then said, 'Come tomorrow to the Hotel Terminus, where the Gestapo is.' And he told me, 'We're going to let you all go, anyway."

She hardly heard this as she hurried down the stairs. Lea came up with a start as another German stepped into her way. She told him the other man had allowed her to leave. "That's impossible," he said. Lea held her breath while he whistled up to the UGIF landing and asked for confirmation. "*Ja, ja*," the other shouted down. "She can go." Lea walked out of the building, breaking into a run as soon as she was out of sight of the Germans, not stopping until she was on a streetcar bound for her neighborhood.

From that point on, Lea Rosen and her mother lived as fugitives, never spending more than a few nights in the same place, dependent on friends for shelter. She dyed her hair, obtained gentile identity papers, and stayed out of reach of the Gestapo for the rest of the war. But the ordeal has permanently marked her. "I'm still afraid," says Lea, a slight woman in her fifties who speaks of the days of the Nazi occupation in a timorous voice. "In my mind, there's always the idea that something will happen and I'll have to run away in the night."

Ω

Maier Weissman and 85 others seized at UGIF headquarters were still under Gestapo arrest. Weissman was an administrator of UGIF, one of those who provided food, housing, clothing, money and advice to the thousands of Jews—mostly foreign—who were crowding into Lyon looking for shelter from the tide of hatred washing across Europe. He was himself a refugee, twice displaced; first from Poland where anti-Semitism had limited his aspirations, then from the eastern French city of Nancy upon the arrival of the Germans.

His daughter, Sylvie Karlin, who still lives in Lyon where she is retired from the practice of pediatric medicine, recalls how their lives became wholly absorbed by his efforts to help foreign Jews arriving in Lyon. "There were Jews from Belgium and the Netherlands, especially, who came through Lyon and asked my father for help," says Karlin. "They came here because we lived not far from the Gare de Perrache. They'd drop off their bags, then go through the paperwork to get money and other necessities. At one point, we had a search by the French police. At the time I had a baby several months old, and I came back from a walk along the quai to find three or four policemen here. They were opening drawers and looking at papers. Well, we had money that had been sent from the United States, and there were a million francs in the cupboard. But it didn't belong to my father, it was for the Jewish organization, intended to help people who were destitute.

"I was afraid when I saw the police, afraid that they might find that money and ask where it came from. So with my baby in my arms, I said to the officers, 'Messieurs, excuse me, I have the little one, I'm going to put her down.' And I went to get the money and I put it in the bathroom, in the tub, and I covered it with the baby's dirty diapers. They went into the bathroom, but they didn't search very well.

"As far as all the luggage was concerned, I told them openly, 'These are people who are fleeing, who want to leave because they stand to go into concentration camps.' We ourselves were Jews, but we were French citizens, so we didn't think we had anything to worry about. I said, 'Look, I don't have the keys, but if you want to force the bags open, put yourselves in the place of those people. What would you do in their place?' The policemen were very humane and very correct." Soon after they left.

But with the arrival of the Gestapo—and Barbie—Weissman was as much at risk as the foreign Jews he aided. On the evening of the Rue St. Catherine raid, Sylvie became concerned when her father had not returned to their apartment at his usual hour of 6:30

or 7:00 P.M. Finally she dialed the number of UGIF only to hear a man's voice, in a hostile tone, come on the line.

"May I speak to Monsieur Weissman?" she asked, the small point of fear in her stomach expanding.

"*Es ist fertig mit den Leuten,*" the man on the other end of the line replied. *It is finished with these people.* The line went dead.

The next day she went to the prefecture for the Rhône *département*, where she talked to a top French official for the region. "We don't know anything," he told her. "We know there was a raid, but we don't even know where these people are." It was only several days later that she learned her father was in Montluc prison, and she heard nothing further until she received a postcard from him, mailed from the concentration camp at Drancy.

Sylvie Karlin saved the cards and letters from her father as they arrived, but they were more distressing than comforting. They recorded the deterioration of an elderly man caught in an inhumane system, trying to maintain his dignity and the fragile belief that a terrible mistake had been made. "Be courageous," he told his family in that first scrawled message from the camp outside Paris that already was the dispatch point for tens of thousands of Jews bound for annihilation. "Let us hope that we will see each other again soon in a free France." That was on February 13. His daughter received the card on February 20.

"Don't worry too much," he wrote from Drancy a few days later. "I am in good spirits and full of hope." But his stomach was empty. "You can send me a package of five kilos each week with bread, biscuits, butter, cheese, jam, etc. But no letters or tobacco. Hurry up and send some, because I urgently need them."

Desperation crept into the next letter. "Hurry with the packages," he wrote, "for one day counts a lot." On March 1 he received his first package and a card from his daughter that had been sent a week before. "The first of March was my first day of joy here. On that day I received your card. I read and re-read it without putting it down. Your first package brought me abundance. You are spoiling me, really."

Eight days later he wrote from another camp, this one called Beaune-la-Rolande, in the Loiret *département* southwest of Paris. "Before Drancy I waited in vain for your letters and packages, but I received nothing. Hurry, because I need it very much. I can't hold out much longer. I am hungry." He was slowly breaking. It was anguishing to Karlin, who was sending as many packages as she could only to learn they were not arriving at their destination.

"About my life here I will say nothing," he wrote from Beaune-la-Rolande. "You would not understand and that's for the best, too. On the other hand, I would love to know how things are with you. What is the weather like there? Has there been much fog? What are you all doing? Say hello to all my friends and tell them not to forget me. I so much want to take up a normal life again."

Sylvie Karlin received two letters after that, but the last one she sent to her father was returned to her unopened, stamped: "Return to Sender, Left for Unknown Destination." Maier Weissman, a naturalized French citizen, had been shipped via Drancy to the Sobibor death camp in his first homeland, Poland.

The fate of the other 85 persons arrested on the Rue St. Catherine—with only one exception—was similar. Back in Lyon, where UGIF was to resume its operations, the Gestapo filed reports with its central office in Paris recording the arrest and forward shipment of the prisoners. They were signed by Der Leiter des Einsatzkommandos, SS-Obersturmführer Klaus Barbie.

Ω

The Jewish community in Lyon counted only about 7,000 members in the early 1930s, but this number was swollen well before 1940 by large numbers of German and Austrian Jews fleeing Hitler's escalating anti-Semitic campaign. They were generally well received: there was room for growth in Lyon, and the Nazi outrages had created a climate of sympathy in much of France. But the German push through Belgium, the Netherlands and France in 1940 turned the movement of refugees into a torrent, as those who had found shelter in Amsterdam, Brussels or Paris fled south ahead of the German advance, aware of what awaited them if caught by Gestapo units working to the rear of the Wehrmacht.

As the Germans and the Vichy government began to apply anti-Semitic measures in the occupied north of France, more Jews began to slip across the Demarcation Line into the Unoccupied Zone. By the summer of 1942 it had become manifest that Vichy was aiding the Germans in the persecution of the Jews. This was true in the southern zone as well as in the north, but to a lesser degree. It was this difference in degree that ultimately made the difference between living or dying. As a result, Lyon was becoming not only the capital of the French Resistance, but the capital of French Jewry.

The arrest of Jews was not a new phenomenon in Lyon, but it had yet to reach the proportions it had long since attained in Paris. The first major operation against the Jews of Lyon was mounted in late August 1942, when the French authorities rounded up more than 4,000 foreign Jews living in the city and imprisoned them in a camp in Venissieux, in the suburbs. The heartrending spectacle of this sweep, beginning August 20, was described in a letter of protest sent to Marshal Pétain by a Lyon resident named Henri Cirange.

"Having fled from their mortal enemies to the sacred soil of asylum in France, these poor refugees have been delivered to their executioners, arrested in the middle of the night, hunted down like criminals, packed like cattle into locked wagons for several days before pitying witnesses who dared not even give them a glass of water." Families were broken up, Cirange told Pétain, and the refugees were transported to Venissieux in groups of men, women and children. Cirange castigated the French officials who had carried out this predatory commission: "People obey, submit, execute these repressive measures with docility, so great and penetrating is the fear of the invader."

French police and prefectural authorities had organized and carried out this first round-up of Jews in Lyon, but it had the side effect of mobilizing public opinion in the city against Vichy. One of the leading figures in this reaction was Cardinal Gerlier, the Archbishop of Lyon, who was to become a heroic, yet controversial, figure in the struggle to save Jewish lives.

For Gerlier's bravery to emerge, however, a catalyst was required. This was provided by Rabbi Kaplan—then a man in his forties—in a confrontation with Gerlier. Before that, the Jewish organizations had exhausted every means of opposition to the arrests. The Consistoire, the highest governing body of the Jewish faith in France, was then located in Lyon, having withdrawn from occupied Paris. When the arrests in Lyon began the council gave shelter to the foreign Jews in the Quai Tilsitt synagogue.

"The Consistoire opened the doors of the synagogue," recalls Kaplan, then a leading figure in the French rabbinate and destined to become the interim Grand Rabbi of France later in the war when his superior was forced into hiding. "They were lodged in the synagogue, they ate in the synagogue, they slept in the synagogue. And to justify their constant presence in the synagogue we said that because of the gravity of events, the Grand Rabbi of France had determined that it was necessary to pray night and day."

When the arrests of foreign Jews in Lyon reached massive proportions, Kaplan decided he needed help from the Catholic Church. In late August 1942, he went to visit Cardinal Gerlier to inform him of the Jewish plight. The cardinal told the young rabbi he would go to see the commissioner of police to try to stop the arrests in Lyon.

"That doesn't interest me," Kaplan told Gerlier. "I haven't come for the Jews of Lyon. I've come for all the Jews in the southern zone." Kaplan asked Gerlier to intervene directly with Pétain, who had received strong political backing from the Catholic leader. He and Pétain were on excellent terms, and Gerlier was obviously reluctant to criticize the French leader. At first, Gerlier attempted to minimize the threat. "They say they're taking these Jews to make them work in Poland," Gerlier told Kaplan. "They say they want to create a region for the Jews, and they're going to work there."

Kaplan shook his head. "No," he told the cardinal. "We know they're going to massacre them."

Gerlier offered to write a letter to Vichy, but Kaplan said that was not enough. "It's too important," he told Gerlier. "This involves the lives of thousands of people, so you must put yourself out."

"What good will it do for me to go?" Gerlier protested. "I can go to see him, because I am on good terms with the Maréchal, and he'll listen to me. But what can I do? Stay one day, two days, and after that I will have to leave, and then my enemies will destroy the work I've been able to do."

"Even so," Kaplan insisted, "you must go."

After an hour and a half of intense discussion, Gerlier relented. He would write a letter to Pétain immediately, then travel to Vichy. Four decades later, Kaplan still wonders at his own temerity. "It took a lot of audacity for a young rabbi to confront a cardinal, the head of the church, the Prelate of the Gauls, to demand that he take action."

The cardinal then took the step that would help counterbalance his earlier strong pro-Vichy stand. He sent a pastoral letter to all the churches of the region, explaining what was happening to the Jews and instructing them to take a position against it. To keep Vichy postal censorship from preventing dissemination of his letter, the Cardinal dispatched it by bicycle couriers who hand-delivered it to parish priests on the evening before it was to be publicly read on Sunday, September 6, 1942, to their congregations.

Gerlier was to take even more courageous positions as the war went on. He authorized all the religious communities under his authority to hide Jews and personally kept the funds and archives of the Jewish Consistoire safe through the entire war. At one point, Gerlier sheltered the Grand Rabbi of France, Isaie Schwarz, who was being sought by the Gestapo. Perhaps the single most humanitarian act to Gerlier's credit was his protection of some 60 Jewish children sought for deportation by the French authorities. An ecumenical religious organization called L'Amitié Chrétienne, Christian Friendship, of which the cardinal and Pastor Marc Boegner, president of the Protestant Federation of France, were honorary co-presidents, had taken the children under its care when their parents were arrested.

Relates Rabbi Kaplan: "Some days after, someone from the prefecture came to the place where they were kept and said, 'We're coming tomorrow to collect them. We have to put them in the trains to reunite the families.' Instead, the priest in charge, Père Chaillet, and Cardinal Gerlier sent the children off to homes in the countryside to prevent their seizure.

"When the French prefect of the Lyon area learned of this, that the children were gone, he was furious," says Kaplan. "Finally he accused Père Chaillet, who had taken them into his charge. He went to Gerlier to complain and Gerlier told him, 'It's not Père Chaillet you should arrest. It is me. The children have been entrusted to me.' Gerlier had prepared forms on which the families signed the children into the care of the cardinal. But they didn't dare arrest the cardinal. They put Chaillet under house arrest in a village near Grenoble. He didn't have the right to leave the village, but he was back in a few months.''

One of the more remarkable instances of Jews being assisted by French gentiles took place in the Protestant village of Chambon-sur-Lignon in the Haute-Loire *département* to the southwest of Lyon. Led by the pastor André Trocmé, the residents of this village protected some 5,000 Jewish children and adolescents during the war. But such courage and generosity were all too rare.

In Lyon, L'Amitié Chrétienne continued to aid Jews, even though many of its members, like René Nodot, were pursued by the Gestapo. Nodot was in close contact with the vice consul of Switzerland in Lyon, Alfred-Georges Berthod, and under cover of a Vichy social service organization, he managed to spirit Jews into Switzerland through the border town of Saint-Julien-en-Genevoix. Nodot and his associates had assembled a network that included local mayors and police officials who provided identification papers that could withstand verification even if the official records were checked.

Nodot, now 67, is a vigorous man who speaks modestly of his role in this wartime life-line and the bravery, which in 1974, won him the Medal of the Just from the State of Israel, a high distinction awarded to gentiles who aided Jews during the years of the Holocaust. "I had an uncle who lived here, in Saint-Julien, on the border," Nodot explained at a table in Lyon's Café de la Cloche, drawing a map of the region around Lake Geneva. "And I knew a *curé* in Collonges. I took the Jewish women and children to Collonges, to the priest. I brought the men across myself, near Saint-Julien.''

Both towns were only a short distance from Geneva and safety. The frontier was marked by barbed wire, but at the time Nodot was working as a *passeur* it was guarded by Italian troops who were either sympathetic to him or indifferent to the anti-Semitic program of both Vichy France and the Nazis. "They weren't against the Jews," Nodot recalls. "It's very curious. The Italians actually saved Jews. In the ten *départements* of France that they occupied, they *protected* the Jews."

There were exceptions, but most local French officials did not share the Italians' sense of decency toward the Jews, Nodot points out. He witnessed the delivery of Jews to the Germans by French bureaucrats in Lyon in August 1942, notably by Prefect Pierre Angeli, who held his post until January 1944. After the war Angeli was arrested, tried and condemned to death, but on appeal, he was tried again and sentenced to only four years in prison, given a 12,000-franc fine and censured with "national indignity for life." Says Nodot, "There were worse collaborators, but he executed orders—blindly."

At the end of 1941, says Nodot, L'Amitié Chrétienne was formed, and although innocent in appearance, it provided the cover for a number of highly illegal activities. "Gerlier didn't know everything," says Nodot. "They told him they were taking care of refugees, but in reality it was a Resistance organization."

Deeply involved in the clandestine activities of L'Amitié Chré-tienne were the priests Pierre Chaillet, who helped save the 60 Jewish children, and Alexander Glasberg. Chaillet, Nodot explains, was a brilliant Jesuit intellectual, while Glasberg, a converted Jew of Russian origin, was "a man of action, a fighter, not a *littérateur*." Together they put out the clandestine publication *Temoignage Chretien*, Christian Testimony, which cautioned in its first issue: "France, take care not to lose your soul."

L'Amitié Chrétienne had learned in advance of the plan to arrest the foreign Jews living in Lyon, and through contacts within the local prefecture had obtained the list of the addresses that were to be searched by the French police beginning August 20. According to Nodot, L'Amitié Chrétienne warned as many as possible and some 1,000 Jews escaped arrest, most by taking refuge in the homes of non-Jews. Nodot cites the case of André Iehle, the director of a Lyon factory, who hid 30 Jews in his home during the sweep by Vichy police.

In all of this, Cardinal Gerlier played a subtle, ambivalent but vital role, says Nodot. Gerlier was a complex personality, a man who had attained success as a lawyer in secular life before entering the priesthood, and who was a figure of great stature in Lyon public life, a close friend of Mayor Herriot and an outspoken *Pétainist*.

Despite having taken a public stand against anti-Semitism in 1938, and having aided some Jews during the occupation, Gerlier was, Nodot believes, "more or less anti-Semitic himself." In a 1941 report by Xavier Vallat, Vichy's first commissioner-general for Jewish affairs, Gerlier is quoted as saying, "No one recognizes more than I the evil the Jews have done to France. It was the collapse of the Union Générale that ruined my family." He was referring to the failure of a Catholic banking house, an event some blamed on Jewish financiers.

Gerlier did speak out against Vichy's collaboration with the Nazis in the round-up of French Jews, but Nodot believes that he condemned Vichy in much milder terms than those used, for instance, by Pastor Boegner or Monsignor Jules-Gérard Saliège, the Archbishop of Toulouse, who, on Sunday, August 23, stated in a pastoral letter that "the Jews are real men and women... [who] cannot be abused without limit." Even as Gerlier condemned Vichy's Jewish policies in defending "the inalienable rights of the human person, the sacred character of family bonds," he underscored his continued support of the regime in stating, "It is not upon violence or hatred that we will be able to build a new order."

But the most significant factor was that Gerlier, as the *Primat des Gaules,* the head of the entire Catholic Church in France, had taken a stand against the persecution of the Jews, Nodot believes. "What is astonishing," he says, "is that it was this protest that carried the most weight. You see, Pastor Boegner reached only the Protestants, or less than a million people. But Gerlier reached all of France. You can't imagine how the collaborators attacked him." The French collaborationist press throughout France, Nodot recalls, accused Gerlier of having "sold out to international Jewry."

Despite the aid of some courageous Frenchmen, the lives of the Jews of Lyon, whether French citizens or foreign refugees, were in jeopardy. Even before the August 20, 1942 sweep in Lyon, Jews in camps in the south of France were being transported by train to Drancy and other centers prior to their transfer to the East; these trains sometimes made stops in Lyon, a major switching point. On August 12, Jewish leaders in Lyon received an urgent telegram from Montpellier, beseeching them to provide food, water and hygienic buckets for 400 Jews coming from a southwestern concentration camp of Rivesaltes in cattle cars and scheduled to stop briefly in Lyon.

Rabbi Jacob Kaplan led a group of Lyon Jews who attempted to deliver provisions to their despairing co-religionists as the train sat in the August heat of the Gare de Perrache. "The platform was closed," Kaplan recalls, "and there were police all around who wouldn't let us get through. Since I couldn't go to the train, I went to the opposite side and was able to board a train that was stopped alongside the other. I could see from the window of this train into the other train." To Kaplan it was obvious that these Jews were not going to work camps. Among them were elderly men who could barely move as they lay on the floors of the freight cars.

"I was so revolted with what was happening there," Kaplan recalls, "that I turned to the French people in the compartment where I was standing, who weren't Jews, and I said, 'Those people are going to Germany, to the camps.' They didn't understand. 'What's going on?' they asked. 'Who are those people?' And so I explained that they had been arrested because they were Jews and that one day, it would happen to them in their turn. They would find themselves in such trains and others would see them and wouldn't understand, either."

The French guards would not permit Kaplan and the other Jews to deliver the provisions, but they were able to toss bread and other goods to the prisoners when some of the guards demonstrated a limited humanity by looking the other way.

Ω

On a hot July night in 1942 a flatbed truck loaded with sacks of coal rumbled through the Loire Valley, bound for the south and approaching the Demarcation Line. It was a regular run for the French driver; there was a war on, and the industries of France had to keep churning out material for the German war machine. But his cargo was not entirely usual, for the stacked sacks of coal concealed a hollowed-out space large enough to accommodate a handful of Jews on their way to what was called the Free Zone of France.

Inside the stifling compartment, Esther Minkowsky and her family bore the jouncing of the truck and held their fears in check. In just a few more hours they would be across the line and in relative safety. They knew there was no alternative; Paris had become forbidden territory for Jews who hoped to escape the Germans. The emotional strain of the last days had been enormous, but the Minkowsky family counted itself fortunate to have avoided Drancy, where the thousands of Jews rounded up in Paris had been imprisoned.

That the Minkowskys were not in Drancy was due to the kindness of one French policeman who had warned them, a few weeks before, that they should not be in their apartment on the Rue de la Roquette near the Place de la Bastille on July 16. That was the day the German and French authorities planned to launch an operation called *Vent Printanier*, Spring Wind, whose aim was the arrest of the entire Jewish population of Paris. The Minkowskys took the warning seriously, for the head of the family, Avram Minkowsky, one of his sons, and Esther's fiancé had already been arrested. They were in Drancy, out of contact with their family but for one pathetic note on a strip of white cloth, written in Hebrew, that conveyed the chilling message: "It is no longer blood that runs in our veins; it is water."

On July 16 Esther's mother and sister hid themselves in the basement of their building with two infants, while she and the rest of her children went to the apartment of a non-Jewish neighbor. Through the open window she could hear the chaos that ruled in the streets of the heavily Jewish neighborhood as French gendarmes and German officers collected their prisoners. "At three o'clock in the morning we could hear them shouting, 'The children too? The children too?' And the Germans were saying, 'Yes, *los, los,* the children, everybody, hurry up!' It was so sad."

As soon as the sweep was over, the Minkowskys set about finding a *passeur*, a professional in the business of smuggling human beings across the Demarcation Line. They found one, at a high price, and within two or three days they were heading south. But even after handing over a bundle of franc notes, the Minkowskys were subjected to one more indignity. "You gang of dirty Jews," he told them. "When are we going to be rid of you? I don't know why I don't just take you straight to the Gestapo!"

Esther's six-year-old brother, already distraught at the collapse of his world, could not understand why this man was mad at them.

In the darkness of their hiding place, the child sobbed and wept uncontrollably. The Minkowskys and the other Jews traveling with them were alarmed. They were soon to cross the Demarcation Line, and the noise was sure to land them in the hands of the German police.

"Will you be a good boy and stop crying?" they pleaded with the child.

"No!" he wailed. "I won't be good. I'm going to cry! I'm going to cry!"

"We were so, so afraid," remembers Esther. "Because we knew what would happen if he was crying when we went past the Germans. And you know, like a miracle, before we arrived at the checkpoint, he fell asleep." The vehicle was cleared and by morning the family was in the town of Vichy and on its way east to Lyon.

The Minkowskys settled into a small apartment in Lyon, where they found a measure of respite from the onerous restrictions that had become part of daily life in Paris. Jews in the southern zone were not obliged to wear the yellow cloth star of David that Parisian Jews had been obliged to pin on their clothing. In Lyon they were not treated like pariahs, nor excluded from parks, museums, theaters, restaurants and other public places. They were as happy as could be expected, given that Avram Minkowsky and the others had been deported from Drancy to an unknown destination in the East.

Ω

The Halaunbrenner family had less luck in resettling in the south, even if they did escape intact from the *Vent Printanier*. Like the Bastille district, the narrow, medieval streets of the old Jewish section of Paris, the Marais, witnessed innumerable human tragedies on July 16, 1942. Thousands of frightened and bewildered people were led by French policemen through the neighborhood south to the Rue de Rivoli to be loaded on buses that stretched out of sight in a long, ominous line. The first transports were pulling out, on the first stage of an ultimately deadly journey, taking their passengers to the unfinished housing project of Drancy in the suburbs.

When Drancy was packed beyond capacity with 6,000, the

buses were directed to the Vélodrome d'Hiver, an indoor bicycle-racing track known as the Vel d'Hiv, where 7,000 were shoved into the spectator stands and onto the banked track to sit and wait, virtually without food, water and adequate sanitation, for five days.

On the Rue des Rosiers, in the heart of the Marais, two of the 9,000 French gendarmes conducting the *rafle* stepped off the street and through a small courtyard, then climbed up a narrow staircase to the two-room apartment of Jacob and Itta Halaunbrenner and their five children who, appearing on a Jewish census list, were to be collected.

Itta Halaunbrenner apprehensively met them at the door, and explained that Jacob was temporarily out of town. This perplexed the policemen. Their list showed an entire family, and if they came in with less than an entire family that would mean more paper-work and besides, the matter would not be properly *reglé*. In their own way, the French authorities were as compulsively bureaucratic as their German counterparts. They came to a decision: they would put the matter off until the next day, when Jacob might have returned and the matter could be properly settled.

But the gendarmes never came back. The 12,884 prisoners already in custody were overwhelming the logistics of the French authorities. Itta and her children began to plan their escape from Paris, while Jacob made arrangements from his place in the small Charente town of Monbron in the Unoccupied Zone. His family traveled across the line with a *passeur* and joined him there at the beginning of October.

The Free Zone, however, was not always as free as the Halaun-brenners had hoped. Just a week after their arrival in Monbron, a local gendarme informed them that Itta and the children stood in violation of the law, having crossed the line after regulations were issued forbidding it. Jacob had moved before the provision came into effect and was safe. The mother and children were told they must enter a residence center, a euphemism for the dozens of concentration camps in the Unoccupied Zone that in 1940 had received unwanted foreign Jews, but which now were also collecting French citizens.

They were first assigned to Rivesaltes, a cement hell in the Pyrenées-Orientales *département* near the Spanish border. Typhus raged, the chilling mistral blew in winter and the summer sun baked the vast collection of ramshackle wooden barracks. They were next transferred to Gurs, a camp in the Basses-Pyrénées that had sheltered Spanish Civil War refugees in the late 1930s, but now was being put to a more ignoble use. By this time, Jacob had been separated from them and assigned to a labor camp. Itta and her children were alone at Gurs. Léon, the oldest at 13, went into the adolescent section. Itta was put in the maternal section with Alexander, 11, Mina, 7, Claudine, 3, and Monique, then just an infant.

Léon found work in the camp and brought his extra ration of soup to his mother, who was nursing Monique. Alexander supplemented their insufficient diet by begging for food in the surrounding countryside after crawling through barbed wire and slithering through drainage pipes to temporarily reach freedom.

Late in August 1943, the Halaunbrenners were released from Gurs through a quirk of the arcane, overlapping bureaucracies of defeated France. In one jurisdiction a Jew could be an outlaw, while in another he might easily obtain residence authorization, complete with the essential ration card. It all depended on the frame of mind of the *département*'s administrators and their attitudes toward Jews. Jacob, who had escaped from his labor camp, took advantage of this confusion to obtain permission for his family to join him at his residence in Grigny, just north of Lyon. The family would be under police control and surveillance, but they would be together, not surrounded by barbed wire.

Their stay in Grigny was short. The Halaunbrenners had seen French gendarmes in action before and had no wish to stay where they were known. A Vichy policeman might come for them at any hour of the day or night. Jacob had a cousin, Joseph Halaunbrenner, who lived in the industrial suburb of Villeurbanne east of Lyon, and he took his family to live there. He knew that Jo Halaunbrenner was active in the Jewish Resistance movement and was aware of the danger involved, but he had no way of knowing that he was entering the sphere of influence of SS Obersturmführer Klaus Barbie.

Ω

As Barbie took charge in Lyon, the death camps of the Third Reich were gearing up for the most methodical massacre in history.

France was no exception to the policy decreed by Adolf Hitler, and with only certain exceptions, the Vichy regime worked closely with the Nazis to seal the fate of over 70,000 Jews. Latent French anti-Semitism paired with Vichy's concessions to the Germans led first to the arrest of foreign Jews and then to that of many French Jewish citizens. French administrators pushed the paper, French policemen made the arrests, French railways delivered the human freight to German hands. And only a few Frenchmen objected.

Whether or not Vichy's leaders knew the slaughter that awaited the Jews whom they were dispatching eastward is a matter of speculation. Vichy policy, of course, demanded that all choose to disbelieve. It was part of *la collaboration*, with one significant difference. Although Vichy haggled obstinately with France's conquerors over financial and material demands, its officials made criminally poor bargainers when human lives were in the balance.

Vichy took its first active step against the Jews in October 1940, less than four months after the signing of the armistice. It instituted the Statute on the Jews excluding *les Israélites* from whole sectors of public life. No longer could Jews hold high public posts, serve as army officers, teach, write for newspapers or magazines, work in radio, film or the theater. A prewar law against anti-Semitism and racism had earlier been repealed, unleashing the ugly prejudices that had lain just below the surface of French public life ever since the Dreyfus affair of the 1890s, in which a Jewish army officer was falsely accused of espionage for the Germans. Even more pernicious than the Statute on the Jews was a law ordering that foreign Jews in France be interned in camps or placed under surveillance by the French police. Another measure withdrew French citizenship from Algerian Jews, who had held this status for three-quarters of a century.

At their postwar trials for treason, Laval, Pétain and others employed the defense that by instituting French anti-Semitic laws, Vichy could forestall or mitigate the effect of harsher German measures. Even if this was their intent, the tactic proved to be simply one more case—and by far the most catastrophic—of Vichy illusions serving Nazi aims.

At the end of September 1940, the German occupation authority began to control the movement of Jews between the Occupied and Unoccupied zones. Jews in the north were registered, and soon after were required to report to their local sub-prefecture to have the word "Juif" stamped on their identity papers. Although Vichy had not yet come under pressure by the Germans, it began to move on its own against the Jews. One authoritative study of this question concludes: "Without any possible doubt, Vichy had begun its own anti-Semitic career before the first German text appeared, and without German order."

Between October and December 1940 the French Jewish affairs officials moved to take control of all Jewish businesses and industries. The situation worsened through 1941 as the Jews were made the scapegoats for France's 1940 humiliating defeat. There was also a general public and official reaction against the estimated 55,000 foreign Jews present in France. The country sealed its borders against refugees in July 1940, but this regulation was ineffective in the great confusion following the defeat. The French tried to deport Jews, but most often the Germans pushed them back into French territory. At that time their policy was one of expulsion rather than extermination. Of course, the Jews needed no encouragement to move south to Lyon and other cities in the Unoccupied Zone.

The yellow star appeared on the clothing of Parisian Jews in June 1942, while Drancy was already housing nearly 4,000 Jews taken in May, August and December raids in 1941. The last sweep took in many of the leading Jewish personalities of Paris. On March 27, 1942, 1,112 Jews in French hands after the 1941 arrests were placed in third-class railroad cars and sent to Auschwitz, where all but 19 of them perished.

In May 1942 another piece fell into place in the French subcategory of the Final Solution. German occupation police power shifted from the Militarbefehlshaber to an SS official, Hoherer SS-und Polizeiführer Carl Albrecht Oberg, who answered directly to Heinrich Himmler in Berlin. The crucial date in fixing the fate of France's Jews was June 30, 1942, when Adolph Eichmann came to Paris. With him he carried orders from Himmler that all French Jews were to be deported, even if they were citizens and ostensibly loyal to the New Order of the Nazi puppet, Marshal Pétain.

When Barbie and the Gestapo came to Lyon in late 1942, their arrival marked an important transition in the life of the Lyonnais Jews. If Barbie and the chief of the SS Jewish section, Erich Bartelmus, did not immediately proceed with mass arrests and deportations, it was because Barbie had more pressing concerns. The Resistance was on the offensive, and he had to counterattack. There had also been a slowing in the rate of deportation of French Jews toward the end of 1942. It translated into a lack of pressure from above for large-scale round-ups in Lyon, at least for the time being. Still, 150 Jews were arrested in Lyon during January 1943. The figures mounted from then on—86 in one raid on the Rue St. Catherine in February—as the Nazis accelerated their activities.

As in his pursuit of Resistance fighters, Barbie counted on an array of French forces for help. Bartelmus, who reported to Barbie in the SS line of command, had no more than a half-dozen officers in his Jewish section to carry out operations in the largest Jewish urban population in France, but Barbie found reliable henchmen in the Milice and the PPF, which attacked Lyonnais Jews with enthusiasm. The profit motive was central, not only for informers who delivered the addresses of Jews, but for the paramilitary groups which financed their activities with plunder extracted from Jewish victims.

But Barbie had another tactic at his disposal. It was not an original one; the Germans had already employed it with success elsewhere in Europe in crushing the Jews. Dangling salvation for the few, Barbie and his Jewish specialist Bartelmus exploited the good intentions of Jewish leaders to lay their hands on a larger number of victims.

His instrument was UGIF, the same organization he had raided within three months of his arrival in Lyon. Without question, UGIF brought aid to many and, to the extent that it was able, sought to frustrate the aims of the Gestapo. But the Jewish organization was cynically manipulated by Barbie and Bartelmus to keep track of Jews in Lyon until such time as the Nazis were ready to collect them for shipment, first to Montluc, then to death camps in the East.

Ω

Despite all the obstacles, survival for a Jew was more likely in

Lyon than in many other places under Nazi control. Here it was essentially a question of chance; there was no pattern, no consistency to the danger. "It wasn't systematic," explains the present Chief Rabbi of Lyon, Richard Wertenschlag. "There were isolated actions, but no steady combing of the Jewish population. The situation was more or less tolerable between 1940 and 1942, until the Germans reoccupied Lyon. It became more serious as time passed. In 1943 and 1944, there were arrests, deportations, murders, hostage-taking."

Jewish life mingled normality with grotesque reality, complacency with justified paranoia. "There was intense anxiety," Wertenschlag explains, "the fear of what lay ahead. People ran the risk of being arrested from one day to the next. There was also the fear of being betrayed. Jewish families were being hunted and there was a constant need to move in order to avoid being denounced by the neighbors."

"Every day there were arrests," recalls Rabbi Kaplan, who lived in Lyon through the entire war. "Sometimes in one neighborhood, sometimes in another. They didn't arrest hundreds, but a little group every day." There were few mass arrests in the early stages of the Gestapo campaign, the Jewish leader said, but many Jews had a certain fatalistic attitude. "A lot of Jews were prepared to be arrested," Kaplan says. "They had made up their bags so as to have the necessary things with them. A lot of Jews did that."

Kaplan himself was arrested on August 1, 1944, on the eve of the liberation of Lyon, by three members of the PPF who rejoiced at having caught "the Pope of the Jews." But Kaplan was finally released by these same men. In part it was through the payment of the money they demanded, but much of the reason for his release was persuasion. After an entire afternoon and evening spent with his captors, Rabbi Kaplan had exerted such a strong degree of moral authority over them that one of them told him in parting, "May the Lord guide you." Kaplan was to save this man's life after the war by testifying on his behalf. The others were convicted of the murder of numerous Jews and executed.

The role of the French gentiles in Lyon varied from open collaboration with the Nazis to aid for the Jews, even if only by closing an official eye. Esther Minkowsky tells of one French policeman who protected members of her family. "There were a lot of people who, when they knew you were a Jew, helped out," she says. "Those were the people whom you could trust. But you couldn't confide in everyone. My sister and my brother-in-law had redone their identity papers and gotten rid of the Jewish stamp. There was a police inspector who knew that they were Jews, but he didn't do them any harm. One day he came to see us and he said, 'You've done the right thing. No one will harm you; just continue with your normal activities and work if you can.' "

With the arrival of the Germans, many Jews desperately tried to make their way to Switzerland or to Portugal, but both routes were difficult and the trips expensive. False papers and clandestine transport had to be arranged. Many Jews settled for migrating to the southeast, to Nice and other cities that were under Italian occupation.

For a great many, however, survival became a matter of simply staying out of the hands of the Gestapo at all costs. "There was an extraordinary solidarity among the Jews," says Rabbi Wertenschlag. "By necessity, if one family was in a dangerous situation, other families put them up. There were a certain number of our Jews, even some French Jewish policemen, who sometimes would warn their Jewish friends, saying, 'Watch out, there's going to be a raid tomorrow in such and such neighborhood, so stay away from there.' "

Jewish religious life in Lyon was strong throughout the war, reinforced by the influx of Jews from occupied France and virtually all of occupied Europe. "There were Jews from all over the north, not only from France, but also from Belgium and the rest of Europe," says Wertenschlag. "The German Jews had come much earlier, in the late 1930s. For all these reasons, there was an active Jewish community in Lyon, as paradoxical as that may seem, an intense Jewish life in Lyon throughout the war.

"The synagogues were open nearly until the end of the war. Until July 1944, the Great Synagogue of Lyon held regular services. There was actually a certain spirit that existed, in which the Jews remained true to their traditions in spite of the persecution. There was a kind of spiritual resistance to the enemy in that people came to the synagogue to pray as they always had, in spite of the prevailing conditions."

But a Jew in Lyon unexpectedly caught in a police cordon could end up in Montluc, his fate sealed. The threat could come from any direction, and without warning. At one point there were as many as 400 "physiognomists" walking the streets of Lyon, pseudoscientific "experts" trained in the art of spotting a Jew by the shape of his nose or the set of his eyes. The greatest threat came from the French paramilitary groups roaming through the city, virtually a law unto themselves, who robbed and murdered Jews with impunity. By 1944 the legitimate police authorities were routinely fishing bodies out of the Rhône and Saône, often those of Jews callously butchered after being robbed by the PPF or the Milice.

The PPF of Francis André was particularly notorious, for its troops were not only virulently prejudiced but possessed the ruthlessness of hardened criminals. The PPF men were authorized to arrest at will any Jewish-appearing suspects, a power they wielded indiscriminately. Bounties were paid for the Jews they turned in to the Ecole de Santé. After the war, André himself recounted a number of his exploits to investigators.

Driving down the Rue Boissac one day, André spotted two men who were, as he put it, "of Jewish allure." He slammed on his brakes and got out of the car to question them. When they fled he gave chase and caught up with the men a few blocks away. Upon examining their papers he decided they were false and brought the men to the Ecole de Santé for questioning. He later searched their apartment, finding a workshop for manufacturing false identity papers. They were thrown into Montluc, from which the only exit was execution or deportation to a Nazi concentration camp.

Other "operations," as André called them, were more profitable. From one of his agents André received the intelligence that a French Jew carrying gold coins was to change trains at Aix-les-Bains in the Savoie region near the Swiss border, on his way to Lyon. André arrested him and seized the 800 gold louis he was carrying, then pried the information from him that his employer was one Hanau, a resident of Annecy in the Haute-Savoie.

Raiding Hanau's home, André found a cache of two million francs in cash, large amounts of precious stones and a pile of negotiable securities. He seized all this and delivered Hanau to the Gestapo. Hanau was later executed in Montluc, officially "while trying to escape." However, André told his postwar interrogators Hanau was murdered because he was suspected of having links to the Free French Army's Deuxième Bureau.

Another time, André took part in a raid on the Lyon home of a fur merchant named Rossner, where the PPF found a room filled with furs and leather goods. They seized these articles, shot Rossner and arrested his wife. The Germans were also involved in this looting.

The Milice, though responsible for many murders, was somewhat less rapacious than the PPF. But this organization still fixed its sights on the Jews, twice sacking the Quai Tilsitt synagogue. The first desecration came in July 1943, the second a year later after the Gestapo had raided Saturday services and the temple was shut down. The Milice took over the synagogue and transformed it into a club for its revels, littering the floor with bottles and firing bullets at the bronze plaques commemorating the French Jewish war dead of 1914-18.

Ω

Through all of this Barbie maintained a sporadic but constantly threatening presence. From time to time Barbie's Einsatzkommando would mount a sweep of one of the market areas frequented by Jews who, barred from their normal professions, eked out a living at small crafts and commerce. "The Gestapo would arrive, Barbie at the head," Rabbi Wertenschlag relates. "Everyone who looked Jewish was picked up and taken to Gestapo headquarters for interrogation. If they were truly Jews they kept them and brought them to Montluc."

Barbie did not bother with day-to-day anti-Jewish activity, unless it involved a large raid or a Resistance connection. The latter was the case with Esther Minkowsky, who was arrested in an outdoor market in the Cours de Verdun, an avenue near the Hôtel Terminus and the Gare de Perrache. In Lyon, Esther had established a new identity, becoming Geneviève Mayer, with a new life history as a Christian and a baptismal certificate to back it up. With her brothers and sisters she tended a stand at the market, selling items people needed in occupation times: pins, fabric, buckles, belts. She ran the daily risk of being denounced as a suspected Jew; this danger was heightened by the Resistance contacts she maintained.

On June 15, 1944, Barbie walked up to her stand, followed by a number of plainclothes Milice members. "German police!" Barbie barked. "Gather up all this stuff and come with us. Quickly!"

Esther, stunned, tried to bluff her way out. "What do you want with us?" she asked. "We haven't done anything. Why are you arresting us?"

"Get moving!" Barbie snapped. "We don't have time to waste on you. You'll be told later."

He gave some orders to the Milice and left. The Frenchmen marched Minkowsky and her brother to an abandoned tobacco factory not far away, where they were met by a Gestapo officer named Joseph Weisel who was part of the Jewish section. Weisel began to interrogate and torture Minkowsky and her brother, passing a lit cigarette across her face and firing shots close to her with his pistol. He insulted them and began to kick and beat them both; meanwhile other German uniformed troops arrived. Finally they were brought to the new Gestapo headquarters on the Place Bellecour, to which operations had been shifted after the destruction of the Ecole de Santé by Allied bombing in May.

There the Minkowskys met up with Barbie again. He strutted before them, a whip in his hands. He lashed out at them, demanding a confession that they were Jews.

"Barbie was there," recalls Esther, now Mrs. Majerowicz, who survived Auschwitz and today owns a women's wear shop in Lyon. "He interrogated us, walking back and forth with his bull whip. Then Weisel went to work. It was Weisel who tortured us. First, he beat my brother terribly, with his fists, with a whip, with rifle butts to the head. 'Say you're a Jew! Say you're a dirty Jew! Dirty Jew!' When he saw that he was practically dead on the ground, he pushed him with his foot and said, 'You're a Jew, right?' And he said, 'Yes, yes, I'm a Jew.'"

After hours at the Gestapo headquarters they were sent to Montluc. Their merchandise was confiscated and Esther was even stripped of her few pieces of jewelry, which were tossed to one of the Gestapo's secretaries. Just before their departure, Weisel hissed at her, "It's finished for you now. You'll never see the light of day again."

This was not Esther's last encounter with Weisel. The train taking her to Drancy stopped in the Gare de Perrache for three hours before leaving, and Weisel was there to see it off. French railwaymen had brought water for the prisoners, but when Weisel saw this, he seized the water and poured it on the ground before their eyes. He swaggered down the platform alongside the train, seizing male passersby at random and forcing them to board the train. He then made them drop their pants so he could see whether or not they were circumcised. Those who were circumcised were arrested and sent to Drancy that day along with the other prisoners.

In some cases, Barbie showed himself ruthless in the pursuit of Jews who had absolutely no connection with the Resistance, even extending his efforts to tracking down Jewish children. Simone Lagrange, then only thirteen, was the victim of one such investigation by the Gestapo chief. After she and her parents were arrested on June 6, 1944, they were brought to Barbie's new office on the Place Bellecour. Barbie knew from the woman who had betrayed them that Simone's younger brothers, Joseph, 5, and Simon, 7, had been sent to a home in the French countryside. He immediately demanded that the Kaddouche family supply the address.

Barbie had come into the office carrying a cat, and as he interrogated the prisoners, he caressed the animal. He looked at Simone's parents without saying a word, then went over the young girl. "He told me I was very pretty," recalls Lagrange, who recounted her ordeal in a barely audible voice. "He turned towards my mother and he said, 'You have other children. Where are they?' "

Mrs. Kaddouche explained truthfully that she did not know where the children had gone. Barbie set the cat down on a desk and asked Simone the same question. When she did not answer, Barbie slapped the young girl across the face. Her father, a large man, stepped forward to defend Simone, but Barbie pulled out his revolver and threatened to shoot him if he moved again. Barbie seized Simone by her long brown hair and again began to slap her as he demanded: "Where are the children?"

"If you give me the children, I'll put all three in the Antiquaille

Hospital," Barbie told the distraught parents. "Otherwise, your daughter is going to go into a concentration camp and she will die there." When the Kaddouches refused to cooperate, they were taken out of his office and locked up in Montluc, the father in the hostage barracks with the male Jewish prisoners, Simone and her mother in basement cells.

That night, through the small window of their cell, they watched as trucks brought in hundreds of Jews, including entire families, who had been arrested in their suburb of Saint-Fons. Simone saw many people she knew. "It lasted all night," Lagrange recalls. The next morning Barbie came to get Simone. "Unless you give me the address of your children," he told her mother, "I am going to take care of your daughter."

At his Place Bellecour headquarters Barbie renewed his assault on the girl. "He beat me with his hands, with his fists," Lagrange recalls. "He beat me all day like that." Barbie came and went on other business, but always returned to question and beat her. "By the evening my face was covered with blood."

Barbie brought the beaten Simone back to Montluc and confronted her mother. "Look at your daughter. You're the one who's responsible." He continued the physical and mental torture of the Kaddouche family for an entire week, after which Simone was kept for days without contact with her mother. They were reunited only at the Drancy transit camp, to which Simone was shipped on June 23, then deported again to Auschwitz with her mother. Her father, she later learned, was deported to the East in a later convoy in August, the last to leave Lyon.

Her mother was gassed to death just two months later, on August 23, in Auschwitz, and her body was cremated. She was just 33 years old. Before her death she was tortured by the infamous Dr. Joseph Mengele for having stolen some cabbage leaves to give to prisoners with scurvy, Lagrange says. Simone was forced to watch and was told a week in advance that her mother was scheduled to die. Each day, Auschwitz's "Angel of Death" told the young girl how many days were left before her mother would die, and at the end of the stated period he kept his word. Lagrange still recalls the twisted, heartless Nazi who is believed to be living in Paraguay today. "He whistled 'Tosca' all day long," she says.

In the winter of 1945 Simone was reunited with her father, briefly, during one of the forced marches to which thousands of concentration camp prisoners were subjected as the Allied armies advanced eastward. "He saw me along the road, in the snow," she remembers. "I said, 'Papa.' A German guard asked me if that was my father. I told him he was, and he gestured for my father to come over. The German told him to kiss me, and just as we were about to embrace, he put a bullet through his head."

Ω

Barbie also entered personally into the lives of the Halaun-brenners. It was in October 1943, not long after they had moved from Grigny to Villeurbanne. At the beginning of October French policemen came to arrest Jacob for leaving his authorized address, imprisoning him in Lyon's Fort de Chapoly. But on October 20 he was released, and Alexander went to the prison to greet his father upon his liberation. Their exhilaration was short-lived, though, for when they returned to the apartment in Villeurbanne Jacob was set upon by Barbie and two other Gestapo agents.

Barbie was after Jo Halaunbrenner, who had been arrested for Resistance activities but had escaped during a prisoner transfer. Barbie began to throw questions at Jacob as he waved a revolver in his face, making threats and demanding to know where Jo was.

"Ich habe keine idee," Jacob protested in German. "I have no idea where Jo is." But Barbie refused to believe him, continuing to stalk agitatedly about the apartment, brandishing the gun and repeating his threats. Time and again he descended the staircase to survey the street.

"The reason why I can be sure it was Barbie is because when I got home with my father, I remember one of them being very much shorter than the others who were with him," says Alexander Halaunbrenner who, with his aged mother, Itta, and his sister, Monique, are the only ones in the family of seven to have survived the Nazi terror. Alexander now lives in a house in a Paris suburb, while Itta has an apartment in a new building near the Place de la Bastille. But they still own the tiny apartment in the Marais, the Jewish quarter, where they lived before the Nazis came. It is maintained as a stable piece of the past, a shrine to their murdered family.

"Barbie had a beret on his head, I'm sure of that, and he wore a raincoat," Alexander relates. "He was impatient, and seemed to move constantly. He said to my father in German—we understood German because we spoke Yiddish—'If you don't tell us something in 24 hours, you'll be shot. You've only got one night left.' He went outside and went down the staircase. The other two that were there waited calmly enough, telling my mother, 'Don't worry, we're just going to take him in for questioning. He'll be released in three days.' They stayed all day, hoping that Jo would arrive.

"Unfortunately, at 6:30 P.M. my brother Léon came home from work," Halaunbrenner continues. "He was only 13 years old, but he was very big, and he looked like a man already. They searched him and they thought he was Jo. It was then that my mother came up to them, saying, 'Leave my son alone, he's just a child, leave him alone!' But they took my father and my brother, and my mother screamed and cried. She pulled at my brother and said, 'You're not going to take him, he's a child!' and while she was pulling my brother away, Barbie took out his revolver and hit her on the hands."

Itta became even more frantic after the Gestapo had left with her husband and her eldest child. She rushed into the kitchen to commit suicide by turning on the gas stove, but Alexander subdued her. The next morning Itta and her children were out on the sidewalk in front of their building, spending hours in a futile wait, clutching at the slight hope that Jacob and Léon might be released after interrogation, as one of the agents had said would happen.

The Germans came back, but not to return the two men. A military truck pulled up and a group of soldiers went into the building to arrest the rest of the family. Itta and the children fled, leaving all their possessions behind. They were fugitives again.

They retreated to a nearby apartment that had been converted into an *oratoire*, a clandestine synagogue where Jewish men, mostly elderly, could come to pray in safety. She explained her plight and was directed to the offices of UGIF, now located on the Montée des Carmelites, a long series of steps climbing the hill of Old Lyon, where they received addresses at which they could temporarily stay. The family was broken up. Itta and Monique, the infant, stayed with one family, while Mina, Claudine and Alexander went to live in another household.

Eventually they were further separated. Mina and Claudine were placed in a home for Jewish orphans. Monique was placed in a nursery and Itta and Alexander returned to Grigny, their first home after release from Gurs, where Itta found work unloading freight cars.

For weeks they had no word of Jacob; then they were informed that he had died in a Lyon hospital. They were incredulous. Jacob had been in perfect health, a man in the prime of life. Itta made the rounds of the hospitals and finally were presented with photographs of Jacob's bullet-ridden body. His death certificate, witnessed by the caretaker of the Quai Tilsitt synagogue, stated he had been executed by a German firing squad at the Ecole de Santé on November 24, 1943. In her mourning, Itta retained the hope that she might again see Léon—though she never would—and she took comfort that her other children were safe. She was not aware that Klaus Barbie was not yet finished with her family.

Ω

UGIF had helped Itta find a home for herself and her children, as they did for thousands of other Jews in France. The justification for the existence of UGIF was that it was able to aid many Jews, particularly foreign Jews, who otherwise would never have survived. UGIF provided housing, clothes, soup kitchens, advice and money, the latter being channeled to them from organizations overseas, most notably from American Jewish charities.

According to the testimony given after the war by one UGIF official in Lyon, these homeless, penniless Jews could obtain between 200 and 400 francs a month, no enormous sum but enough to make the difference between survival and starvation. Other sources say that UGIF also provided a cover for a number of clandestine groups that supplied forged identity papers and other essential documents, and provided the means of escape from France overland through Switzerland or Spain or by sea from Marseille.

But certain Jewish groups have harshly criticized UGIF's role in France during the war. The Gestapo had compelled UGIF officials to maintain lists of the Jews they were assisting, lists which the Gestapo seized and used to find and arrest Jews. At a postwar

Jewish exposition held in Paris in 1947, one exhibit proposed to show the "pernicious work" carried out by UGIF. The French Zionist leader Marc Jarblum, following the Liberation, even demanded that UGIF's leaders be tried for their actions. During the war, some Jewish Resistance groups bitterly opposed UGIF, going so far as to kidnap Jewish children that were in UGIF custody.

On the other hand, UGIF had many supporters who believed the organization did the best it could with a complex political problem: how to keep Jews alive in a nation conquered by the Nazis. American historian Zosa Szajkowski, writing in the journal *Jewish Social Studies*, stated: "In studying the activity in France of Jewish Resistance groups, one constantly encounters UGIF, under the cover of which operated a vast network of illegal Resistance; there is no doubt on this issue."

Nazi-hunter Serge Klarsfeld recognizes that UGIF was in many ways compromised with the Nazis, but he believes that there are too many factors involved for any easy judgment to be passed. "It's very difficult to sum up UGIF," says Klarsfeld, who has thoroughly researched the fate of French Jewry in the war. "UGIF helped many Jews by giving them money, enabling people who had nothing to stay out of the street. Also, there were Jewish Resistance organizations which aimed to save the children, and which were camouflaged within UGIF." He adds, "UGIF itself saved children. There were children's homes that were administered by UGIF which were still in operation at the end of the war. If the children weren't in these homes, where would they have gone?"

He criticizes UGIF on several points, such as the failure to disperse children's homes in the Paris region more effectively and the fact that in some cases UGIF officials helped certain Jews at the expense of others. Also, he says, there came a point when UGIF should have dissolved itself but did not, which he attributes to "poor judgment." But he still maintains that "altogether, the role of UGIF was not a negative one."

Forty years later, Rabbi Wertenschlag of Lyon echoes the mixed emotions Jews felt toward UGIF. He applauds the "humanitarian vocation" of UGIF. "But," he adds, "UGIF was also obliged to give a certain number of lists of Jews to the Gestapo. Of course, the leaders of UGIF did not know what was going to be done with these lists. But, by this means, the Gestapo was able to have the addresses of our co-religionists.''

Rabbi Kaplan, a leader of the Lyon Jewish community during this controversial period, says that although UGIF provided valuable assistance for a number of Jews, it was opposed by the Consistoire, the highest governing body of French Jewry. "UGIF had a lot of merit,'' says Kaplan. "It provided assistance for a number of Jews. But the Consistoire was against UGIF because it was seen as a German creation.'' He adds, "They had hard responsibilities to assume, because at times they had to give their accord for the arrest and deportation of such and such group. The Consistoire was against UGIF, and one of my responsibilities was to tell those who were going to join UGIF that we were against it.''

Ω

Raymond Geissmann, the director of the Lyon branch of UGIF, realized that in Barbie he was faced with a man who was violent in his detestation of Jews. He was aware that Barbie frequently ordered Jewish prisoners held in Montluc to be shot, not even bothering with the fiction of deportation for "resettlement'' in the East. "I remember seeing Barbie froth at the mouth as he vented his hatred of the Jews,'' Geissmann said years later. Geissmann once had tried to intervene for a group of Jews condemned to death before the firing squad, pleading with Barbie to deport them instead. But the Gestapo leader was unmoved. "Deported or shot,'' he said, confirming Geissmann's supicions of what was happening in the camps, "there's no difference.''

Although UGIF was one of Barbie's first targets in his assault on the Jews of Lyon, there was nothing contradictory in the fact that he tolerated its existence until the last days of the war. Barbie had every reason to allow UGIF to operate relatively freely in Lyon; it was useful to him and Bartelmus when orders came down from Paris that more Jewish bodies were needed to fill out a convoy heading East.

In reality, it had been a Nazi who first came up with the idea of creating UGIF. Jewish leaders were aware that their organization was a Vichy creation inspired by SS-Hauptsturmführer Theodor Dannecker, who at the same age as Barbie was the director of the overall Nazi anti-Jewish campaign in France. Dannecker, a veteran of Nazi anti-Semitic affairs, knew that the most effective way to control and monitor Jewish populations was the Judenrat system of Jewish councils. Whether in the ghettos of Poland or in the affluent, intellectual Jewish community of Vienna, the Judenrat had successfully been used to maintain and administrate these captive populations, to raise the funds extorted from them and to deliver them up when the time came for their annihilation.

The French Jews at first resisted when Dannecker, upon his arrival in Paris in the summer of 1940, tried to force the Consistoire, an assembly of rabbis and laymen, to set up an organization the Nazis could control. When Dannecker persisted, the Consistoire established a committee coordinating all the Paris-area Jewish relief organizations.

When Dannecker brought in two Austrian Jews who had been involved in the Vienna Judenrat and put them in key positions on the coordinating committee, its members were accused by Parisian Jews of helping create a local Jewish ghetto and of encouraging Nazi arrests. The protests culminated in a massive demonstration by 5,000 Jewish women in July 1941 in the street outside the committee's offices, provoking the resignation of many members.

Vichy also became involved at this time. Xavier Vallat, head of the Commissariat-Générale for Jewish affairs created in March 1941, began to negotiate with French Jewish leaders for the creation of an umbrella Jewish organization. Faced with a rapidly deteriorating situation and heavy pressure from Vichy and the Germans, they finally accepted the creation of the Union Générale des Israélites de France.

France's chief rabbi, Isaie Schwarz, and Jacques Helbronner, vice-president of the Consistoire, would have nothing to do with this organization. Jews in the Unoccupied Zone, where they lived, still retained many rights stripped from the Jews in the north, and they resented the high-handed tactics of Vallat, refusing to permit their Committee for Aid to Refugees to participate. But Vichy moved ahead without them, and in the fall of 1941 UGIF came into existence throughout France, by law replacing and absorbing all other Jewish organizations.

As the war progressed, a higher and higher degree of self-deception became necessary for UGIF officials. The Jewish community had learned of the massacre of Jews in Eastern Europe and it required only a small leap of logic to conclude that the French Jews leaving on packed convoys were heading for the same fate. The leaders of the Consistoire, which had retreated to Lyon in October 1941 due to arrests in Paris, wrote to Pierre Laval in August 1942 to protest Vichy's collaboration with the Germans in the collection of the Jews.

"A program of extermination has been methodically applied in Germany and in the countries it has occupied, since it has been established by precise information that several hundred thousand Jews have been massacred in Eastern Europe," the Consistoire told Laval. "The fact that the people delivered by the French government have been collected without any regard as to their physical abilities, that among them are the ill, the elderly, women and children confirms that it is not for labor that the German government is demanding them but with the clear intention of pitilessly and methodically exterminating them."

By 1944, the UGIF office in Lyon was being compelled to turn over children to the Gestapo. The Jewish Resistance group raided UGIF offices not only to carry off files and equipment but to kidnap Jewish children entrusted to the care of the organization. A glimpse of the Jewish Resistance in Lyon, and its antagonism to UGIF, is provided by the postwar testimony of a man identified only as Monsieur C. After the Paris *rafles* of July 1942 he and his fellow Resistance members fled to Lyon and formed the Groupe de Combat Juif de Lyon, the Jewish Combat Group of Lyon. They obtained arms from the Franc-Tireurs et Partisans, a communist Resistance group that originated in the north and eventually moved into the southern zone.

The Jewish *résistants* also developed links with the mainstream Resistance movement, and by the beginning of 1944 they were receiving equipment and instructions from the Mouvements Unis de Résistance (MUR), carrying out sabotage missions and military attacks. "We also carried out an operation at the offices of UGIF on the Rue St. Catherine and on the Montée des Carmelites," said C. "We took away all the files as well as their duplicator, which we found good use for later. In addition, we saved seven children from UGIF, who were being kept at the Antiquaille Hospital. One of our comrades, dressed as a nurse and with false papers from UGIF, went to get them and we placed them in Lyon and in the countryside."

By this time UGIF was obliged to maintain regular contacts with Bureau IVB-4 of the SS, the Jewish section run by Bartelmus. After the war, a woman employee of UGIF gave a statement detailing how this relationship worked. In February 1944, ten months after she came to work with UGIF, her superiors asked her to accept an assignment that another woman had no longer been willing to fill: liaison with the Gestapo.

On a regular basis the Gestapo telephoned her after they had made arrests of adult Jews and ordered her to take custody of these children. She would place them in the temporary care of other families. Later, the Gestapo would come around to collect the children, assuring her that it was against their procedures to separate children from their families. Of course, they did not reveal that the entire family would be murdered once it had been reunited.

After the Jewish Combat Group kidnapped the children from the Antiquaille Hospital, she was the one who had to go to the Gestapo and explain what had happened. The resulting interrogation, as well as the arrest of two people involved in the care of the kidnapped children, heightened her fears of what would happen to her if she lost children given into her care by the Gestapo.

In September 1944 following the liberation of Lyon by the Allies, she testified about UGIF at length. "At the beginning, my work consisted of distributing money to foreign Jews who received a monthly stipend of between 200 and 400 francs," the woman stated. "Many Jews were afraid to come up to the office. Those who didn't want to come were paid by money orders, and their addresses were entered into a notebook. We had a certain number of files concerning these people, and these files I brought home with me after a certain date.

"Beginning in February 1944, of my own free will, I went to the Gestapo with a woman who took care of children. One of the [UGIF] directors had asked me to take care of this business because Mme. Z. didn't want any more of it. I was in contact with Bureau 4B of the Gestapo where, among others, worked Erich Bartelmus, Joseph Weisel, Bruckner, Heinrich, Boeckerle.

"The Gestapo telephoned me to come and take the children whose parents had been arrested. I placed them with families who were paid to keep them and whom I instructed not to let them leave and to release them only to persons designated by UGIF.

"The Germans came to my home on June 15, July 29 and August 17, 1944. The Gestapo then telephoned me to tell me to bring in the children. I brought them to them. They put them back with their parents. They sent them to Drancy. The Gestapo assured me that they didn't separate children from their parents. I don't know what they did with the parents.

"After the Antiquaille affair, where six children were kidnapped by the Resistance, I went on my own to tell the Gestapo, who told me to come in the following day. I was brought to the Antiquaille, then brought back to the Gestapo with the manager and an employee. These two were arrested. I was released, and I don't remember what questions the Germans asked me. They continued to place children in my care.

"My superiors, naturally, were aware of what was happening. Only July 29, 1944, the Germans gave me a child of 20 months of age whose parents I knew. When the Resistance came to my house to kidnap the child, I told them there was no child at my home that they could take. I said that if they took the child from me I would go to Montluc. My maid alerted the police. After the men from the Resistance left, I immediately placed the child with the Antiquaille so as not to have the responsibility, afraid of another Resistance visit.

"I did this work from February 4 until August 17, 1944, and 79 children came into my care. UGIF was doing social work. I didn't know that Jews had been seized in the UGIF offices. I knew that there was a question of disbanding UGIF because its employees were in danger, but the directors never talked about it to the employees. Personally, I had no opinion on the matter.

"I never considered arranging the escape of a single child; I was obliged to surrender them to the Gestapo."

Ω

But despite the Gestapo's manipulations, the work of saving Jewish children went on. One effort was so successful that it came to the attention of Klaus Barbie.

It seemed the ideal refuge from a war that had already brought pain into the children's lives. The huge farmhouse overlooking the rugged countryside of the Ain *département* east of Lyon was ideally suited to the needs of the Jewish organizers who in 1943 were looking for a place to hide some 40 Jewish children, many of them already orphaned by Hitler's policy of murder. In the small farming village of Izieu, strung along a remote hillside at the end of a winding mountain road, the children would be safe.

They were, for eleven months. Miron and Sabrina Zlatin found the farmhouse through friends, and they moved in with the children in May 1943. The Italians were occupying the region at the time, and the Jews in France knew that one stood a much better chance with the Italians than with either Vichy or the Germans.

Izieu was easy to ignore. It was an obscure village two kilometers up a steep, winding road from the slightly larger village of La Bruyère. It had only about a hundred inhabitants, and the Zlatin farmhouse was outside the village proper, set in a hillside field just above the point where the road made a loop, then straightened out for the final slow climb toward the cemetery and church at the entrance to Izieu.

The farmhouse was ideal, large enough to accommodate two-score children plus their guardians and teachers. It had roomy attics that could be used for schoolrooms, a number of large bedrooms that could be turned into dormitories, and a barn next door that could provide additional sleeping space. Food was available from the farmers in the region, which meant that the children would be eating far better in Izieu than in Lyon, where food was rationed and expensive.

The Zlatins had previously established their boarding school in the town of Palavas, in the Hérault department to the west of Lyon. But after the occupation of the southern zone by the Germans, Hérault was no longer safe. Then the Zlatins managed to rent the old, 12-room farmhouse in Izieu, which belonged to a family from the larger town of Belley, 15 kilometers away.

The presence of the Jewish children was technically not legal, but they followed a daily routine that was normal in most respects. They attended classes on all official French school days, taught by a schoolteacher assigned to the home by the regional educational authorities in Belley, a sub-prefecture of the Ain department. The teacher, Gabrielle Tardy, bicycled each Sunday evening from her home in Belley to Izieu, where she rented a room in a farmhouse near the boarding school. Monday through Saturday she taught the children in the mornings and afternoons and ate lunch with them. Those between the ages of 5 and 14 were taught in one group at home; the older ones attended classes at the high school in Belley.

It was an awkward assignment for an inexperienced teacher 21 years old. "They were very difficult, but I became attached to them. You couldn't help but become attached to them," Gabrielle says today in her apartment in Belley. "Yet these children were different from others their age, in certain subtle ways. They never talked about themselves, about their families, or about their lives. They never said anything; they were very secretive. They were used to being distrustful. They explained nothing, they said nothing."

The photo that Mme. Tardy pushed across the table in her living room shows children who look like any others their age. All are smiling, some have their arms around each other. "They were happy to be alive," she recalls. But, she adds, "they had a maturity that others don't have at their age. They were children who had already lived; some had already been in concentration camps."

The children lived in the farmhouse in Izieu for almost one year. But in the spring of 1944, Mme. Zlatin began to get worried. Following the Italian capitulation to the Allies the Germans had taken over the occupation of the region, and it was no longer safe. A major garrison of German troops was now located in Belley, just 20 minutes away.

Shortly before Easter, in April 1944, Mme. Zlatin left for the south of France to seek another shelter for the children. She was to return on Good Friday. The last time Mme. Tardy saw her charges they were preparing a surprise for Mme. Zlatin's return, but she never received it. On Holy Thursday, at 8:00 A.M., two trucks rumbled up the winding road to Izieu and stopped in the driveway of the "Children's Colony of Izieu," as it was called. The soldiers, members of the German Flack Batallion Abteilung 958 based in Belley, leaped out and began the operation. Directing the morning's work was Obersturmführer Klaus Barbie.

Julien Favet, a farm laborer, witnessed the proceedings. He had been working in one of the fields below the boarding school, but his employer had not yet brought him his customary morning meal. He began to walk back up toward the village, stopping at the school where the two trucks he had earlier seen driving up towards Izieu were now parked. He had assumed that they were coming to pick up two loads of firewood.

"I was walking back up toward the village, and that's when I saw the Germans, about 15 of them, pushing the kids in the trucks." Favet, now 63 and still living in Izieu, could hear the children crying inside the trucks, which had been requisitioned from a Belley construction company. "The littlest ones, who didn't know what was going to happen, had been frightened by all that violence when they had just woken up. But the older ones—13 or 14 years old—knew well where they were going. The *rafle* lasted two hours."

There were 43 children at Izieu that day; the older ones had come to the farmhouse from Belley because of the Easter school holidays. Also arrested were Miron Zlatin, 40, Marie Friedler, 36, Lucie Heiger, 30, and Suzanne Reifmann, 38, the school's doctor. Barbie also arrested Reifmann's husband's parents, Moise and Mova Reifmann, who had come to visit. The only one to escape was Suzanne's husband, Léon Reifmann, who had been in an upstairs room when the German arrived. Reifmann, who was already wanted by the Germans, jumped the 15 feet to the garden below, leaped a wall and made his way to a neighbor's house, where he was hidden until the Germans had left.

In the yard in front of the house, the Germans were collecting the children. "When I turned in the driveway, I had a machine gun in my stomach, and I saw the entire school assembled in front," Favet recalls. "There were German soldiers all around, and two civilians. An officer was talking, and then he made them get into the trucks.

"I was bare from the waist up, because it was very hot. My boss said to me, 'They're asking for you.' A German held me, and an officer questioned me. I only understood the word 'terrorist,' and they motioned toward the countryside. Finally, they let me go. I think they were asking me if there were 'terrorists' on the mountain. One of the children, the one called François, made a motion as if to jump from the truck. He was struck with a rifle butt full in the face."

One of the neighbors began to approach the group, but Miron Zlatin told him, "Stay where you are." For that, Favet says, Zlatin was kicked and beaten with rifle butts.

Favet today is certain that it was Klaus Barbie who directed the operation. "He even saved my life," the farm laborer later explained. "One of the SS officers took me for Dr. Reifmann, and wanted to push me into the trucks. It was Barbie himself who ordered him to let me go. During the search Barbie stood leaning against the stone fountain in the driveway. He was dressed in civilian clothes and spoke sometimes in French, other times in German."

Soon the two trucks were loaded with their frightened cargo, and they pulled away. "At the first turn," Favet said, "you could hear a vague noise, then a song, stronger and stronger." The Jewish schoolchildren were singing as they were carried away to their deaths. Their song was a popular patriotic French melody of the era, called, "You Won't Have Alsace and Lorraine." The sound of the song, which the children had learned from Sabrina Zlatin, died away as the trucks descended the hill.

Five German soldiers stayed on in the terrified village, pillaging the schoolhouse and eating at the homes of the nearby residents, their machine guns resting on the table during meals. The day after the children were taken away they shot a pig that had been raised at the school, and spent the afternoon machine-gunning the carcass. Once the Nazis left, the stunned villagers picked up their normal lives.

"We had ended up by adopting those kids," Favet says. "Nobody really expected such a raid; we had reassured ourselves by thinking that the *maquis* could be warned in time to intervene. It was a month before I dared to go into the farmhouse of the children's colony. On the table in the kitchen I found baskets of bread and 43 bowls, with the coffee and the milk that they never had time to drink that morning."

Ω

Most of those taken in the raid were sent to Drancy, but Miron Zlatin, who had helped the *maquis* in the area, was executed at the medieval fortress of Revel, near Toulouse in the southwest, along with two of the older boys. Traces of the other children have been found in lists of the death convoys sent to Auschwitz. The three Benguigi children, Jacques, 13, Richard, 8, and Jean-Claude, 6, were shipped to Auschwitz in convoy number 71, which left Drancy on April 14, 1944. That convoy comprised 1,500 people including 624 men, 854 women and 22 others not identified. There were 148 children under the age of 12, and 295 under the age of 19. Seventy women survived at the end of the war, as did 35 men. None of the children lived.

Another convoy, shipped on June 30, included Mina and Claudine Halaunbrenner, aged 4 and 5, respectively. From this convoy, 398 men and 223 women were selected to receive tattooed numbers and be kept in the work camp at Auschwitz. In 1945, 100 women and 67 men were still alive. But those not selected for labor—including all the children—were immediately gassed and cremated.

Ω

The raid on the children's home in Izieu stands out as a particularly barbaric act, one of the most telling indictments against Barbie today. Documents exist that establish beyond any doubt that Klaus Barbie played a principal role in the affair.

The telegram sent from Gestapo headquarters in Lyon to the Paris Gestapo headquarters told the story in concise terms, as if it were a military dispatch. The cable was addressed to Barbie's superiors in the occupation security forces, the Befehlshaber der Sicherheitzpolizei und des SD in Paris. In one terse paragraph, the fate of the Jewish children and their adult companions was sealed and filed away in the Nazi archives. At the end of the war, the vast majority of Gestapo files were destroyed to prevent them falling into enemy hands, but this telegram survived to bear witness against Barbie.

It was headed: "Concerning: Jewish orphanage in Izieu-Ain."

"In the morning hours today the Jewish orphanage 'Child Colony' in Izieu-Ain was shut down. A total of 41 children, aged from 3 to 13, were arrested. In addition, the entire Jewish personnel, consisting of 10 persons, including five women, has been arrested. It was not possible to seize either money or other valuables.

"Transport to Drancy follows 6-4-44."

The telegram, dated April 6—the day of the raid—was signed: "Barbie, SS-Obersturmführer."

THE MAKING OF A NAZI

"**H**E WAS THE SOUL OF THE GESTAPO."

This comment about Barbie by a fellow SS comrade does much to explain the mentality of a 29-year-old whose enthusiasm for violence caused the death of thousands. A more difficult task is to trace the early history of such a man and describe the personal and national environment that shaped him.

The political and social forces that drew the German nation down a precipitous spiral to war, genocide and self-destruction have been minutely examined. They include a humiliating defeat in World War I; crushing reparations and military occupation imposed by the victors; massive unemployment and deep social upheaval; and strong threads of militarism and anti-Semitism in the German culture. It was in this environment that Barbie grew to manhood.

Born on October 25, 1913, in Bad Godesberg, near the present-day West German capital of Bonn, Nikolaus "Klaus" Barbie was the result of an unsanctified union between a 25-year-old clerical worker and a 27-year-old woman from a family of small land-owners. It was not until three months after his birth, in January 1914, that the father, Nikolaus Barbie, married Anna Hees in the Saar town of Merzig, where the Barbie family's roots went back several generations. That summer, World War I erupted and the elder Nikolaus entered military service, surviving the war after sustaining a wound in the neck and being taken prisoner by the French.

By 1919 he had obtained his freedom and a schoolmaster's post in the village of Udler, in the Eifel region of Germany, near the border with Belgium and Luxembourg, north of his native Saar. The Barbies had now attained a modest gentility even though Nikolaus raised pigs and goats and worked five acres of land in addition to his teaching job. He is said to have been a stern schoolmaster and a heavy drinker; at times his wife was obliged to turn for financial assistance to her family in the nearby village of Mehren. Chronically ill, Nikolaus took a leave of absence from his post in 1925 and never returned.

In 1923 young Klaus was sent off to the city of Trier, south of the Eifel region on the Mosel River, to begin his secondary studies in the Staatliches Friedrich Wilhelms-Gymnasium on the Jesuiten-strasse near the center of the town. Together with the city of Koblenz further to the east, Trier was a center of the rather poor, heavily Catholic Mosel region. Although a provincial community, Trier was founded in 15 B.C. by Romans under Emperor Augustus. The city had another distinction: it was the birthplace, in 1818, of the political philosopher Karl Marx. Ironically, the dedicated Nazi and the communist philosopher were graduates of the same secondary school.

For Barbie, the change from Udler, where he had been taught by his own father, to Trier, where he lived as a boarding student, was exhilarating. "Thus an entirely new period began for me," Barbie was to recall a few years later in an essay written shortly before his graduation in 1934 at the age of twenty. In Udler, he explained, "as the son of the teacher I had to set an example for the others." But in Trier, he wrote, "I found myself left to my own devices for the first time."

Barbie lived with a minimum of supervision in his boarding

situation, which apparently was not directly connected with the school. This independence, he says, "became the major aspect of my education." But within a few years his father retired and Barbie's parents and younger brother, Kurt, moved to Trier. "Again," he recalled, "I had to live with my mother and father. My joy was great, but so was my disappointment."

Barbie's home life was clearly unhappy in this period. "The terrible sufferings that I had to endure during the years when I passed from the upper third level to the upper first must forever remain my secret and a warning for my future," he wrote. "I can say that these years made me a wise man. These years taught me how bitter life can be, and how terrible destiny."

Despite his inner turmoil Barbie, in the eyes of his peers, was an ordinary young man. One fellow student and close friend was Konrad Jacobs, now a retired civil servant in Trier. The two studied together for seven years and graduated in the same class in 1934. Barbie, Jacobs says, "was a very good comrade and a good student, though not outstanding." He was well liked, but was not a leader of the student body of the Gymnasium. He played handball and soccer, excelled in languages—a talent that proved invaluable in Lyon years later—did poorly in mathematics and was, with Jacobs, a member of the Catholische Jugend, a religious youth organization. He was well-behaved and rarely earned demerits. Jacobs went to Barbie's home only once or twice, where he could see that the family was not, as he expresses it, "in the roses."

The unhappiness Barbie had alluded to in his essay undoubtedly was connected with a dual tragedy that struck the family in 1933. His father developed cancer of the neck, which ended with his death on October 3, 1933, only a few months after the death of Barbie's brother, who suffered from a chronic illness. "The year 1933 brought great disturbances in our country," Barbie writes, "but also changes in our family. In June my only and dear brother died (I have no other brothers or sisters), and just a few months later I lost my father, who departed this life too early due to the effects of a war wound."

The autumn of 1933 was a turning point for Barbie; he found in the political turmoil of Germany a parallel with the disruption of his own life. Nazism was his anodyne. "This was a terrible blow for my mother and me," Barbie wrote of his double loss. "The events of this year have not left me a moment of rest. The powerful national upsurge attracted me, as it did every true young German, and today I can serve among all those who follow the Führer." This was written on November 30, 1933; since April of that year Barbie had been a member of the Hitler Jugend, the Nazi youth movement. Like millions of other Germans, Barbie was swept up in the wave of nationalism and demagoguery that followed Adolph Hitler's appointment to the Reichschancellor post on January 30, 1933.

While Barbie had been seduced by Nazism by the end of 1933, former classmate Jacobs insists that in earlier years at the Gymnasium he was initially unsympathetic to students attempting to organize a Hitler Youth group at the school. In his autobiographical essay, Barbie makes no reference to his Hitler Jugend involvement, speaking only about another organization called the Deutsche Jugendkraft, and to a group which assisted travelers and prisoners. Possibly Barbie believed that his Hitler Jugend membership would be negatively viewed by his teachers and decided to omit mention of it from his essay.

The National Socialist Democratic Workers party, later known as the Nazi party, was slower to develop in Trier and the Mosel region than in many other parts of Germany, according to Dr. Reinar Nolden, who now heads the Trier municipal archives. In early 1933, when Hitler came to power as Reichschancellor, there were only 120 committed Nazis in the entire Mosel region, Nolden says. This number included "the young, the active ones who would also use their fists." Nor was the subsequent growth of the Nazi Party a spontaneous phenomenon: the party's central office sent a Dr. Simmer to the region to organize it.

Even at the moment of the Nazi triumph on a national level in 1933, the party remained weaker in Trier than the Center party, which was dominated by the Catholic Church. In the 1930 Reichstag parliamentary election, the Nazis drew only 16 percent of the city's vote compared with the 43.1 percent polled by the Center party. In the two 1932 Reichstag elections, the Nazis fluctuated between 23 and 20 percent, while the Center held a steady 48 percent. In the March 1933 election that consolidated Hitler's power, Trier's Nazis attained only 32 percent compared to the 44 percent held by the Center. Still, on a national level Hitler received less than 38 percent of the vote; the success of the Nazis was more the result of ruthlessness and intimidation than mastery of the democratic process.

Under the provisions of the Versailles Treaty, the region had been occupied by the French Army from 1920 until as late as 1930, a fact that probably contributed to Barbie's command of French, a language he studied in the Gymnasium. The French troops had been preceded by the Americans, who occupied Trier and the rest of the Saar from the end of 1918 until relieved by the French two years later. But the American presence never provoked as much resentment as did that of the French.

By 1923 the French occupiers faced major public disturbances in Trier and throughout the region, mainly in reaction to their move to occupy the Ruhr, the industrial heartland of Germany to the north. The people of Trier particularly resented the Spahis, Algerian colonial troops who were considered brutal. An issue of the *Trierischer Volksfreund*, celebrating the July 1930 French withdrawal, displayed political cartoons with strongly racial overtones showing mounted Spahis wreaking havoc in the Hauptmarkt as German civilians flee their swinging scimitars.

This was the political climate in which Barbie spent his formative years. It is not surprising that he harbored antipathies toward the French; he once told one of his victims in Lyon that he hated the French because they had imprisoned his father. Whatever the reason, Barbie became active in Nazi organizations soon after Hitler took power. He was no exception, for the popularity of the Nazis in the region soared after their national victory. From the 120-man core in the Mosel region at the beginning of 1933, the party grew rapidly; by the end of the year it had 120,00 members out of a regional population of 1.2 million.

"All these people wanted to get the new jobs," says Dr. Nolden, adding, "after they came to power there was a huge turmoil. You wouldn't believe how quickly the Nazis took over all possible fields of life." After the March 1933 Reichstag election, the Sturm Abteilung, the Brown Shirts, stormed the Karl Marx House in Trier and ejected the Social Democrats who were headquartered there. The

SA renamed the building Braun Haus and turned it into the head-quarters of the *Trierer Nationalblatt*, the local Nazi newspaper.

Barbie rose rapidly in the Nazi movement. By late 1933 he had already attained the rank of a Jungvolkführer, or Youth Leader, in the Hitler Jugend. In March 1934 he was graduated from the Friedrich Wilhelms Gymnasium with mediocre marks, receiving the grade of *genugend*, or "sufficient," in eight of fourteen subjects, with a "good" in the remainder. He received his diploma, but according to Jacobs did not receive the Hochschulereife, the endorsement to go on for higher studies.

Barbie had already known that he would not be attending university: "I must say that destiny, through the death of my father, has reduced my most cherished hopes to nothing. I wanted to become a philologist, but my present situation forbids this." Jacobs says that the Barbie family—now only Klaus and his mother—could not afford higher schooling for the young man.

With his options limited, Barbie entered the Freiwilligen Arbeitsdienst, or Volunteer Work Service, a public works project sponsored by political parties and churches for youth, which had existed before Hitler took power. Like every other aspect of German society, it too came under the control of the Nazis. Barbie joined a detachment that was sent to work in Niebull, in Schleswig-Holstein on the North Sea coast, from April to November 1934.

Returning to Trier afterwards, he became a volunteer leader in the local Hitler Youth group, a move Barbie later claimed he made to obtain party help in continuing his studies. He developed a close association with a man named Karl Horrmann, leader of the Trier center Ortsgruppe, or Nazi party political unit. It was Horrmann, Barbie said, who in February 1935 asked him if he were interested in joining either the Gestapo or the Sicherheitsdienst, explaining that members of these police services received free training in law.

Barbie immediately applied for membership in the Nazi secret service, but not until September was he interviewed by Reinhard Heydrich (as Barbie later claimed), then chief of the SD, at 102 Wilhelmstrasse in Berlin. On September 26, 1935, Barbie was accepted into the SS, though he was not formally inducted until October 1, when he was assigned the SS identification number 272 284. Klaus Barbie's career as a professional Nazi had begun.

By the time Barbie joined its ranks, the Schutzstaffel, or Protection Detachment, was firmly established as a powerful state within the Nazi police state. Formed in 1925 from an earlier paramilitary group called the Strosstrupp Hitler, the SS was intended to serve as an elite corps of bodyguards for the party leaders. The role of the SS began to expand in 1929 when it came under the control of Heinrich Himmler, Reichsführer-SS, destined to become the most feared man in Nazi Germany. When Himmler took control of the SS it had only 280 members, compared with the 60,000 troops of the Sturm Abteilung, the Brown Shirts who were then the strongest paramilitary arm of the Nazi party. But by the end of 1930 the black-shirted SS had almost 3,000 members and was rapidly gaining on Ernst Röhm's SA in size and power.

Himmler, who shared Hitler's obsessive hatred of Jews, injected his racist and Aryan elitist theories into his recruitment of SS men. By 1931 candidates were being screened to ensure that they were of pure Aryan stock; the same genealogical requirements were imposed on their brides. Himmler's SS soon became the blind instrument of Hitler's will. Each recruit had to swear "loyalty and valor" to the Führer, pledging "obedience unto death, so help me God."

There is evidence that Barbie took this ideology deeply to heart; long after the war had been lost he would maintain his pride in being a member of the brutal organization. "I am a member of the SS," Barbie said nearly forty years later. "Perhaps you think that any fool could become a member of the SS. Do you really know what an SS soldier is? He is a superman. He is a professional chosen personally by Hitler. A soldier whose antecedents are analyzed for four generations back before he is given the honor of being allowed to join this elite organization."

The Sicherheitsdienst or SD, the intelligence arm of the SS, was formed in 1932 and placed under the command of Reinhard Heydrich. There were other intelligence organs within the SA and the Nazi party apparatus, but the SD rapidly expanded its influence and by 1934 it was the principal intelligence and counterintelligence service of Nazi Germany, rivaled only by the Wehrmacht's Abwehr.

Even before Hitler claimed the office of Reichschancellor, these unofficial police groups were imposing his will in Germany's streets. But after assuming official leadership of Germany, the repressive capacities of Hitler's police forces were strengthened. In April 1933, Hermann Göring, then Prussian minister of the interior, created the Geheime Staatspolizei, or Gestapo, which came under the central control of Himmler the following year. At the time of Hitler's rise to power, the SS had 50,000 men, but it still shared power with Ernst Röhm's SA.

Both participated in the witch hunt that followed the Reichstag fire of February 27, 1933, but in June 1934, the SS vanquished the Sturm Abteilung in the "Night of the Long Knives," when Röhm and other SA leaders were assassinated and the SA was permanently put in a subordinate position. That month also brought a reorganization of the German police forces, dividing them into Ordnungspolizei, or regular police, and the Sicherheitspolizei, or security police, further legitimizing the power of the SS and its Gestapo.

Barbie entered the SS during a period of great opportunities for advancement. Barbie, as an SS-Mann, or private, was initially stationed at the SD-Hauptamt, the main office in Berlin, but then in October 1936 he was transferred to Düsseldorf, where he worked in the SD-Oberabschnitt West, the western regional office, as a *Referent* or specialist. His SS personnel file gives no indication of what his duties were in Düsseldorf, but he evidently performed them satisfactorily, for by April 1939 he had been promoted to the rank of Oberscharführer, or non-commissioned officer. He had also become a member of the Nazi party, receiving the matriculation number 4 583 085 in 1937. Between September and December 1938 Barbie went through basic training in the army, serving in the 39th Infantry Regiment, but this duty was foreshortened because of his SS status.

In early 1939 Barbie and his fiancée, Regina Willms, 23, entered the complicated bureaucratic process of obtaining permission to marry. Regina, who met Barbie in 1937, was the daughter of a postal clerk in the town of Osburg near Trier. She had not finished high school, but in 1934 and 1935 she took courses in housekeeping and cooking in her native region. In 1936 she went to Berlin as an *au pair* girl, caring for children in a private household, and in

1937 she moved to Düsseldorf to work in a nursery run by the Nazi women's organization.

In order to marry with the Führer's blessings, the 25-year-old non-com and his fiancée had to submit genealogical charts giving data on 62 ancestors going back five generations to the early eighteenth century, establishing that they were racially pure. Regina Willms also had to obtain character references, which were conveniently provided by other SS officers; both had to undergo medical examinations and fill out questionnaires on family health history. Although Barbie and his wife were both born into the Catholic faith, the couple gave their religious affiliation as *Gottgläubiger*, or "believer in God," a term adopted by Nazis who had rejected formal Christianity.

In October 1939 Barbie was assigned to the SD's regional office in Dortmund, which was also in the west of Germany. This office was to remain his Dienstelle, or administrative base, throughout World War II, even though his actual assignments took him to several countries in western Europe. On April 20, 1940, Barbie was promoted to Untersturmführer, or second lieutenant. His promotion papers indicate that he was a *Referent* for SD sections that gathered intelligence on individuals and organizations falling within the suspect categories of "liberalism and pacifism."

Barbie and Willms were married on April 25, 1940, in Berlin, with two SS officers as witnesses. The couple returned to Dortmund and established what seemed the ideal Nazi household, even to their address at 28 Horst Wessel Strasse, a street named after the Nazi "martyr" and pseudo-patron saint killed in February 1930 in street-fighting with communists in Berlin.

Ω

In the early days of May 1940, Klaus Barbie was probably aware of the Blitzkrieg attack that Hitler was preparing to launch on the West. In the weeks preceding it the entire western region of Germany had seen a massive buildup of forces preparatory to the invasion of the Netherlands, Belgium, Luxembourg and France. At 4:30 A.M. on May 10, the 1st Panzer Division, commanded by General Heinz Guderian, crossed into Luxembourg, while to the north the 7th Panzer, under the command of General Erwin Rommel violated the Belgian frontier. The ground offensive was covered by a massive air assault, and within hours the entire world knew that the so-called Phony War, what the French called the *Drôle de Guerre*, which had prevailed since the German invasion of Poland in September 1939, was over.

The Netherlands capitulated to the Germans on May 15; Belgium surrendered on the 28th of that month. France withstood the onslaught only slightly longer. By June 22 at 8:50 P.M. the French had signed an armistice with the Germans in the same clearing at Rethondes, and in the same railway car, where the Germans had acknowledged defeat after World War I in November 1918. The cease-fire took effect early on the morning of June 25; the entire battle had lasted just 46 days, and in that short length of time the French Army had been thrown into chaotic retreat and the British Expeditionary Force driven off the beach at Dunkirk.

The Germans wasted no time consolidating their hold on the new territories; on May 29, Barbie was assigned to the SD office in Holland. The SD's main branch was in The Hague, the capital, but Barbie himself was posted to Amsterdam. After five months in Holland, Barbie was recommended for promotion to Obersturmführer, or full lieutenant. A superior officer wrote that Barbie was an "especially hardworking and responsible" SS officer who devoted himself "completely and intensively to SD work," adding that Untersturmführer Barbie's "SS bearing on duty and off was irreproachable." The same officer wrote that Barbie was "a lover of life and truth, and a good comrade." On November 9, 1940, Barbie's promotion to Obersturmführer was made official. At home in Dortmund, Barbie's family was thriving as well; on June 30, 1941, Regina Barbie gave birth to a baby girl, who was named Ute Barbie.

In his personnel file Barbie is technically described as a *Hilfsreferent*, or assistant specialist, for the Amsterdam SD branch office in the area of culture. He was responsible for investigating anti-Nazi tendencies in the domains of science, education, religion, sports or entertainment. However, his actual duties were not always as cerebral. Other evidence indicates that Barbie was involved in political police activities, including anti-Jewish actions.

The Nazi campaign against Dutch Jewry was initiated on February 12, 1941, with the formation—through German coercion—of the Joodsche Raad, or Jewish Council. The Jews of the Netherlands opposed the plan, correctly suspecting that the organization would become an instrument of Nazi control. The issue was forced in mid-February 1941, when violent confrontations between Jews and Dutch Nazis broke out in the old Jewish section of Amsterdam. Hans Rauter, Nazi SS and Police commander, summoned Jewish leaders and demanded that the council be formed and accept responsibility for maintaining order in the Jewish community.

A week later, in south Amsterdam, another violent incident took place between a German police patrol and Jews. It was shortly followed, on February 22 and 23, by the German seizure of some 400 Jewish men between the ages of 20 and 35 years. Their deportation to the Mauthausen camp in Germany provoked a general strike by the residents of Amsterdam on February 25 and a subsequent German crackdown. But despite Dutch civilian support for the Jews, it was the beginning of the annihilation of the Jewish community in Holland.

According to Dr. David Barnouw, a research associate with the Rijksinstituut voor Oorlogsdocumentatie, the Netherlands State Institute for War Documentation, Barbie was not then with Section III of the SS, as some documents suggest, but with Section IV, the Gestapo. Citing the work of Dutch historian Jacob Presser and the memoirs of Jewish community leader David Cohen, Barnouw says that Barbie was directly implicated in at least one anti-Jewish action in Amsterdam, the round-up, subsequent deportation and eventual murder of nearly 300 Jewish men in mid-1941.

The incident began in a Zionist colony in the Wieringermeer region of the Netherlands, an area near the Great Dike that had been reclaimed from the North Sea in the early 1930s. The Jewish colony, called the Werkdorp or Work Village, had been established in 1934. On March 20, 1941, German troops came to Werkdorp and rounded up all the young men. "These boys were afraid that they would be sent to a concentration camp," says Barnouw. Instead, the youths were placed with Jewish families in Amsterdam through the auspices of the *Joodsche Raad*. They remained there, Barnouw says, until June 9, 1941, when Klaus Barbie paid a call on the head of the Jewish Council.

"He said to this man, David Cohen, 'We want to bring these

boys back to the working farm. Will you give me the list of their names and addresses?"' The Jewish leader was inclined to cooperate with Barbie because the Werkdorp had earlier implored the Germans to allow its work force to return. Not realizing the consequences, the head of the Joodsche Raad gave Barbie the list.

"Two days later," Barnouw says, "there was a raid on the places where they were staying." The Germans did not limit their arrests to those on Barbie's list, many of whom were no longer at the addresses indicated. Instead they took all Jewish males between the ages of 20 and 30 from the households, a total of 278 men. They were first sent to a transit camp north of Amsterdam, called Schoorf, then shipped to Mauthausen. All died there, the last of the group surviving only until September, 1941.

The Germans claimed the deportations were carried out in reprisal for Resistance activities in Amsterdam. "They said it was the youths who did it, which was nonsense," says Barnouw, who is categorical about Barbie's involvement in the deportations. He cites the memoirs of David Cohen that have appeared in a Jewish publication in Holland and a book on the fate of Dutch Jewry under the Nazis by the late Jacob Presser. "We have it from other sources, also," says Barnouw. "There weren't many German officers here, at least at the beginning."

The deportation of the Wieringermeer Jews was only a prelude to a broader attack begun in the summer of 1942. Large numbers of Dutch Jews were deported to the East via the transit camps of Westerbork and Vught. German immigrant Jews were the first to go, Barnouw says, and were followed by the native Dutch Jews. In all, some 110,000 Jews had been deported from Holland by the end of the war, mainly destined for the camps of Auschwitz and Sobibor; only 5,000 survived. Another 30,000 went into hiding and escaped deportation, but by 1945 about 75 percent of the Jews in the Netherlands had been murdered.

Ω

After Barbie's assignment in Holland ended, he spent some time in Belgium before being posted to France. But before that, he returned to Germany to attend a special training school in counterinsurgency tactics, then later participated in a counterespionage operation on the Swiss border in France.

"It happened that in the regions we were occupying, not only in Russia, but also in France, Belgium, Holland, Yugoslavia, Norway, guerrilla resistance movements arose," Barbie explained. "The response to this was the establishment in Germany of a center for the preparation of commandos specially instructed to oppose such groups. I was one of the first to be called up for this center.... In the middle of 1942, around June, I finished my preparation and received orders to travel to France to establish my first commando. But before taking on this responsibility, I was put in charge of an intelligence operation in Switzerland."

As Barbie related it, his assignment was to uncover a Soviet spy ring that was operating in Switzerland and which was funneling such vital information out of the German High Command that it was undermining the Nazi offensive on the Eastern front. In charge of this spy ring, Barbie says, was a mysterious person code-named Werther.

"Werther, Werther. Who was Werther? It was never known. He operated, we knew, under the cover of the German High Command, in Berlin. He shared vital information with the Russians. Even today, I am convinced that it was he, in large part, who led us to disaster on the Soviet front. Our service knew that he operated across the Swiss border, led by the German Roessler, but his sources were located in the High Command. The decisive battle of spring 1943 ended with the German rout at Kursk: Werther's actions were decisive."

Barbie and his commando never tracked down the Werther ring. The Swiss government moved first and broke up the network, though Barbie maintains that the key members escaped and continued to serve the Soviets throughout the war and even in the postwar era. He may have exaggerated the role of the spies he was pursuing on the Swiss border, but his next statement is accurate and telling. "From Switzerland I was sent to my original destination, which was also my first command, where I became involved in my principal activity of the war: chief of the SS in Lyon."

It was in that capacity that Barbie was to meet the great challenge of his Gestapo career, the search for Jean Moulin, the head of the French Resistance.

BARBIE AND MOULIN

Even in exile, the general infused his every action with distinctively Gallic solemnity, a mood that prevailed one February evening in 1943 as Charles de Gaulle called a handful of men to attention in the living room of his Hampstead, England, home. "Corporal Mercier," he pronounced slowly as the man before him threw back his shoulders, "we recognize you as our companion in the liberation of France, with honor and through victory." De Gaulle inclined his lofty frame to place upon Mercier the Cross of the Liberation, the highest honor his shadow government could bestow.

Mercier, a solidly-built man in his early forties with wisps of gray in his dark hair, was moved by the ceremony. De Gaulle's intelligence chief, André Dewavrin, could see a tear streaking the cheek of Mercier—or the man living under that *nom de guerre*. Dewavrin and the others present were aware of the man's real identity, just as they knew the origin of the ugly scar etched horizontally across his throat. Not even in the besieged safety of

England could Jean Moulin, code-named Max, step fully out of the shadows.

Moulin would be moving east across the Channel again in just a few days, back to occupied France and the furtive round of concealment he had pursued for the past 13 months. On this trip Moulin was to bear a responsibility more weighty than any previously entrusted to a member of the Resistance. The degree of his success, or failure, would have profound implications for de Gaulle and France.

De Gaulle was already heavily in the debt of Moulin, who had laboriously united the disparate units of the French Resistance in southern France into a coherent organization. It had been Moulin's vision from the start, an audacious strategy he had outlined to de Gaulle when first ushered into the leader's office in the Carlton Gardens headquarters of France Libre in London in December of 1941.

General de Gaulle later wrote in his memoirs, "In October 1941 I learned of the presence in Lisbon of Jean Moulin, who had arrived from France and was seeking to come to London. I knew who he was." De Gaulle contacted the British to ask that Moulin be sent along, but he had to wait for two months to see him. The British were also trying to recruit Moulin into their intelligence service for France.

Moulin, de Gaulle writes, was a man extraordinarily suited for the work he was to undertake: "Full of judgment and seeing things and people as they were, he would be watching each step as he walked along a road that was undermined by adversaries' traps and encumbered by obstacles raised by friends."

De Gaulle had sent agents back into France beginning in July 1940, just a month after the defeat. He had already established an intelligence network, but he had been slow to appreciate the potential of the Resistance, perceiving it more as an espionage web than a fighting force behind enemy lines. Qualifying himself as a "simple messenger," Moulin impressed on de Gaulle that it was imperative to create direct forms of liaison with these groups, and to support them materially and politically to maximize their combat potential. "It would be insane and criminal not to use these soldiers," Moulin argued in a written assessment he handed the general, "who are ready to make the greatest of sacrifices in the event of large-scale operations undertaken by the Allies on the continent."

Moulin was not a military man, nor had he organized his own Resistance network. Although he informed de Gaulle on the status of Resistance organizations in Lyon and Marseille, he had little knowledge of the French opposition to the Germans in the occupied capital of Paris. The only document Moulin could produce to back his proposal was an identity card sliced into eight pieces. When assembled, it showed that Moulin had been an official of the French government before the war, the prefect, or district administrator, of the Eure-et-Loir *département* of France.

The mutilation of his card reflected the precautions he took before crossing from France into Spain and Portugal the previous September on a forged passport in the name of Joseph-Jean Mercier. The pieces were concealed both in a travel clock and in the grip of his valise, stitched and glued securely away. Moulin had another credential to prove his sincere opposition to the Nazi conquerer. It was the prominent gash across his throat, irrefutable evidence of his will. His reputation had made its way to London even before Moulin flew into England and landed at an airfield in Bournemouth. De Gaulle already knew the story of Moulin's first stand.

Ω

Moulin was prefect of the Eure-et-Loir province in June 1940 when the Germans were completing their Blitzkreig defeat of the French Army and the British Expeditionary Force. Paris had yielded without a fight and the Nazi juggernaut moved on south and west, towards Chartres, capital of Moulin's *département*. Chaos ruled in the streets of the cathedral city, which lay in the path of millions of frantic French and Belgian refugees fleeing ahead of the German advance. Moulin did his best to maintain public order and supply the most desperate of the fugitives with food and, until supplies were exhausted, fuel for their vehicles.

The Germans arrived in the open city on June 17, 1940. Moulin acknowledged its conquest while demanding that the invaders respect the rights of noncombatants. The ranking German officer agreed, and it was not until the following day that Moulin learned the Nazis had already committed a series of atrocities. In the nearby village of Luray German troops had commandeered the home of an 83-year-old woman. When she vigorously protested, they dragged her into her garden, tied her to a tree and shot her before the eyes of her daughter—who was then forced to dig the grave. As a warning, the woman's body was left tied to the tree for 24 hours.

Before Moulin could seek out the commander to protest, German soldiers came for him. They escorted him to German military headquarters in a Chartres hotel, where they laid a document before him. In a crude attempt to divert suspicion from German atrocities and blame them on black French troops, the paper stated that a Senegalese unit of the French Army had gone on a barbaric spree during the disorderly retreat, raping women and killing indiscriminately. His signature was demanded on the spurious deposition to record these "facts." Moulin flatly refused, and his own ordeal began.

Two German officers pushed the paper before him, but Moulin continued to object. "Do you really imagine that a Frenchman who is a high public official responsible for representing his country before the enemy could agree to sign such an outrage?" he asked.

The ranking Nazi officer flew into a rage. "It is unacceptable," he shouted at Moulin, "that you should make a mockery of the army of Greater Germany. You are going to sign! Do you hear me? You are going to sign!"

Moulin demanded proof that the alleged atrocities had been committed by the African colonial troops. "There is no doubt as to that," the German officer responded. "The victims were examined by German specialists. The violence they suffered shows all the characteristics of crimes committed by Negroes." Moulin could not resist smiling at the absurd response. Suddenly one of the German officers took out his revolver and stuck the barrel in Moulin's back. Pushing him toward the table, he ordered him to take the pen another held out. "Sign," he snarled, "or you'll find out what happens when people fool with German officers."

When Moulin did not move to comply, he received a sharp blow from the barrel of the gun between his shoulderblades. The session deteriorated into a cruel beating; Moulin was hit in the kidneys with a rifle butt, and struck in the face. The Germans dragged him out of the hotel and pushed him into the back of a command car which drove out of the city. After ten miles they arrived in the village of Taye and pulled up in front of a farm-cafe near the train station. They showed him a shed in which nine disfigured bodies, including those of children, were laid out, contorted in the grotesque postures of sudden and violent death.

"Look at what your wonderful Negroes have done," a German exclaimed. "I hope now you won't keep making difficulties for us in signing the statement."

"Either you've been misled," Moulin responded, "or this is a macabre scenario of some kind. Anybody can see these poor people are simply bombing casualties."

The enraged Germans attacked Moulin, beating him again before leading him across the farmyard to another shed. Inside, Moulin was confronted with further horror: the mangled, blood-drenched corpse of a woman whose limbs had been torn off by the force of the explosives dropped by the Luftwaffe. They abruptly shoved him onto the cadaver and walked out, locking him inside.

Moulin could feel his will draining as the smell of death filled his nostrils. Night was falling by the time he was let out of the shed by the Germans, who again pushed the paper in his face. When Moulin refused to sign, his wrists were bound and he was driven back to Chartres for another round of physical abuse.

At 1:00 A.M. he was taken to a building he did not recognize and shoved into a room with a Senegalese prisoner. "Tomorrow, we will make you sign," the Germans assured him as they bolted the door.

Seven hours of beatings had brought him down to his last ounce of fragile force. "I know that today I have gone to the limit of my resistance," he later recorded. "I know also that tomorrow, if it starts again, I will finish by signing." The African soldier offered him the single mattress that lay on the floor amidst shards of glass scattered by the German bombing of Chartres. Moulin threw himself down, emptied of strength, and considered his position. He came to a decision: "I already understand what I can do with this debris of broken glass that litters the floor. I think they could cut a throat in the absence of a knife."

He seized a jagged splinter and drew its razor edge across his throat. Four hours later soldiers found Moulin covered with blood but still alive and rushed him to the hospital, where he was given emergency treatment by a German field surgeon. Instead of a propaganda coup, the Nazis had a potential public relations disaster on their hands. A dead French official would hardly lend credibility to their widely announced claims that the German army was the friend of the abandoned French population.

His throat enveloped in a thick bandage and his voice hoarse, Moulin was back at work at his prefecture four days later. The Germans never again brought up the question of the deposition, but Moulin's opposition to collaboration with the occupier had been made abundantly clear. It became more evident when he advised local mayors not to post German propaganda notices within their communities. Moulin's attitude angered the Vichy regime, which was already intent on cultivating excellent relations with the Reich, and he was relieved of his post on November 2, 1940.

A period of reflection followed by months spent collecting intelligence on the nascent Resistance movement primed Moulin for his encounter with de Gaulle. "He was exactly what de Gaulle was looking for," recalls Resistance leader Christian Pineau. "That is, he was loyal, courageous, and he represented a point of view that was politically centrist, balanced. This enabled him to deal with the socialists and the communists as well as with the people on the right. He was slightly to the left of center, but that was a good position, given that the Resistance was more to the left than the right." On a personal level, Pineau says, Moulin conveyed an impression of solidity and reliability. "He wasn't someone for the podium, he wasn't an orator, not at all a striking person in the political sense of the word. But he was a solid man."

His sister, Laure Moulin, adds to this portrait, depicting Moulin as a prudent man, the perfect secret emissary in those dark days of intrigue and betrayal. "Even with his intimates, Jean never gave himself completely," Mlle. Moulin wrote of her brother. "If he opened to friends, he often guarded, even with them, a secret corner to shelter his deepest feelings and thoughts." Part of this behavior was, of course, dictated by necessity. When Moulin returned from his first visit to London, Laure asked him if he had seen a mutual friend working at the BBC. "I kept well away from him," he told her. "I fled journalists who talk too much. My mission had to remain secret, since, contact made, I was going back to France."

Ω

Jean Moulin was born in the city of Béziers near the Mediterranean coast of France, the youngest child of Antoine Moulin, a French and Latin professor active in local politics. As a child, Moulin showed more talent in art than in studies. Summers were spent at the family's second home in Saint-Andiol, in the countryside of the Midi.

In 1918, young Moulin was mobilized and sent to the front in September, but the war was soon over. He finished his army service a year later at the age of 21, and began his career in the French civil service. Through his father's political connections, he was named an attaché in the office of the prefect of the Hérault department.

Moulin proved to be a natural politician. In 1922 he concluded his studies in law and was assigned to the city of Chambéry, in the Savoie *département* near the Swiss-Italian border. At the age of 26 he became the youngest sub-prefect in France. A year later he married Marguerite Cerruty, a young woman from Savoie; two years later the couple divorced.

Moulin became involved in national politics in 1928 in the National Assembly campaign of Pierre Côt, who in the years ahead would become one of his closest friends. Moulin's contribution took the form of political caricatures that eventually made their way into the Parisian press. They were printed over the pseudonym Romanin, a name later used in his wartime undercover operations.

Côt would reward Moulin for this support. In December 1932, the independent socialist Paul Boncour came to power in one swing of the perpetual right-left power struggle that paralyzed France during the decade Hitler was preparing his war. Moulin's patron was named to a high post in the Quai d'Orsay, France's Foreign Affairs Ministry, and Côt called his protégé in from the provinces as his top aide. When the Boncour government fell, Côt moved to head the Air Ministry under four premiers—Edouard Daladier, Maurice Sarraut, Camille Chautemps and again Daladier in the musical-chair politics of the 1930s. Throughout, Moulin was at Côt's side.

The French left closed ranks in the turbulent years of the mid-1930s. Socialist leader Léon Blum and Communist party secretary Maurice Thorez signed a solidarity pact in 1934, clearing the way for the left-wing Popular Front, which came into power in June 1936. With the coming to power of the Popular Front, Côt returned to head the Air Ministry and Moulin accompanied him. It was 1936, and the Spanish Civil War had begun. Left-wing France rallied to the Republican cause, and the Air Ministry provided planes and volunteer pilots to Spain's left in its ultimately losing battle against Francisco Franco's Nationalist forces. Moulin oversaw the shipment of planes to Spain, enlisting French pilots to ferry them over the Pyrénées.

During the late 1930s, the governing left coalition, the Front Populaire, continued its ineffective course in the face of the growing Nazi menace. When power shifted from Léon Blum to Daladier in April 1938, Côt and Moulin were temporarily out of a job. Moulin, however, learned that the prefecture of the *département* of the Eure et Loire, whose capital was the city of Chartres, not far from Paris, was about to become vacant. He applied for the job, using all his accumulated political contacts in Paris, and was appointed prefect in Chartres, the scene of the personal drama that two years later brought him to the attention of Charles de Gaulle.

Ω

De Gaulle recruited Moulin immediately. On New Year's Eve 1941, the dismissed prefect was flying back to France across the English Channel in a twin-engine Whitley plane to be parachuted with two other men into southern France. Antiaircraft fire rocked the small craft and fixed it in the glare of German illumination rounds, but Moulin and his companions floated safely to the ground close to the village of Andiol, near Marseille, home territory for Moulin. The operation was flawless but for two points: they were ten miles off target and Moulin landed up to his thighs in the middle of a swamp.

As Moulin struggled out of the cold mud of the Rhône River delta he faced an immodest agenda. He had to evade arrest by the agents of Vichy and the Gestapo and track down the scattered soldiers of the emerging Resistance. His next task was the most demanding: Moulin had to persuade them to submit to a higher but invisible authority thousands of miles away in London, submerging their identities in a unified front.

Moulin had not approached his mission empty-handed. He carried with him a microphoto of a letter from de Gaulle. "I designate M. Jean Moulin as my representative and as the delegate of the French National Commission for the occupied zone of the mainland. M. Moulin's mission is to unify the action of all elements resisting the enemy and his collaborators. M. Moulin will report the results of his mission directly to me."

The letter was intended to dispel any reservations of the underground, for whom de Gaulle was a disembodied voice of hope on the British airwaves. But Moulin had more than patriotic symbolism to offer. At his early January meeting in Marseille with Henri Frenay, then head of a Resistance group in the Unoccupied Zone that was soon to become Combat, Moulin gave Frenay 250,000 francs in cash, half the money he had carried with him from London.

But Raymond Aubrac, second-in-command of Libération, was less impressed with Moulin at their first encounter. "My first rendezvous with Moulin was beneath the columns of the Théâtre Municipal in Lyon," Aubrac recalls in his Paris office, his measured speech reflecting the precise manner of a career civil engineer. As was Aubrac's cautious habit, he reserved judgment about Moulin until he knew more about the man. "I didn't know that his name was Jean Moulin. He was called Max. He took me to an apartment that he had available, and he took out a box of matches, which he emptied. There was a false bottom, and beneath it there was a photocopy of instructions signed by de Gaulle. I told him he should destroy it. I wasn't very convinced by it, but I knew that the police would be very interested in it."

Political rivalries within the Resistance complicated Moulin's task. Two of the leaders, Frenay and d'Astier de la Vigerie, were undecided to what extent they should cooperate with each other in opposing the Boche. Frenay was politically conservative, an attitude shaped by a career in the tradition-bound French Army. D'Astier's Libération group stood moderately to the left and was aligned with numerous socialists and trade unionists.

The ideological schism widened late that January when Frenay was drawn into ultimately unfruitful negotiations with high Vichy officials. Dozens of his people had been arrested in mid-January after a courier was seized while foolishly carrying a list of contacts. Frenay responded to a Vichy overture in hopes that the French government could be seduced into a tacit arrangement of toleration for the Resistance. But the discussions were unsuccessful and served only to put d'Astier on his guard against Frenay.

The arrests within Frenay's network yielded one benefit: they lent force to Moulin's arguments that tighter organization was required. Paramilitary elements had to be organized separately from those involved in propaganda, intelligence, recruitment and other activities. A breakthrough came late in March when Frenay and d'Astier, at Moulin's bidding, named regional military chiefs for their respective networks and took a coordinated step toward a hierarchical, unified Resistance.

The fusion Moulin had sought came about in September 1942. Frenay's Combat, and d'Astier's Libération merged their lower-level military units. But it was a forced arrangement in which both parties harbored growing resentment toward the organizer. On their arrival in London later that month, both Resistance chiefs complained bitterly to de Gaulle about Moulin's high-handed direction of their affairs, d'Astier referring to him as a "petty appointed bureaucrat." The complaints failed to sway de Gaulle. He saw only that Moulin had produced results and wanted more of the same.

Ω

There was soon no time for squabbling. On November 11, 1942, the Germans reacted to the Allied landing in French North Africa by reinvading the Unoccupied Zone of France. Everyone's appreciation of the need for a unified front was heightened. Resistance soldiers in the south were now confronted with Panzer tanks and an expanded Gestapo presence. For de Gaulle in London, it had also become a matter of political survival that an organized Resistance—under his sole command—be established.

The November 8 Allied landings had liberated Morocco and Algeria, but this had come about without de Gaulle's aid. In fact, until the American and British task force hit the beaches, de Gaulle was not informed of the operation. Once the Allies had subdued the last traces of Vichy opposition in Africa they began engaging in political maneuvers that de Gaulle saw as perverse: making deals with the same Vichy officials and officers who had attempted to thwart the landing. The Allies, particularly the Americans, were resolved to keep lines open to Vichy, hoping eventually to woo it away from the German embrace.

French Admiral Jean Darlan, an overt Vichy collaborator, was appointed to the top political post in North Africa. A rival to de Gaulle also emerged: General Henri Giraud, only slightly tainted by Vichy involvement and renowned for his Houdini-like escape from the Koenigstein Fortress in Germany. Giraud was named to head the French military forces in North Africa. As President Franklin D. Roosevelt told an angered Free France envoy during a White House conversation: "The important thing for me is to get to Berlin; I don't care about the rest. Darlan gave me Algiers: *Vive Darlan!* If Laval gives me Paris, *Vive Laval!*"

The cynical double game enraged de Gaulle, held at arm's length by the Allies, who continually questioned his right to leadership. The rivalry between de Gaulle and Winston Churchill had sprung up early in the war, beginning with the creation of separate and often competing espionage services for occupied France, and extending to de Gaulle's resentment of his logistical dependence on the British.

Roosevelt made it clear that he disliked and distrusted de Gaulle, as well. It was he who had insisted that de Gaulle be kept ignorant of the North African landings. When the two men met at Casablanca in January 1943 FDR refused to acknowledge de Gaulle's claim to preeminence among the French. The Frenchman tried to explain that in times of historical crisis leaders sometimes arose spontaneously, citing the story of Jeanne d'Arc. The remark was leaked to the Anglo-Saxon press and de Gaulle found himself the butt of numerous jokes, an insult the future president of the French Republic was ill-disposed to suffer and unlikely to forget.

In this high-stakes game of Realpolitik, de Gaulle needed a trump to throw on the strategic table. It was the French Resistance. If Moulin could turn the widely disparate movements inside France into a disciplined fighting force, de Gaulle would obtain his leverage for an expanded role in the Allied command. He would have an army of his own, already in place to the German rear and intimately familiar with the terrain.

As the Germans rolled into Lyon on November 11, 1942, and the Place Bellecour once more filled with tanks, trucks and armored vehicles, de Gaulle's hopes were assuming a measure of reality. On that day General Charles Delestraint, once a superior officer to de Gaulle and a man who held his implicit trust, took command of the French Secret Army. Its coordination committee, composed of representatives from the three groups—Combat, Libération and Franc-Tireur—met in Lyon for the first time on November 27. Between that date and the end of the year Moulin was to complete the first phase of his mission.

Resistance leader Christian Pineau stresses that Moulin's mission in France had little to do with the actual military struggle going on between the Germans and the Resistance. "It was purely political," explains Pineau. "De Gaulle had problems with the English and the Americans, especially with the Americans' intrigues in Algiers where they were trying to put someone else in his place. He needed to have the movements unanimously behind him so that he could tell the Anglo-Saxons, 'I represent the Resistance.'"

The Resistance, which was united militarily, was soon fused politically as well through an entity entitled the Mouvements Unis de Resistance, or MUR, an acronym that spelled out, meaningfully, the French word for "wall." Soon the three letters began to appear widely in street and building graffiti, giving the Resistance a political identity it had not possessed to date.

But communications between Lyon and de Gaulle's London base remained slow, even chancy. The Resistance was growing but it was being frustrated by the failure to meet logistical and material needs. Moulin's answer was *la Délégation*, in effect a travel agency, delivery service, telephone company and news network for the Resistance. It was to handle radio transmissions, parachute and airplane movements and the distribution of propaganda and political dispatches to the underground newspapers. Moulin placed it under the direct authority of London, through himself, and recruited its staff with painstaking care. He relied on close personal contacts—including his sister, Laure—to build the staff of *la Délega-tion* up to approximately 50 by the following spring.

In mid-February 1943, Moulin was back in London via air-plane to report to de Gaulle. The general recognized Moulin's achievements not only through the award of the Croix de la Libération but by appointing him to a top London political post and expanding his Resistance authority from the southern zone to the entire occupied territory of France.

On March 21, Moulin was ready to return to France to resume his mission. Christian Pineau, then in charge of intelligence work in southern France, was on the same night flight with Moulin. Pineau had extensively briefed Moulin in London on the persona-lities in the French trade union movements he would be meeting as part of his effort to bring the various elements of the Resistance closer together. Their Lysander plane left England and set down on a landing strip in the Loire Valley. "The car was waiting for us, fortunately, because the Germans arrived a few minutes later," Pineau recalls. "We spent the night on a farm, hidden in the barn. The next morning they took us separately, Moulin and Delestraint in one car, myself in another, to the railroad station at Mâcon. We went to Lyon and we split up there."

Ω

Max. The name, so simple and so tantalizingly anonymous, was rattling about in the head of Obersturmführer Klaus Barbie. Within a few months of his taking command of the Lyon Gestapo, Barbie had received reports from his agents and informers that a personal envoy of Charles de Gaulle was quietly making the rounds of the subterranean world of the Resistance, urging its leaders to create an anti-Nazi alliance. Barbie wanted Max.

By April 1943 Barbie could sketch a satisfyingly precise chart showing the organizational structure of the insurgent movement in the southern region. It radiated outward from Lyon, and "Max" stood at the top, above the elusive MUR and the local operations that directed the clandestine parachute drop and airplane landing apparatus.

Leaky Resistance security provisions were responsible for Bar-bie's comprehensive understanding of the movement. Some Resis-tance member, impelled by the deeply ingrained French desire for formalized classification, had drawn up a report outlining Moulin's activities and movements over the past year. Within days a copy of the paper arrived in the hands of Barbie at Gestapo headquarters in the Ecole de Santé in Lyon.

"The Vichy police and the Gestapo are perfectly aware of my identity and my activities," Moulin wrote to de Gaulle in May 1943, just three months after his return to occupied territory. "I have decided to hold out as long as possible, but if I were to suddenly disappear, I wouldn't have time to bring my successors up to date." This disquiet was not a recent concern: In his first radio message back to London after his safe arrival, Moulin told de Gaulle that arrests by Vichy and the Gestapo were striking the Resistance with an alarming frequency.

But Moulin, traveling discreetly between Paris, Lyon, Marseille and other major cities, still held a precious, if dwindling, edge over Barbie. The Nazis did not know his true identity. Barbie knew that Max was a former prefect, but he did not have his name or a physical description. He needed a break, an informant close to the top of the Resistance hierarchy.

Max carefully covered his movements in the trap-strewn world of German-occupied France. Dissimulation became a way of life, as he cloaked himself in the bourgeois protective cover he had developed in his years as a French bureaucrat. Moulin wore tasteful but undistinguished suits and a dark overcoat, with a scarf wrapped about his neck to cover the identifying scar. A gray fedora was pulled down low to further obscure his features.

One of Max's first tasks was to unite the various military groups of the Resistance. Despite friction, by April 1943 the military forces of the communists were finally incorporated into the Secret Army organized in the north. It too was under the command of General Delestraint, who outlined the orders sent by London. The Secret Army was to be largely held in reserve, its forces built up and trained until the day when the Allies, ready to launch an invasion of the French mainland, would give it orders to attack from the rear. The communists, who had embraced a philosophy of "immediate action" and harrassment of the Germans despite the civilian reprisals this often caused, objected but eventually acquiesced.

One more step was required to fulfill Moulin's master plan. He needed a symbol, a political body that could stand as concrete evidence of the Resistance's willingness to follow the orders of de Gaulle in a unified formation, one that would place General Giraud, the American's great hope in Algiers, permanently in the wings. Moulin needed a structure that could pull errant Resistance groups and individuals into line by the influence of their peers and smooth over differences before they flared into divisions. Moulin and de Gaulle had come up with the design of this body, and its name, even before Moulin left London. It would be the Conseil National de la Résistance, the National Resistance Council.

Moulin's mission in this second phase was far more delicate and complicated. His expanded powers now required that he knit the northern Resistance groups into the fabric he had already woven in the south. But conditions in the north were far different, much more tenuous than in the south. The Gestapo had ravaged the Resistance groups in the Occupied Zone to such an extent that most were fragmented and limited. On the other hand, these northern groups were usually more politicized along prewar lines and less straightforwardly nationalistic. But Moulin was not starting alone. Pierre Brossolette, sent by de Gaulle's London intelligence network, had long been working in the north and had laid a foundation for Moulin's structure of unity.

Moulin never attained the same level of activity in the north that he had in the south. One measure of the difference is that between January and May 1943 he distributed 50 million francs to the southern zone networks, while those in the north received only 6 million francs. Politics were a factor. The strongest group in the north was the Front National backed by the Communist party; its shock troops in the Franc-Tireurs et Partisans Français were vigorously conducting attacks and sabotage operations against the Germans. But other Resistance groups had strong reservations about the communists. Though they were highly effective fighters, they had not begun their struggle against the Germans until after the rupture of the Soviet-Nazi nonaggression pact in June 1941 when the Nazis invaded Russia.

A constant traveler, Moulin spent his days and nights in trains and cheap, nondescript hotels, under the identity of Jean Martel, an itinerant artist and decorator who ran an art gallery in Nice. This was less than a complete fiction. Moulin had shown a talent for drawing in his youth and in addition to political cartoons he had illustrated a number of fine literary editions even as he rose in the French prefectural service. The gallery actually existed; it had opened on February 9, 1943, just before the "artist" secretly flew to London for his second meeting with de Gaulle. Notables of Nice were in attendance at the opening of Moulin's gallery, where, with the utmost of correctness and not a little irony, a portrait of Pétain was displayed prominently on one wall.

In Lyon, Moulin kept a room under the name of Marchand, but he was rarely there. When not making the rounds of contacts throughout France, he stayed at his family's summer residence in Andiol, near Marseille, or visited his mother and sister at Montpellier, a city on the Mediterranean coast. In the southern coast region, where he was personally known, he kept the name Jean Moulin.

Moulin was a shadowy figure even for those in the Resistance with whom he dealt. Confiding completely in no one, he gave those under him only the minimum of information needed to carry out their assignments. He scheduled his rendezvous in parks and public establishments by preference, but rarely twice in the same place. He listened more than he spoke.

Within the Resistance, Henri Frenay of Combat had now become a major adversary of Moulin. Although he had backed the earlier efforts at coordination, Frenay bridled at the notion of becoming just one voice in a committee dominated by Moulin. He felt that the Resistance was becoming top-heavy, to the detriment of those on the front lines. The obstinate personalities of the two men had clashed before, and the issue of the Conseil National de la Résistance (CNR) brought them into open conflict.

They met in person to talk about it, walking along the riverbank in Lyon just blocks from the Gestapo headquarters where Barbie was energetically working at unveiling Moulin's identity. Later, as the tensions between Frenay and Moulin mounted, they exchanged long, formal letters with vitriol just below the surface. Frenay would become increasingly bitter in tone, referring to Moulin in a letter to a London officer as "the grave-digger of the

Resistance.''

Despite this divisiveness, the Conseil National de la Résistance convened for the first time as 16 delegates representing the country's major Resistance and trade union movements took their seats around a table in the heavily-guarded apartment of one René Corbin at 48 Rue du Four, in the St.-Germain-des-Près area of the Left Bank of Paris, on May 27, 1943. Moulin presided and outlined the purpose of the group, following his remarks, significantly, with a message from General de Gaulle. At this point Moulin had effectively completed his mission.

Ω

Barbie, however, was still working at the completion of his. In the latter half of May 1943, as Max strained to bring French communists under the same umbrella as conservative Republicans, the investment of time and manpower Barbie had placed in the infiltration of the Lyon Resistance networks was starting to bring rewards.

French turncoats, especially those who had once been Resistance members, made the most effective agents, Barbie had found. Toward the end of May he came into the possession of two French agents, Jean Multon and Robert Moog, who went by the names of Lunel and Bobby. Multon was a former Resistance man who had been turned to a Nazi agent by the Gestapo. On May 24 Barbie received Multon as a gift from the head of the Marseille Sicherheitsdienst. After Multon had infiltrated the Resistance and led the Gestapo to some 100 *résistants* in the Marseille region, he was dispatched to Barbie in Lyon.

Once in Lyon, Multon made contact with the local Resistance and proved himself as effective an agent for the Gestapo there as he had been in Marseille. Multon was delivering top-drawer intelligence that led to a second series of arrests jeopardizing Combat at its very heart. As a result of Multon's information, Frenay himself was almost netted by the Gestapo.

On May 28, Bertie Albrecht, a female aide of Frenay's, had boarded a train in Lyon bound for a meeting with Frenay and several others in Mâcon, 40 miles to the north. The rendezvous was set for the morning in the Hôtel de Bourgogne in the center of Mâcon. Through Multon's efforts, the hotel had been staked out by the Germans. Albrecht, whose *nom de guerre* was Victoria, arrived early and took a seat on a bench in a small square in the center of the city, where she began to thumb through a newspaper.

Suddenly she was approached by a woman who addressed her by the name of Victoria. Albrecht ignored this greeting, but moments later, when the Gestapo swarmed around her, she knew she had been betrayed. To warn others headed for the meeting, Bertie screamed at the top of her lungs, *"Alerte! La Gestapo! Attention! La Gestapo!"* as she was taken away to the Hotel Terminus in Mâcon, the local Gestapo headquarters. She was last seen leaving the building under heavy guard, in handcuffs and showing the evidence of a brutal beating. She died in the Fresnes prison south of Paris, either murdered or a suicide.

Moog, an Alsatian who spoke fluent German, had helped the Abwehr destroy a British-run espionage ring in the Savoie region near the Swiss border. The central figure in the British spy ring was named André Dévigny. Barbie's Einsatzkommando played an active role in this operation and Dévigny subsequently was tortured at the Ecole de Santé before becoming a Resistance legend. He became the only prisoner, of some 10,000, to escape from Montluc in the entire course of the war.

Dévigny had found a way to disassemble his cell door in a wooden puzzle of eleven pieces. At night, he would let himself out of his cell and walk the silent corridors of Montluc, cheering up his fellow prisoners and helping them out in one significant way: He erased the chalk marks on their cell doors left by the guards to instruct the following watch what punishments to deliver. Condemned to death one Monday in August, he was scheduled to be executed the following week. He worked feverishly every night to improvise equipment to scale the prison walls. On the following Saturday he made his agonizingly slow progress across roofs, courtyards and walls to freedom, but only after he had spent five hours immersed in the Rhône River to evade the German guard dogs tracking him down.

Dévigny had escaped both Barbie and Moog, but he was an outstanding exception in Nazi-controlled Lyon. Barbie set Multon and Moog to work in tandem to help him find Moulin and break the Resistance. The team was put onto one of Barbie's most promising leads, a letter-drop on the Rue Bouteille in Lyon, a piece of information given to the Gestapo by a tortured Resistance member. The mailbox was used by a Combat unit for railroad sabotage known as Résistance-Fer, Rail Resistance. In its first sweep the Gestapo arrested the secretary of Résistance-Fer and the owner of the house. The members of the group still at large were alerted that the box was "burned"; instructions were issued for no one to use or collect mail from it.

Barbie of course knew that the box was burned, but he asked Multon to watch it, in case the Resistance committed an oversight. In a startling lapse in security precautions among the top Resistance ranks, someone did. General Charles Delestraint, commander-in-chief of the Secret Army, met near the end of May with his chief of staff, Henri Aubry. He asked him to set up a meeting for June 9 in Paris with René Hardy, head of Résistance-Fer, who was developing a master plan for the derailment of the French train system. Aubry, preoccupied with his ailing wife in Marseille, told his secretary to draft and dispatch a letter to Hardy. She wrote the letter "in clear," or uncoded French, then deposited it in the burned letterbox. When she returned from this errand and told him what she had done, Aubry expressed concern, yet did nothing to warn Delestraint or Hardy.

When Barbie read the letter he was exhilarated: Vidal, code-name for the head of the Secret Army, was to meet with Didot, code-name for the head of Résistance-Fer, at a Paris Metro station on the morning on June 9.

Late on the evening of June 7, 1943, the Gare de Perrache hummed with activity and blared last calls for the night train to Paris. René Hardy, a lanky man with blond hair and a thin, youthful face, arrived well before train time with his ticket and his sleeping car reservation in hand. There were German sentries throughout the station, but Hardy felt confident and at home. He had worked for the Société National de Chemins de Fer, the French railway system, for years before entering the Resistance, at one point serving as a stationmaster of the Gare de Lyon in Paris, at the other end of the line. He knew the ways in and out of the station and how to avoid document checks and other obstacles set up in the station by the Gestapo. He was going to Paris, but not for the meeting with Delestraint. He had never picked up the letter from the box on the Rue Bouteille, but he had another appointment in the capital, also for June 9, with a member of his sabotage unit.

Walking along the platform next to the train, Hardy's heart started to race. Coming toward him was Multon, whom he knew as Lunel from the days in Marseille before the man had turned. Hardy knew about Multon's work for Barbie since then, and he braced himself for escape. It was clear Multon had recognized him as "Carbon," the name Hardy had once used in Marseille. There was no way to bolt out of the station; that would surely draw attention from the Germans on guard. But Hardy spotted another Resistance member on the same platform and moved up to him on the pretext of asking for a light. "If something happens to me," he murmured, "it's Lunel's fault." Hardy then boarded the train.

Hardy, in another unlucky twist, had been assigned a bed in the same car as Multon, who was traveling with Moog. As the train rolled north through the summer night toward Paris, Hardy was uncertain what to do. But Moog, who had observed the startled expressions of both Hardy and Multon, had no such hesitation. When the train halted at Chalon-sur-Saône at 1:00 A.M., Moog led the German police back to the *wagon-lit* to arrest Hardy. The two informers continued on toward Paris and their next prey.

General Delestraint was arrested with ease outside the La Muette station and yielded a bonus for the Gestapo. In another security lapse, he confided in the double agent who met him at the station that he had another rendezvous 30 minutes later at a nearby Metro station. Delestraint was shoved into a car, which took him to Gestapo's national headquarters on the Avenue Foch, a short walk from the Arc de Triomphe. The Gestapo team then moved along to arrest two other Resistance men at the Pompe Metro station.

Ω

Obersturmführer Barbie was elated as he drove out of Lyon on the afternoon of June 10 and headed for Chalon-sur-Saône 80 miles to the north. He had Delestraint, head of the Secret Army. At least he had received credit for the arrest, even if the top Gestapo officials were doing their own interrogation of the French general in Paris.

He was now ready to move on to Max. He was not sure of the identity of Hardy, who had been caught at the Chalon train station by Multon and Moog, but he was determined to learn his place in the Resistance scheme. Barbie signed for the prisoner with the police in Chalon, and returned with Hardy to Lyon, to the Ecole de Santé.

What Hardy said or did not say to Barbie during interrogation has perplexed historians and jurists ever since. Two postwar military tribunals listened to Hardy's version of the story. One declared him innocent of the charge of treason leveled at him for possible collaboration with the Gestapo, while the second resulted in a hung jury.

Hardy has said that Barbie was totally unaware that he was sitting across from Didot, head of Résistance-Fer; evidence suggests this is so. Traveling under his own name, Hardy had been arrested simply because of his unlucky encounter with Multon. But in the belief that he was dealing with a Resistance member, Barbie began to apply pressure, using a letter Hardy had written to his fiancée but had not mailed before his arrest. Barbie threatened to take her family hostage if Hardy failed to cooperate with the Gestapo.

Hardy maintained that Multon had been mistaken; he had nothing to do with the Resistance. He worked in the farm machine business and was on his way to Paris to pick up some spare tractor parts when he was arrested. Besides, he assured Barbie, he sympathized with the German cause. Hardy played up his distinctly Nordic features, and mentioned a German Army general he had met before the war while on his honeymoon.

Hardy later claimed that he had posed as a cooperative prisoner, but had not divulged any significant information. "I try to play their game," he later stated. "I endorse their political tirades between questions...I declare myself ready, if able, within my means, to render them service, although not being involved in militant politics."

Barbie, however, gave an entirely different account of the meeting, both when interrogated by French officials after the war and in subsequent statements. Hardy, he said, was known at the time of his arrest to be Didot, and was handled accordingly. Hardy admitted his role in the Resistance, the Nazi alleged, and briefed

Barbie on his extensive plans for the sabotage of the national rail lines in the event of invasion from England. Then, Barbie said Hardy in his deposition, agreed to work with him, promising to provide him with information on the Resistance, a charge which two French juries later rejected. Barbie also claimed that he then wired Paris and Berlin to obtain approval of his plan to use Didot to lead him to Resistance higher-ups, particularly Max.

Hardy was released at 11:00 P.M. on June 10, after being informed by Barbie of General Delestraint's capture in Paris. He reestablished contact with the Resistance but decided not to reveal that he had been captured by the Gestapo. "I wanted to make my own investigation," he later explained. "I could not open up to anyone, given that the blow sustained by General Delestraint had to have come from high up. I therefore chose silence."

No link, Hardy claimed, remained between himself and the Gestapo after his release. "Contrary to the claims of Barbie, I was neither followed nor accompanied, and I was not living at Gestapo headquarters," he later insisted. Hardy assumed that if his Resistance comrades knew he had been in Gestapo custody they might conclude he had helped betray Delestraint. He went about his normal routine after meeting with friends in Nîmes to establish an alibi in case questions should arise. Hardy suppressed the fact of his arrest by Barbie until after his first trial for treason following the war; it was because of this disclosure that Hardy was tried again despite his acquittal.

His message passed to a Resistance colleague on the platform of the Gare de Perrache did produce queries from above, but Hardy explained that he had jumped from the speeding train near Mâcon, then had boarded train after train to throw any pursuer off the track. The leadership was less concerned with Hardy than with the arrest of Delestraint. It was essential to act quickly to minimize the damage.

The news of Delestraint's arrest had badly shaken Moulin and confirmed his worst fears that the Gestapo was closing in. He made preparations to convene the leaders of the Resistance networks: a successor to Delestraint would have to be chosen and new arrangements for security would have to be made. Aubry, second-in-command to Delestraint, had returned by June 19 from Marseille, where he had been attending his sick wife. A meeting was set for June 21, in the afternoon, but as a precaution no location was given in advance. Nevertheless the lapses in security continued.

When Aubry returned from Marseille, he found a message from Hardy saying that they had to get together. The two men were close friends, and Aubry agreed to see him the next day, Sunday, at 11:30 A.M. at the Pont Morand, a bridge over the Rhône in the northern section of Lyon. Before they parted, Aubry committed another breach of security by telling Hardy of the upcoming meeting with Moulin.

The next morning Aubry kept his rendezvous with Hardy. Before this he had seen a Marseille Resistance leader, a young socialist named Gaston Defferre, later to rise to national political prominence like so many surviving members of the underground. Aubry arrived late for this first appointment and found Defferre about to leave.

The two men strolled along the Rhône quai, talking as they went. By the Pont Morand, they came to the square where Hardy was sitting on a bench. On the same bench sat a man whom neither Aubry nor Defferre recognized, reading a newspaper held up in front of his face. Only later would they discover that the man on the bench at the Pont Morand that day was Klaus Barbie. The Nazi's bodyguard, Harry Steingritt, kept watch not far away.

Aubry and Defferre finished their conversation a short distance away, and Defferre left. Then Aubry and Hardy rode into the center of Lyon on a streetcar, to a restaurant. As they ate, Aubry explained that if Hardy wanted to come to the meeting with Moulin, he should meet him the following day at a restaurant across from the bottom terminus of a funicular that connected the main city of Lyon with a plateau high above. From there, a man named André Lassagne was to lead them to the site chosen for the crucial meeting.

Lassagne, a Lyon professor and friend of Moulin, had made arrangements for the session. He had telephoned to a long-time friend, Dr. Frédéric Dugoujon, a physician practicing in the northern suburb of Caluire-et-Cuire. Dugoujon said the meeting could be held in his combined home-office. Only Lassagne, Moulin and another man named Bruno Larat, head of Moulin's parachute and airplane section, knew the location of the meeting beforehand. They were to meet the others at various points around Lyon and lead them to Caluire. Lassagne instructed Aubry to meet him at the *ficelle*, as the funicular was called, at 1:45 P.M.

On Sunday, June 20, the day before the meeting, Raymond Aubrac met with Moulin in the Parc du Tête d'Or, a large park in the northeast part of Lyon. They had come together to discuss how best to repair the damage wrought by Delestraint's arrest. The two men strolled and talked for over two hours, occasionally taking a seat on a bench. Moulin, Aubrac says, proposed to divide the Secret Army into two sectors. "He asked me to take responsibility for the northern zone," Aubrac recalls, adding that André Lassagne, another top *résistant*, was to take command of the southern sector.

Moulin was upset at Delestraint's arrest, and the situation was complicated by the fact that no one knew how the capture of the Secret Army commander had come about. "Delestraint's arrest hadn't been explained," Aubrac says today. "We were worried."

Still Moulin did not seem to feel personally threatened. "We thought there was a very serious security problem," he explains, "but we didn't feel like we were being tracked down."

Sunday evening Moulin met in a Lyon bistro with Claude Serreulles, a member of the London intelligence group who had arrived by parachute only a few days before. Moulin confided to Serreulles some of his plans intended to repair the damage done by Delestraint's arrest.

Moulin and Serreulles met again the following morning, and around 10:00 A.M. Moulin kept a rendezvous with Aubry. In spite of the crisis facing the Resistance, the old political divisions were still unresolved. As the two men walked through the center of Lyon, each holding an umbrella to ward off the constant drizzle, they argued about an issue that had driven another wedge between Moulin and Combat, the group Aubry was to represent at the meeting later in the day. Aubry's men had taken parachuted arms from a cache without authorization; Moulin threatened to break off relations with Combat if such undisciplined acts continued. They separated, agreeing to talk again at the meeting in a few hours.

Given the arrest of Delestraint, Moulin had misgivings about the meeting he was about to attend. Besides, that morning he had been urged not to go to the meeting by Gaston Defferre, who had an intuition it might end in disaster. "I had a long conversation with Jean Moulin, in the Place Jean-Mâcé, in Lyon," Defferre recalled many years later. "I told him I was wary of the rendezvous in Caluire. For more than an hour, I tried to convince him not to go. I didn't have any precise reasons, just the impression that things hadn't been well arranged, that there was a risk." But Moulin had decided to go through with it. The leaders of the three main networks—Frenay, Lévy and d'Astier—were in London, and the responsibility for holding things together in this time of crisis fell to Moulin.

Ω

That afternoon André Lassagne was surprised when Aubry showed up with Hardy at the *ficelle*. He did not think Hardy had been invited, but since Hardy was highly placed in the Resistance hierarchy he thought little of it. It was almost two o'clock when Aubry and Hardy boarded the funicular and slowly rode to the top of the hill. They waited there a few minutes until Lassagne, who had taken the next car, arrived. Lassagne told them to take the No. 33 tramway, which began at the funicular terminus, and ride it to the center of Caluire, about a mile and a half away. He followed on his bicycle and, once in Caluire, led them to Dugoujon's house, a three-story stuccoed house that overlooked a wide square and, downward, a long, steep hillside ending at the Saône River. Larat and an Army colonel named Lacaze had already arrived when they were ushered into the house by Dugoujon's housekeeper and mounted the staircase to a second-floor room overlooking the courtyard surrounding the house.

Their nervousness grew as the minutes ticked by and Max did not show up. They were all familiar with Moulin's insistence on punctuality at clandestine meetings. It was an essential tenet of Resistance protocol: one never arrived early or late, and one never stood around too long in one spot waiting. Moulin was breaking both of these rules as he met for the second time that day with Raymond Aubrac in the Place Carnot at 2:15 P.M., a quarter of an hour after the Caluire meeting was to have begun. They lost 15 more minutes as they waited for a third man to join them.

All were totally unaware of the desperate efforts of a woman named Edmée Deletraz to pass a message along to Moulin that he was about to walk into a Gestapo trap set by Klaus Barbie. Deletraz had entered the Resistance at the start, in 1940, working with the English before joining a French intelligence network. Arrested by the Gestapo, she was released on the promise that she would work as a Nazi informer. But upon gaining her freedom Edmée immediately informed the chief of her Resistance network of what had happened. He instructed her to maintain contact with the Gestapo, and to learn what she could about the Gestapo's operations in Lyon.

It was through Deletraz that the Resistance learned that the Gestapo had uncovered the drop on the Rue Bouteille in which Aubry's secretary placed the letter leading to Delestraint's capture. Her exact position between the Gestapo and the Resistance remained unclear until after the Liberation when a French military tribunal examining her actions failed to charge her.

On this day of June 21, 1943, as Moulin was on his way to Caluire, Edmée showed up at a clandestine Resistance office in the Croix-Rousse section of Lyon with startling news. Minutes before, she had seen a highly-placed Resistance member at Gestapo headquarters. He had come to notify the Germans of a major Secret Army meeting to take place that afternoon, at which he would be present. Edmée had been assigned by the Gestapo to follow the Resistance member to the meeting, whose location he still did not know. Resistance security now began to work to disadvantage. No one in the office knew how to reach any of the principal officers of the Secret Army. One tried to get a message to Lassagne, but could not immediately reach him.

It was 2:45 P.M. when Max arrived at the house in Caluire, three-quarters of an hour late, with Aubrac and another Resistance leader. The three men took seats in Dr. Dugoujon's waiting room, settling onto the imitation Louis XV furniture amid the doctor's patients. As a precaution, Moulin had brought with him a letter from another doctor referring him to Dugoujon saying he was suffering from chronic rheumatism. Moments later the Gestapo closed in.

Today Dr. Fréderic Dugoujon still lives in that house overlooking the Saône, retired from medical practice and the office of mayor of Caluire, which he held for thirty years after the war. "Lassagne came over to my house that Sunday and asked me if he could have a meeting here the next day," he says, seated behind an antique desk in his consulting office. "He thought that a doctor's office would be a good place for it, since the comings and goings of strangers wouldn't arouse suspicions. I gave him my permission and the next day I told my housekeeper that I was expecting Lassagne with some friends and would she show them up to my office?"

Busy with patients on the ground floor, Dugoujon noted the arrival of Lacaze, then Lassagne with Aubry and Hardy, and a short time later opened the front door of the house to Larat. Nearly an hour later, the 29-year-old physician was just seeing a young patient and her mother to the door when he glanced out into the yard and saw a group of men coming up to the entrance.

"I opened the door and saw two pretty big fellows, each holding a revolver," Dugoujon recalls. "One of them told me in a low voice, 'German police. You have a meeting in your house?' I said no, but they didn't believe me," recalls Dugoujon. "They pushed me out of the way and went upstairs without any noise." Others had come in by the French doors to another room and followed the first pair. Then there came a clatter and shouts.

Five of the Resistance leaders on the floor above the waiting room had spotted men in leather jackets entering the courtyard. Aubry, who had glanced out the window upon hearing the squeak of the gate, knew at once what was happening.

"We're cooked," he told the others. "It's the Gestapo."

Hardy drew his pistol, but the others told him to put it away. There were too many Gestapo to attempt to shoot it out. A moment later the door to the room opened and Klaus Barbie walked in. "Hands up," he snapped in excellent French. "German police."

Barbie rushed at Aubry, covering him with blows and knocking him against the wall. He handcuffed him. "Well, Thomas," Barbie said triumphantly, using Aubry's cover name, "you don't look so good. You seemed a lot happier yesterday at the Pont Morand. I was reading my paper, but the weather was so nice I thought I'd let you have that beautiful day since we would meet again today."

Barbie seemed to know everything. Aubry was shocked, not only by the reference to the Pont Morand, but by the Gestapo chief's use of Thomas, a code-name Aubry had only recently assumed.

Downstairs the Germans had burst into the waiting room, forcing everyone up against the wall, then handcuffing the prisoners with their hands behind their backs. While the Germans were occupied elsewhere, Moulin passed some papers to Aubrac. Both men chewed and swallowed them.

Dugoujon, in the hallway, told his housekeeper to advise another doctor that he wouldn't be seeing any more patients that day. A German punched the doctor in the stomach, handcuffed him and pushed him into the waiting room. "Just at the entry," Dugoujon says, "there was a man who told me in a low voice, 'My name is Jean Martel.' That was Jean Moulin. Nobody knew he was Max." For the Nazis, Moulin produced the letter referring him to Dugoujon, but it did no good. Only the female patients were released.

Barbie came downstairs and ordered the prisoners in the waiting room to be taken upstairs to join the others. Aubrac and the others were shocked to see Hardy, who had not been called to the meeting. "We all had the same reaction," Raymond Aubrac remembers. "Stupefaction. Indignation. Why was he there? Our concern increased when the SS put handcuffs on everyone, with the exception of Hardy."

While everyone else was searched meticulously, the Gestapo failed to take the gun Hardy had hidden in his sleeve. After separate questioning in an upstairs room the prisoners were led out to the waiting cars one by one. It was during this transfer operation that Hardy made his break.

As Hardy's German guard opened the door of the car, Hardy pushed him off balance, tripped him and slammed the car door in his face. The guard fell against the car and let go of Hardy's chain. Hardy took off across the square in front of Dugoujon's house, which abruptly dropped off in a long rugged slope leading down to the Saône River.

Hardy later said that as he zig-zagged across the Place Castellane, he could hear bullets whistling around him. He was hit in the arm by one shot. He almost fell, recovered, then pulled out his pistol and fired over his shoulder to cover his escape.

As Hardy ran down the steep slope known as the Mont Castellane, the Germans abandoned their pursuit to attend to the other prisoners. This gave Hardy time to throw himself into a ditch and attend to the wound on his arm. He crawled along the ditch, then ducked into a street leading off the side of the hill. Since he did not know exactly where he was, Hardy decided to head down towards the Saône by following the line of steepest descent.

By this time several of the Resistance leaders were suspicious that Hardy had betrayed them to Barbie. "I was convinced as soon as we were arrested," Aubrac later said. "He was the only one who didn't have handcuffs, he escaped, he crossed the square without anyone firing an automatic weapon at him, and then, when the Germans captured him again, he escaped again."

Hardy was arrested later that day by the police after he was brought to the Grange Blanche hospital in Lyon for treatment of his arm wound. The next day he was transferred to the prison ward of the Antiquaille hospital, and on June 28 given over to Germany custody and interrogated at the Ecole de Santé. After that he was placed in the prison section of the German hospital in the Croix-Rousse section of Lyon.

While he was in the hospital, some members of the Resistance sought to execute Hardy without a trial. Lucie Aubrac anonymously sent Hardy a food package that included a small jar of preserves that had been dosed with cyanide; but Hardy was suspicious and did not eat the condiment. On August 3 Hardy escaped from the hospital by climbing over a garage roof and mounting a wall. He immediately left Lyon with his fiancée, Lydie Bastien, and went to Paris, where once again he became involved in Resistance activities. Eventually he and Bastien made their way to North Africa, where Hardy remained until the end of the war in France.

After the Liberation Hardy was arrested by the New Resistance-led government. In January 1947, Hardy was tried for treason before the Court of the Seine in Paris and acquitted. But two months later new evidence from German sources disclosed the arrest of Hardy at Chalons, a fact that he had kept secret from the Resistance. He acknowledged that he had lied, but explained that he knew that if he had revealed his capture, he would have been summarily executed for having presumably betrayed Delestraint, even though he was not involved.

The second trial, which was held in April 1950, focused on *l'affaire de Caluire*. The star witness was Klaus Barbie, who testified *in absentia* through depositions just as he had been condemned to death *in absentia* by French courts. That Barbie was allowed to offer evidence at all was deplored by Hardy's lawyer, Maurice Garçon.

Barbie's was not the only evidence weighing heavily against Hardy. Also submitted by the prosecution was a Gestapo report written by Ernst Kaltenbrunner on June 29, 1943, specifically naming Hardy as having been the source of information leading to the Caluire arrests.

But this evidence was weakened by inconsistencies, particularly in Barbie's testimony. Barbie had informed French investigators that Hardy had told him Max was actually Jean Moulin; however, it was established that Hardy did not know this at the time. The Kaltenbrunner report also had flaws. The Gestapo officer had claimed that "the Jew Heilbronner, alias 'Arel,' thanks to the help of Hardy, was arrested at a rendezvous." But Max Heilbronn, the correct name of Hardy's co-worker in the rail sabotage network, testified at the trial on behalf of Hardy. He told the court that following his arrest on June 12 he had been tortured for hours by the Gestapo, who wanted him to admit he was Didot, an obvious inconsistency in Kaltenbrunner's story.

Reporting on the trial, *Le Monde* described "a note of apparent sincerity" in Hardy's demeanor at the trial. Even tribunal member and former Resistance leader Claudius Petit—whom *Le Monde*'s reporter described as one of those most hostile towards Hardy—admonished his fellow jurists: "If there remains the thousandth part of doubt in his favor, you must acquit him."

The court failed to convict Hardy. Of the seven members of the tribunal, three voted for acquittal, while four voted for conviction. The state could not muster the five votes needed for conviction; the result was a hung jury, and freedom for Hardy. The court found there were simply too many other means by which Barbie could have learned of the Caluire meeting: Aubry's indiscretions; the excessive number of people who knew a meeting would take place that day; the fact that one of Aubry's subordinates later was revealed to be a Gestapo spy.

This is the only known picture of Barbie in a Nazi uniform. As a 29-year-old SS lieutenant, he wielded enormous power over the city of Lyon.

Ten thousand Resistance members and Jews were imprisoned here at Fort Montluc by Barbie. Thousands died, thousands of others were deported, and only one man ever escaped. Montluc, plus the headquarters at the Ecole de Santé, where Barbie interrogated the prisoners, made up the Gestapo universe of Lyon.

Jean Moulin, a former prefect of Chartres, was de Gaulle's deputy who headed the Resistance in France. A man of great courage, Moulin was captured and beaten to death by Barbie, but not before he had finished unifying the Resistance.

After the war, Resistance leader René Hardy was twice charged with treason for having betrayed Moulin to Barbie, but juries failed to convict him.

General Charles de Gaulle, here speaking from England over BBC radio during the war, was the spiritual voice of the French Resistance. De Gaulle united Combat, Libération, Franc Tireur, and other Resistance groups under his banner.

Heinz Hollert was Barbie's superior in the Lyon SS, but Barbie operated autonomously. Hollert was killed in an Allied bombing raid.

Erich Bartelmus was head of the SS Jewish Section under Barbie. Convicted of war crimes, he went to prison but is now free.

Barbie's official SS portrait. He often dressed in civilian clothes while on duty at the Ecole de Santé, where he personally beat many prisoners.

Nazi troops in the Place Bellecour, at the heart of the city of Lyon. Because of its location and the fact that it was unoccupied for two and a half years, Lyon became the center of the French Resistance. It was reoccupied by German troops on Armistice Day, 1942, after the Allied invasion of North Africa.

Pierre Laval and Marshal Philippe Pétain, the hero of Verdun in WWI, took over the French government after the *débacle* and adopted a course of collaboration with the Nazis. Although the Vichy government was less severe than the Germans, it aided them in sending many Jews to their deaths. The Vichy paramilitary force, the Milice, was feared and detested because of its brutality.

Rabbi Jacob Kaplan, who headed the Lyon Jewish congregation, convinced Gerlier to help the Jews. Now 88, he lives in Paris.

Pierre Cardinal Gerlier, above, was a close friend of Pétain's and supported Vichy, but he also heroically aided the Jews of Lyon.

Despite the Gestapo and Vichy, the Quai Tilsitt Synagogue held services until July 1944. It was the subject of grenade attacks, raids by Barbie's Gestapo, and finally pillaged.

These are the Jewish children of the Izieu orphanage. One of the major charges against Barbie is that he personally ordered them, and the adults supervising them, arrested and deported to Nazi death camps in the East. All of the children died there.

Of the seven members of the Halaunbrenner family, shown above, four were killed on Barbie's orders. Two of the daughters, Mina and Claudine, aged 4 and 5, were deported from Izieu. Husband Jacob and son Léon were arrested by Barbie and subsequently killed. After the war, Mrs. Halaunbrenner went to Bolivia to help identify Barbie and will be an important witness at his trial in Lyon.

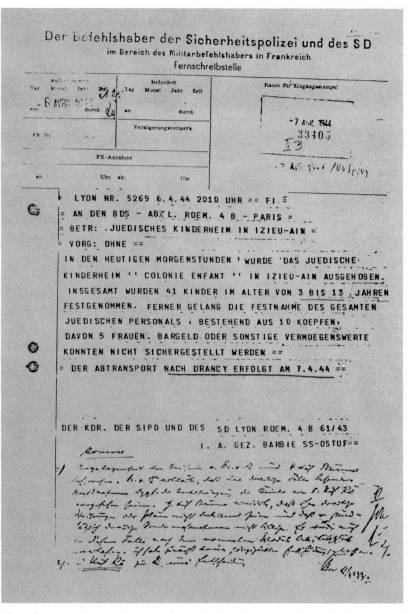

Der Befehlshaber der Sicherheitspolizei und des SD
im Bereich des Militärbefehlshabers in Frankreich
Fernschreibstelle

LYON NR. 5269 6.4.44 2010 UHR == FI =
= AN DEN BDS - ABT L. ROEM. 4 B - PARIS =
= BETR: JUEDISCHES KINDERHEIM IN IZIEU-AIN =
= VORG: OHNE ==
IN DEN HEUTIGEN MORGENSTUNDEN WURDE DAS JUEDISCHE
KINDERHEIM '' COLONIE ENFANT '' IN IZIEU-AIN AUSGEHOBEN.
INSGESAMT WURDEN 41 KINDER IM ALTER VON 3 BIS 13 JAHREN
FESTGENOMMEN. FERNER GELANG DIE FESTNAHME DES GESAMTEN
JUEDISCHEN PERSONALS , BESTEHEND AUS 10 KOEPFEN,
DAVON 5 FRAUEN. BARGELD ODER SONSTIGE VERMOEGENSWERTE
KONNTEN NICHT SICHERGESTELLT WERDEN ==
= DER ABTRANSPORT NACH DRANCY ERFOLGT AM 7.4.44 ==

DER KDR. DER SIPO UND DES SD LYON ROEM. 4 B 61/43
I. A. GEZ. BARBIE SS-OSTUF==

This telegram to Gestapo headquarters, signed by Obersturmführer Barbie,
confirms the arrest and deportation of more than forty Jewish children at Izieu. It
is a damaging piece of evidence against Barbie and will be introduced at his trial.

General de Gaulle shakes hands with rival General Henri Giraud, formerly head of the Vichy army in North Africa. Giraud joined the Free French and led the French troops in the invasion of southern France in August 1944.

In July 1944, prior to the German evacuation of Lyon, Nazi soldiers and Barbie's men killed hundreds of civilians throughout the Lyon region. This massacre took place near the village of Villars les Dombes, northeast of the city.

Karl Oberg was head of the Gestapo in France and was responsible for thousands of deaths and deportations. Originally sentenced to death, his term was shortened, and he was released in 1962. He now lives in Germany as a retired insurance salesman.

Kurt Merk, a German officer in France and friend of Barbie's, brought Barbie together with the American CIC after the war.

Erhard Drabinghaus, an American counterintelligence officer, was Barbie's "handler." He was instructed not to reveal Barbie's whereabouts to the French.

This passport, in which Barbie is called "Klaus Altmann," was secured in 1951 by American counterintelligence agents through a Vatican contact. It permitted Barbie and his family to escape from Germany to Bolivia.

Once in Bolivia, Barbie became a powerful advisor to various military dictators. As shown here, he generally walked the streets of La Paz with his armed bodyguard.

Hans Ulrich Rudel, famed German flying ace, was a contact for Barbie with the proto-Nazi communities of South America.

Serge and Beate Klarsfeld are a prominent husband-and-wife team of Nazi hunters, who live in Paris. He is Jewish, she is Protestant. It was Beate Klarsfeld who first found Barbie living as "Klaus Altmann" in South America ten years ago.

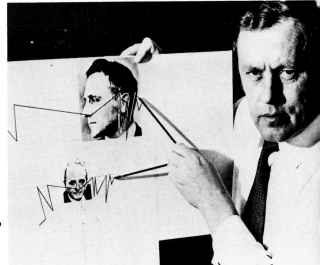

An anthropologist demonstrates how he compared a picture of "Altmann" taken in Bolivia to a WWII photo of the Lyon Gestapo chief and positively identified him as Barbie.

An abrupt change in the Bolivian government resulted in Barbie's loss of power and his imprisonment on a supposed charge of debt fraud. The new government arranged for his secret expulsion to France.

At a Bolivian airport, Barbie was smuggled onto a plane, accompanied by agents from the Ministry of the Interior. Flown to French Guyana, he was met by French authorities, placed under arrest, and taken to Lyon, where he will be tried.

Barbie is brought back to the same prison at Fort Montluc in Lyon where he ordered and supervised the deaths of thousands. A stone plaque at the gate commemorates the fact that 7,000 prisoners died there during the war.

Having accused Hardy of collaborating with him in postwar interrogations by French security officials, Barbie again made the charge in a series of interviews published in *France-Soir*, the Paris daily in 1972, after the Klarsfelds had unmasked the Nazi in South America. Once again, Hardy felt obliged to rebut the accusations point for point in a series of articles in the same newspaper. Hardy also granted an interview to the *Nouvel Observateur*, a Paris weekly magazine, in which he stated, "I have proven in two trials that the accusations brought against me are false." Asked if he thought Moulin and the others had been betrayed by someone in the Resistance, Hardy responded, "No. I don't think so. I think that, as often happened in the Resistance, some among us did not take enough precautions."

For the French, *l'affaire Hardy* seems destined to remain, much like *l'affaire Dreyfus*, a matter resolved by law but forever unresolved in national opinion. By the time Barbie had been returned to France and justice, Hardy was an old man, living quietly in a small village in the Deux Sèvres *département* in Western France. "Barbie's return?" he would respond to an interviewer seeking his reaction. "I heard about it on my radio. What do you think my first thought was: It's all beginning again."

Ω

The top leaders of the French Resistance were now in the hands of the Gestapo. But Barbie still did not know which of his prisoners was Moulin—Max—though he was sure Moulin was among them. He set to work to cull out the top *résistant*. At the Ecole de Santé, each of the prisoners was interrogated once, then again, but by nightfall Barbie still had not identified Moulin. At 11:00 P.M. they were loaded onto a truck and brought to Montluc prison where they signed their names in the notebook. The last to sign was Moulin, using his cover name, Jean Martel, and his Nice address.

The next day, the tortures and beatings began, with Barbie both supervising and participating. On Aubrac, Barbie personally used his fists. He pounded away at the man, demanding an answer: Who is Max? Aubrac was beaten by the Gestapo chief every day for a week. The others underwent a similar treatment, including Moulin himself. Aubry, Lassagne and Bruno Larat, whose Resistance activities were known to Barbie, were most cruelly punished. Aubry's shoulder was dislocated during one session; three times he was subjected to a mock firing squad in the courtyard of Montluc. Lassagne also took heavy punishment: for a full 48 hours, Barbie thought he was Max.

By sometime on Wednesday, Barbie had finally singled out Jean Martel as being Moulin, the man he wanted. Barbie was to later claim that he used no duress on Max; that their sessions were carried out in the spirit of respectful adversaries. "All the newspapers, books and publications that write about the matter always claim that I tortured Moulin. This is not true," Barbie claims. "All this is literature conceived on a basis of pure fantasy. There were no witnesses. The only ones who saw were my secretary and one or two men of the highest confidence."

During the first interrogation session, Moulin insisted on his identity of Jean Martel. "I'm an artist, a painter and decorator, and you have all my documents in front of you," Moulin told Barbie. "I am not Moulin."

Barbie called for a pencil and some paper. "You're an artist, aren't you?" he said to Moulin. Then he handed the Resistance suspect the drawing materials, instructing him to demonstrate his talents. Moulin calmly began to sketch as Barbie watched. Barbie began to laugh and claimed that "as soon as he put the point of the pencil to paper it was obvious that he couldn't draw anything. He was particularly incompetent at sketching." According to Barbie, he took the drawing and wrote on it, "done by Max." Barbie says that he saved the sketch until after the war when his wife burned it along with other incriminating papers.

In reality, the interrogation of Max went quite differently according to a member of the Ecolé de Sante staff. Gottlieb Fuchs, a French-German interpreter working at the Ecole de Sante, relates another version of Barbie's test of Moulin's drawing ability. In his memoirs, he states that Barbie handed Moulin the pencil and paper so he could draw a diagram of the Resistance networks. Instead, after sketching for a few minutes, what Moulin handed Barbie was not the scheme he wanted, but a grotesque caricature of the Gestapo chief. This, combined with Moulin's persistent silence, infuriated Barbie.

The following evening, seated at his receptionist post at the main entrance to the Gestapo headquarters, Fuchs witnessed the result of Barbie's anger. "I heard a stamping noise upstairs, then the sound of someone running down the stairs while pulling a load that was bouncing on the steps," he relates. "I looked up toward the staircase that led to the second story. I was seated just across from it. Barbie, in shirt-sleeves, was dragging a man by the feet. Arriving in the hallway, he breathed heavily, his foot on the inanimate body."

It was Moulin. Barbie had dragged him down from his office by a rope attached to his bound feet. "The prisoner's face was swollen, and his jacket was in shreds," Fuchs, who now lives in Switzerland, recalls. When Barbie came up from the cellar he was still in a rage, Fuchs says. "If that guy doesn't break tonight," Barbie swore, "I'll finish him off tomorrow in Paris!"

Those arrested with Moulin could also see the evidence of Barbie's brutality on the Resistance leader's tortured features. Dugoujon had been placed in cell number 129; Moulin was diagonally across the corridor in number 130, and the doctor could easily see the other's cell door from the small opening in his own. "On Wednesday they knew that Max was the resident of cell 130," Dugoujon recalls. "I saw two Gestapo men in civilian dress come to get him. They took him away a little before noon and brought him back that evening, at nightfall. This was June, so it was late. He had bandages on his head, he was limping and he was in a poor condition.

"Early Thursday morning they took him back to be interrogated at the Ecole de Santé on Avenue Berthelot, and they brought him back that night in a pitiful state," Dugoujon continues. "He could no longer walk and he was almost carried by the two guards, his legs dragging, his face all disfigured. They lay him out on the mattress in his cell and left him there all night, the door open, the light burning, with two guards watching. Friday morning they came to get him again."

Barbie had been beating Moulin, knowing that if Max could be persuaded to talk, the arrest would make his career. He used the whip, the truncheon, and his favorite weapon, his own fists. He worked over the Resistance leader for days, but Moulin, who once tried to take his own life to avoid talking, did not break under the punishment.

From his own cell, Raymond Aubrac could see the stairs leading down into his section of the prison. He saw Moulin being brought back, barely conscious, badly beaten, virtually carried down the stairs by two SS guards supporting him under each arm. "He was in very bad shape," Aubrac recalled. But Aubrac knew that the severity of the torture also meant that Moulin had scored a moral victory over Barbie. He had not talked.

Ω

Christian Pineau, who had flown back to France from London with Moulin in March, recognized Moulin with shock when the leader first appeared in the exercise yard of Montluc Prison where Pineau had been imprisoned weeks before Moulin was captured. Pineau was called out of his cell one night later that week. He was the only prisoner to possess a safety razor, which for some reason had not been confiscated when he was arrested in May. As a result, he became the prison's de facto barber. That night, a German non-commissioned officer told Pineau to follow him and bring his razor.

Pineau followed the guard through the silent corridors of the prison. It was late evening; all was still. The German officer led Pineau out into the north court, between the front gate of the prison and the entry to the main building. Another soldier stood there, a gun slung over his shoulder. On a bench nearby a man was stretched out, immobile.

"Monsieur, you shave," said the officer to Pineau, gesturing at the man lying on the bench.

Pineau took a closer look and realized with horror that this wreck of a man was Moulin. Unconscious, his eyes were sunken as though someone had punched them back into his head. There was a livid black-and-blue welt on his temple. Through his swollen lips came a faint rattling breath. As the German urged him to begin, Pineau was struck by the absurdity of the situation. "There I was, my little razor in my hand, in front of a man who was barely alive and whose face I had to shave," he later recalled. But he asked for soap and water, which the officer went to obtain.

Pineau bent closer to Moulin and took his ice-cold hand. But there was no reaction; the man was in a coma. The soap and water arrived, and Pineau painstakingly began to shave Moulin, trying to avoid the most damaged parts of his face. The blade was blunt from use, but Pineau managed to shave about Moulin's lips and cheeks.

The task perplexed him. "Why this macabre attention to someone who had been condemned to death?" he asked himself. "Why take such ridiculous pains after the horror of torture? This was inexplicable, having something to do with the Nazi mentality."

Suddenly Max opened his eyes and stared up at Pineau. It seemed that Moulin recognized Pineau. He whispered one word. "Drink." Pineau asked the soldier for water. The German hesitated for a moment, then went for water at the single tap in the prison yard. He rinsed out the soapy cup Pineau had used to shave Moulin and brought it back filled with fresh water. Meanwhile, Pineau leaned over Moulin and tried to comfort him. The battered man spoke five or six words in English, but Pineau could not make sense of what he was trying to say. Moulin took several gulps of water, then lapsed back into unconsciousness.

Pineau stayed by him until 10:00 P.M., apparently forgotten by the officer who had brought him there. Finally, the German NCO came back and took Pineau to his cell. "As the NCO climbed the stairs behind me, shaking his keys, Max lay stretched out on his bench where, undoubtedly, they would leave him all night. I never saw him again."

Pineau had been mystified by the shaving of Moulin, but there was a simple explanation. Moulin was being shipped to Paris, to the custody of Barbie's superiors, and he had to be made as presentable as possible. Due to Barbie's excesses, Moulin was in desperate shape. Not only had Barbie failed to get any information out of Max, but Max could no longer talk to anyone. Barbie wanted to disguise the damage he had done, which was the reason for the bizarre shaving chore.

Moulin was transported to Paris, where he was first brought to Gestapo headquarters at 84 Avenue Foch, the main Nazi torture center. But when the Germans realized that Moulin was now of little use, he was transferred to the villa of a Gestapo officer named Boemelburg in Neuilly, an upper-class western suburb of Paris, where other Resistance leaders were also being held. There, Delestraint and Lassagne saw him stretched out on a couch, his skull wrapped in bandages, his face yellow and deathly. He was barely breathing; only his eyes seemed to be at all alive. When Delestraint was asked to identify Moulin as Max, the officer drew himself up and, with the utmost in Gallic coldness, told his captors: "Military honor forbids me to recognize Max in the pitiful man you have presented to me."

One of the last men to see Moulin alive was a German policeman named Heinrich Meiners, who in the first days of July 1944 went to the Neuilly villa to pick up a prisoner. After the war, he told French investigators what he observed there. "In one cell I saw a prisoner who made a bizarre impression on me. He was lying down, then he sat up and I saw him walking once in the room supporting himself on the furniture and the walls. He was suffering and he was holding his stomach. He seemed like a very sick man who did not have long to live. He had a blank, haggard expression in his eyes. I asked a guard who the prisoner was. He told me he was an important Frenchman, a former prefect, Jean Moulin."

Meiners added, "A few days later, an SS medic that I knew told me he had been ordered to transport Moulin to a police hospital in Berlin."

In early July Moulin was put on a train heading east toward Berlin, but shortly before the train reached Frankfurt he died. The body was taken out of the train in the Frankfurt station and sent back to Paris, where it was cremated on July 9, 1943, at the Père-Lachaise Cemetery.

The cause of death was given in a certificate obtained later that month by Laure Moulin. It read: heart failure. The place of death was given as Metz, in the province of Lorraine, inside what had been French territory before the war. The date of the death was given as July 8, 1943. Moulin was only 44 years old.

Barbie had gotten his man, but too late. By June 1943, de Gaulle's resistance movement had been fully organized by the courageous Frenchman and was securely in place, ready to back the Allied landing that was to come a year later.

In a September 18, 1944, report of the SS head office, it was stated that SS-Reichsführer Heinrich Himmler had sent a personal letter expressing gratitude to Barbie and others in the Lyon SS for their "high efficiency in the pursuit of crime and their indefatigable devotion to the battle against Resistance organizations in France." In addition, Barbie received the Iron Cross, First Class, with Sword on November 9, 1943. In a recommendation for promotion to Hauptsturmführer, a rank Barbie received in 1944, a superior officer stated that, "his most meritorious accomplishment has been the cleaning out of numerous enemy organizations."

A report on the events of June 1943 filed by Obergruppen-führer Ernst Kaltenbrunner, Berlin chief of the RSHA, the Security Police, praised the Lyon Gestapo capture of General Delestraint, but significantly failed to mention the arrest and subsequent death of Jean Moulin at the hands of an overzealous Klaus Barbie.

THE FINAL MASSACRE

It WAS NOON ON A THURSDAY IN JULY 1944 AND THE PLACE Bellecour was crowded with Lyonnais returning home for their midday meals, when a platoon of German soldiers halted traffic along the northern edge of the vast square and cordoned off the sidewalk in front of the Café Moulin-à-Vent.

As a gray military vehicle pulled up in front of the empty cafe and drew to a halt, a group of SS men got out and took up positions around the truck, warning back the growing crowd. A wan and unshaven Frenchman stepped onto the sidewalk from the back of the truck; seconds later one of the Gestapo men leveled a pistol at the back of his neck and squeezed the trigger. The crowd watched in shock as the prisoner dropped into a motionless heap on the sidewalk, blood pouring from the wound in his head. As the horrified civilians looked on, four more men met the same fate in the next minutes. Klaus Barbie was serving notice on the city of Lyon that a new wave of butchery had begun.

The atrocity was intended to demonstrate to the population of

Lyon that although the Allies had landed in Normandy in June and were moving east toward Paris, the Germans had no intention of either gracefully accepting defeat or tolerating a popular uprising.

An incident in the Moulin-à-Vent the night before had provided Barbie with the opportunity. The cafe-restaurant was located diagonally across the Place Bellecour from Gestapo headquarters. Requisitioned by the Germans, the cafe was a popular evening gathering place for the Gestapo and Wehrmacht officers. But it was also open to French civilians, which enabled Resistance members to place a package of explosives on a shelf in the restaurant during the evening of July 26. It was timed to go off five hours later, but the bomb intended to kill leading members of the German occupation force instead exploded an hour after the restaurant had closed.

The intent was perfectly clear to the Germans. The next morning the Gestapo went to the prison of Fort Montluc and took five hostages from among the Resistance inmates. One of these was Albert Chambonnet, 41, alias Didier. Although the Gestapo was not aware of his rank, Chambonnet was chief of the Secret Army in the Lyon region. There was also Gilbert Dru, 24, and Pierre Chirat, 24, both members of a Christian Resistance network who had been arrested together the previous June 17; Léon Pfeiffer, 22, apprehended in possession of machine gun clips; and Pierre Bernard, 40, another Resistance member.

They were taken to the Moulin-à-Vent, where one after another they fell before the Gestapo executioner's bullets on the street in front of the cafe. When the shooting stopped one of the men was still moving, but those who sought to go to his aid, including a Red Cross nurse, were pushed back. The Gestapo and the Wehrmacht left the murder site after ordering that the bodies remain under the hot July sun for three more hours. The French police stood by to see that the German command was carried out.

Word of the shootings filtered quickly through the city, reaching Dominique D'Ermo within the hour. D'Ermo lived just a few blocks away from the Place Bellecour and was at home when he received a telephone call from a fellow Resistance member informing him of the reprisals. D'Ermo and his friend had returned to Lyon only the day before, having escaped with their lives from a massive Wehrmacht assault on the *maquis* stronghold on the Vercors plateau near the city of Grenoble.

About 5,000 French partisans had gathered in this mountainous redoubt, preparing for the day when they would break out
in support of an Allied advance. On July 14 Allied aircraft had
dropped a massive quantity of arms, ammunition and other supplies, but on the following day the Germans launched an attack on
their camp spearheaded by glider troops who landed on the very
airstrips the *maquis* had prepared in hopes of French Army rein-
forcements from North Africa.

The Vercors became a trap; hundreds of *maquisards* died in the
ensuing battle. Then only seventeen, D'Ermo was taken prisoner
and interrogated, but escaped to the city of Bourg-en-Bresse, where
he and a comrade caught a train home to Lyon to regroup. Today a
restaurant owner in Washington D.C., D'Ermo recalls the panic
that was in his friend's voice that day in Lyon. "He said, 'Dominique, we've got to get out of here.'" His friend told him of the
executions at the cafe and they agreed to meet at the Place Bellecour.

"I saw five bodies on the sidewalk and they were shot in the
neck," recalls D'Ermo. "They cordoned the sidewalk, all the blood
was still fresh running on the sidewalk, and they wouldn't let
anybody pick up the bodies. They wanted to leave the bodies all
day there on the sidewalk. I recognized Pfeiffer, whom I had
known for two years. He must have been 20, 21 years old. The
Germans and the French Milice were taking pictures. Barbie and all
the Gestapo were also there taking pictures and having a good
time. It was a great celebration for them."

The next morning, notices headlined: "The Rapid Punishment
of an Attack" appeared in all the Lyon newspapers, written by the
German-controlled French press agency Havas. "A bomb exploded
in a Lyon restaurant, at the Place Bellecour, in the night of July
26-27, 1944," they read. "This establishment was frequented prin-
cipally by a German clientele. A rapid operation allowed the arrest
a short time later of five persons belonging to the terrorist group
responsible for the attack. They were executed on the spot of their
deed the very day after the explosion."

The executions profoundly shocked the occupation-weary populace of Lyon, but the event was soon overshadowed by further

atrocities as Barbie ordered and participated in the massacres of hundreds of Jews and Resistance fighters. It was his final orgy of killing before the inevitable retreat. It was in August 1944 that Klaus Barbie earned the name that would follow him for the next four decades: The Butcher of Lyon.

Ω

Barbie's capacity for cruelty was already well known in the Haut Jura, the mountainous region to the northeast of Lyon that had witnessed a massive anti-*maquis* operation in which the Gestapo lieutenant participated during the month of April 1944. The military operation launched by the Germans was largely unsuccessful, but Barbie extracted civilian reprisals for the German losses, turning homes into ashes and women into widows in villages throughout the area. It was thereafter called "Black Easter" in the Jura Mountains.

The *maquis* developed in the Jura department much as it did throughout southeast France, both as a form of resistance and as a response to the forced labor program the Germans and the Vichy government had initiated. Frenchmen had been going to work in the factories of Germany ever since the Armistice was signed, at first through volunteer recruitment, then through a program called *la relève,* by which one French prisoner-of-war was released for every three laborers who went from France to Germany.

Finally, in February 1943, Frenchmen were forced to work in German industry through a labor draft, the Service de Travail Obligatoire, or STO. To avoid the conscription, young Frenchmen by the thousands took to the forests and the highlands. The STO had become an effective Resistance recruiter, pushing thousands into the *maquis,* and reinforcing the guerilla opposition to the Germans in such mountainous regions as the Jura, the Alps, the Massif Central and the Pyrénées. At first, the new recruits were poorly equipped and trained, but cadres were formed, military discipline imposed and supplies received through Resistance channels and Allied parachute drops.

The *maquis* of the Haut Jura were largely provisioned from the industrial town of St. Claude, which lay at the bottom of a valley formed by five rugged, stubby mountain peaks typical of the region. The area was perfect for *maquis* activities. St. Claude, with

15,000 inhabitants, was large enough to provide material assistance to the insurgents encamped in the hills, out of easy German reach but within striking distance of rail lines and military outposts.

Several hundred strong, the Haut Jura *maquis* was not one of the largest Resistance groups, but it was effective enough to draw the attention of the German command. During the month of March 1944 the *maquis* cut six train lines; destroyed two locomotives; severed a high tension line in a rugged region; and killed 20 enemy troops, including members of the French Milice.

In early April a contingent of German troops, including a small group under the command of Barbie, moved into the Haut Jura with the aim of eliminating the *maquis*. The operation, which began on Good Friday, 1944, went poorly for the Germans from the start. A column of troops moving north into the Juras from the Ain department was ambushed at a spot called Champravelet, where the *maquis*, armed with machine guns and grenades on the sides of a narrow gorge, waited. As the Germans came through, the *maquis* killed 200 of the enemy, losing only 22 men in the process, then faded back into the hills.

Infuriated at their military losses to the French guerrilla army, the Germans took vengence on the nearby village of Larrivoire, where they tortured residents, burned 27 homes and executed six men suspected of *maquis* activity or sympathies. Between April 7 and 18, the German troops moved through the region, burning homes and executing civilians either for suspected guerrilla activities or simply in reprisal.

The deaths in Larrivoire were followed by executions in other villages as the Germans unsuccessfully sought to destroy the elusive *maquis* forces. Civilian deaths constituted the majority of the nearly 60 victims of the Germans and their French auxiliaries in Jeurre, Rogna, Sièges, Les Bouchoux, Coyrière, Les Moussières, Molinges, Vaux-les-Saint-Claude, Ravilloles, Grand-Rivière, Lonchaumois, Prémanon and Prénovel. The mayor and other prominent local figures were usually selected by the Germans for reprisal executions, often after severe beatings and torture.

That Barbie was present and took a leading role in many of these atrocities was established after the war, when war crimes investigators collected evidence to be used at his trial. On April 12, 1944, the husband of Germaine Clément was shot by Germans under the direct command of Barbie. At 8:00 A.M. that day, she told investigators in 1950, a machine-gun vehicle pulled up in front of her house, followed by an armored personnel carrier, out of which stepped Klaus Barbie. The widow identified the Gestapo agent from a photograph shown her by the French Sûreté National.

"As soon as he came into the house," Mme. Clément testified, "he demanded to know where my husband was. I told him he was in the woods. A few moments later two Germans brought my husband in to this officer. Barbie interrogated my husband and demanded to know if it was correct that he had housed and fed *maquisards*. My husband denied this. Immediately, Barbie started to torture him, striking him with a stick, and when this broke, with a whip. Not being able to extract any information, Barbie had all the men of the village assembled on the square and interrogated them about the movements of the *maquis*. In this way he picked out six young men, one of whom was forced to confirm Barbie's information, but he was executed anyway a few minutes later in front of our house. My husband was taken on the machine-gun vehicle and shot at the spot called Le Fournet in the community of Moussières."

Another widow, Julie Perrier, told the Sûreté what she had witnessed in the village of Larrivoire on April 13, 1944. After identifying Barbie from a photograph as the officer in command, Perrier told of the torture of one Gaston Patel, a resident of nearby Molinges, by the Gestapo lieutenant.

"At one point I went into the dining room and through the windows I saw Patel, who was guarded by Germans. I saw Barbie strike him with a stick on the head and in the back. He also kicked him in the lower abdomen. Then he gave an order and Patel was taken away by a firing squad. A few minutes later I heard firing and I learned later that this was the execution of Gaston Patel, who died 50 meters from our house."

St. Claude itself was taken over by the Gestapo on April 6 with the assistance of regular German Army units that established a *cordon sanitaire* at a radius of five kilometers around the town, leaving it to Barbie's Einsatzkommando to conduct a sweep of the area inside the ring. Throughout the operation, the residents of St. Claude were terrorized by Barbie's Gestapo unit, which established a torture center in the Hôtel de France on the main street of the town. Upon his arrival, Barbie proceeded with the immediate arrest of the employees of an agricultural cooperative called La Fraternelle, which had been denounced by informers as a major supplier of food to the region's *maquis*. A dozen of its employees and managers were deported.

Few in St. Claude were less comfortable with the presence of the Germans than René Aimé Chorier, whose home was directly across the street from the technical school where the German troops were billeted and where the bodies of soldiers killed in mountain skirmishes with the *maquis* had been brought. Chorier was a fugitive wanted by the Vichy government for his failure to present himself in 1943 for forced STO labor on the German coastal fortifications in Normandy. Before that, he had been a soldier in the impotent French Armistice Army until its dissolution in late 1942.

When the STO draft order came, Chorier headed into the mountainous countryside of the Haut Jura and found a job working in a mill, where he ground flour for the area's peasants. Surreptitiously, he provided flour to the *maquis*. In October 1943, when he returned to St. Claude to take care of his aging father, Chorier worked at odd jobs and kept out of sight of the police, who came to his home fifteen times to search for him.

From the windows of his home, Chorier anxiously watched the comings and goings of the Germans. At one point he sent his younger brother to see if it was feasible for him to escape from St. Claude by a steep path, the Chemin de la Rochette, which wound up Mont Bayard directly behind the town center. The boy returned with a negative report. The Germans had set up a machine gun at the base of the path, making flight by that route impossible. All other exits out of the town were similarly guarded; Chorier could only watch and wait.

On Easter morning the word came. The Germans ordered every man between the ages of 18 and 45 to assemble on the village square. "They said that anyone found in the houses would be shot," Chorier, who still lives in St. Claude, recalls. "And maybe his

family with him, *hein*? We had to go down to the Place du Pré."
Chorier, who carried false identity papers in the name of an uncle,
René Aimé Coquet, who had been killed in the First World War,
decided to obey the order. The alternative was to risk reprisals
against his family and certain death for himself if he were found
hiding in the house.

"The square was encircled by troops, with machine guns on all
the street corners so as to rake with fire if anyone tried to escape.
They were everywhere," recalls Chorier, a restrained man who
recounted his story as he sat over coffee in the home of Maurice
Emain, another former Resistance member in St. Claude. "We
were all assembled on the square and then they started to make
their selection. They wanted 118 hostages, although in the end
they took more, but at first they wanted 118 for the Germans who
had been killed in the mountains."

The Germans first inspected identity papers and took as hostages anyone who might be able to help the *maquis* with provisions
or other material assistance. But the Nazis then started to choose
the men arbitrarily. "They took one, they skipped one, they took
one, they skipped one," says Chorier, who was one of the unlucky
ones. He was pulled out of the lineup and placed with the other
hostages.

When the selection was over, 302 men from St. Claude had
been placed to one side. Uncertain of their fate, they waited all day
in the town square until evening, when they were placed in the
technical school. The following morning, the hostages of St. Claude
were shipped by train to the town of Bellegard to the south, on the
first leg of their deportation to Nazi concentration camps. In Bellegard the Jews, or suspected Jews, were removed from the main
body of the prisoners; the rest were sent to the transit camp of
Compiègne, near Paris. From there, Chorier was shipped first to the
camps of Dora and Buchenwald, ending in a complex at Hellrich, in
Germany, where he worked at digging tunnels until he was freed
by the Russians in 1945. Of the men deported from St. Claude, just
over 100 returned. The rest died or were executed.

Ω

Two months earlier, in February 1944, Barbie and his Einsatzkommando had taken part in a similarly bloody operation of

shorter duration in the Ain *département* to the south. Five thousand German soldiers drew a net around a mountainous region some 50 miles northeast of Lyon and attacked the Hauteville and Brenod plateaus where the *maquis* had established camps. In two days of heavy fighting over the 5th and 6th of February, the *maquis* were forced to abandon their positions. But the Nazis were not satisfied with military targets, and devastated the villages of Corlier, Nivollet-Montgriffon, Evosges and Petit-Abèrgement. Now, in April, they and Barbie were back in the Juras, only this time they were concentrating their forces 30 miles further north. This offensive would be far longer and bloodier.

During their sweeps of the area, the German troops captured seven of the Resistance fighters, who were brought back to a hotel in St. Claude. They were placed in the dining room to be interrogated by Barbie and his unit, which consisted of two other SS officers and three Frenchmen in German uniforms without insignia of rank. All the prisoners, dressed in civilian clothing, were kept face to the wall with their hands held high. One German army officer remained in the room, in which there were several tables and a piano.

"It was known that there was, among the prisoners, a prominent leader of the local French Resistance," the German officer recalled after the war. "The word was that it was the chief of section, named Kemmler, an Alsatian. Kemmler was the oldest of the prisoners; in my opinion he was between 40 and 55 years of age."

Barbie did not come into the dining room until the prisoners had been assembled. "I remember that they were visibly frightened when they saw Barbie enter," the German army officer recounted. "He was satisfied with briefly interrogating the civilians before turning quickly to Kemmler. He interrogated him in French; Kemmler responded only with the word, 'Never.' Upon that, Barbie struck Kemmler in the face with his gloved fists; he repeated his questions, then struck him again. After having hit Kemmler this way three or four times, the prisoner began to bleed from the nose and the mouth. Barbie walked over to the piano, a few steps away, and with his gloved and bloody fingers played the first few bars of 'Talk to Me of Love.'

"Then he came back to Kemmler and asked additional questions. When he received no response other than 'Never,' Barbie hit Kemmler again and again. The session lasted for a half to three-quarters of an hour. Meanwhile, night had fallen; Kemmler was kept at the hotel while the rest of the prisoners were brought elsewhere."

From another German officer, the Wehrmacht witness learned that Kemmler was taken to one of the upper floors of the hotel, where he was alternately plunged into scalding hot and freezing water, then bound and thrown on the landing of the third floor of the hotel, where he lay until the following day.

"In the morning Kemmler was brought down to the dining room, where his interrogation was to continue," he continues. "The interrogation took place in a part of the dining room separated from the other part of the room, where I was working with other members of the headquarters, by two glass partitions."

The German officer witnessed the entire proceeding that followed. "In the back of the dining room were Barbie, two of the uniformed Frenchmen, and Kemmler. Kemmler was standing up and he was struck alternately by each of the Frenchmen, who used a piece of rope. They hit him only in the torso, in the area between the shoulders and the thigh, and not once in the head. You could see that Barbie was asking questions, but because of the glass partitions, you could not hear any of the questions, nor the responses eventually given by Kemmler.

"Kemmler received about five blows. Then Barbie again asked some questions, which were followed by more blows. This situation continued for about a quarter of an hour, then Kemmler collapsed for the first time." The Frenchmen put Kemmler back on his feet, and the interrogation continued. The record indicates that the questioning lasted for over an hour. When Kemmler could no longer stand on his feet, the two Frenchmen assisting Barbie dragged Kemmler to a chair, whose arms kept the Resistance leader from collapsing. Shortly after, Barbie and his aides went to lunch.

"Kemmler could see everything," the Wehrmacht witness recounts. "His head was still lifted, leaning slightly forward. His eyes followed our movements. At the end of about a half-hour, his eyelids fluttered, he closed his eyes and his head leaned forward a bit. About five minutes later a puddle of urine formed beneath Kemmler's chair. For me it indicated that he was dead.

"About a half-hour after Kemmler's death three or four SS men came in—without Barbie—and they carried the body out of the hotel. The fact that the SS had left Kemmler only a half-hour before his death and came back only when he was dead made me conclude that they assumed Kemmler would die after the treatment he had endured and had precisely calculated when death would come. It was said at the time that Kemmler's body had been transported with others to a farm located in Saint-Claude or in the area, which they later burned."

Ω

By June 1944, two months after the operation in the Haut Jura, the position of the German occupying forces in France had deteriorated considerably. The Allied landings at Normandy and the subsequent move inland triggered actions by Resistance and *maquis* forces all across France in a coordinated effort to harass the Germans from the rear. Lyon itself had been hit at the end of May by a massive Allied bombing raid, which leveled the Ecole de Santé and heavily damaged the rail lines converging in the city. Unfortunately, the attack also left hundreds of civilians dead. It also killed Hollert, the SS second-in-command, and moved Barbie up in the SS hierarchy.

The Allied military success accelerated reprisals by the Germans, who knew it was their last opportunity. In the days immediately following the Normandy landings, a total of 122 French Resistance members held prisoner at Montluc were executed at Neuville-sur-Saône, Saint-Didier-de-Formens and other areas around Lyon. On June 29, 1944, a convoy of 724 prisoners was sent to Germany from the prisons of Montluc and Saint-Paul. On July 9, 30 prisoners from Montluc were executed at Porte-les-Valence, while 28 more were gunned down at Toussieu on July 12. On July 13, 197 were executed throughout the countryside surrounding Lyon, in lots of between 15 and 52 at a time; seven were murdered on July 14, the French national holiday, Bastille Day. Five days later, another 52 were killed.

One of the prisoners executed at Neuville-sur-Saône (also called Villeneuve by the Lyonnais) that June was a man named René

Leynaud, a journalist, poet and close friend of *Combat* writer Albert Camus. Camus later described the death of Leynaud, who was arrested on May 16, 1944, in the Place Bellecour at Lyon. When he fled he was wounded in the leg by the Vichy Milice, and after hospitalization he was placed in Montluc prison.

On the early morning of June 13, nineteen Resistance prisoners were chosen by the Germans and assembled in the courtyard. "One by one, they climbed into a truck, which took them to the Gestapo headquarters in Place Bellecour," Camus wrote. "They waited three-quarters of an hour in the cellar of the building. When they were finally called, their handcuffs were removed and they were made to climb into the truck again with some German soldiers armed with machine guns. The truck drove out of Lyon in the direction of Villeneuve ....

"Just beyond Villeneuve, opposite a grove of poplars, the truck stopped, the soldiers leaped to the ground and commanded the men to get out and go toward the woods. A first group of six left the truck and started toward the trees. The machine guns immediately crackled behind them and mowed them down. A second group followed, then a third. Those who were still breathing were put out of their pain by a final shot. One of them, however, though frightfully wounded, managed to drag himself to a peasant's house. From him we learned the details."

The pattern was clear; if the Germans were aware that the Normandy landings had signaled the end of their occupation of France, they had no intention of taking the defeat with grace. In spite of these killings, it was not until the July 27 execution of five men on the Place Bellecour that the ruthlessness of the Lyon Gestapo was publicly revealed to the French.

After that atrocity, Cardinal Gerlier went personally to see Knab, the SS commander, to protest the murder of five men who were in jail at the time and could not have had anything to do with the Moulin-à-Vent bombing. "It was a very stormy interview," a monsignor who accompanied Gerlier later reported, "Commander Knab pounding on the table, overturning his chair. I wondered if we were going to get out of there."

The tide then turned even more decisively against the Germans with the Allied landing on the southern Mediterranean coast of

France on August 15. Some 575,000 American and Free French troops, led by French General Henri Giraud, established beach-heads under the cover of heavy offshore and aerial bombardment, then moved to take the ports of Marseille and Toulon. Ashore, the Resistance harassed the Germans, cutting rail lines and blocking roads by ambushing convoys. By August 20, the Germans were in retreat from the Mediterranean, and Marseille and Toulon fell a week later.

The U.S. forces moved up the east bank of the Rhône, while Free French forces followed on the opposite shore, as the Germans retreated to the north. After liberating Grenoble, to the southeast of Lyon, on August 21, the Allies launched a pincer movement on Lyon. By August 28, the Germans were withdrawing their gun emplacements on the approaches to the city, and the last of the Germans withdrew on September 2.

Throughout this fateful month of August, however, Barbie and the Gestapo had been indulging in a final, systematic massacre of the prisoners left in Montluc. On the morning of August 17, the Germans removed 50 prisoners from the so-called "hostage bar-rack" at Montluc that housed the Jewish prisoners and loaded them onto trucks. They were driven out to an airfield at Bron, in the near suburbs of Lyon, which had been heavily damaged in August 15 bombardments. The prisoners were set to work repair-ing the bomb craters on the runways of the Bron airfield. One witness to what took place at Bron was Otto Huber, who was brought there by the Germans to serve as an interpreter.

"Around noon," Huber later told investigators, "one prisoner escaped. The commander said that if the man was not found, all the prisoners would be shot. In the evening, the prisoners got back in the truck that was to take them back to Fort Montluc. But at that point, a major arrived and gave the order to take the prisoners out of the truck and to lead them over to another work site where no one had worked yet." That was all Huber saw before leaving that day.

Upon his arrival the following morning Huber asked the com-mander at the site if the prisoners had worked late the night before. He was told that it was none of his business; the matter was closed. A short time later, prisoners arrived from Montluc, but there were only 23 this time and none were from the group of the previous day. As they worked on the Bron runways, Huber noted that one of the prisoners had both hands swathed in bandages, from injuries received at Montluc. Huber told the adjutant on the field that the prisoner was wounded and that it was painful for him to work. The German officer looked at Huber and smiled, telling him that by night the man would be feeling no more pain. He added, ''Do you understand now where the others are?''

At six o'clock that evening the adjutant ordered 20 German soldiers to accompany the prisoners. According to Huber's account, the German soldiers volunteering for the detail came forth laughing and enthusiastic, joking about going ''to make music.'' The Jewish prisoners were loaded into one truck, which took off in the same direction as the previous day's workers; the truck filled with soldiers followed. The next morning Huber returned to the airfield and saw the adjutant talking to a sergeant, making gestures that clearly indicated he was talking about shootings.

No prisoners came to Bron that day, Saturday, August 19, but according to Huber, he went with the adjutant to bring a truckload of dirt to a bomb crater in the area where the Jewish prisoners had been brought the previous evening. The truckload of dirt was dumped into the bomb crater, and although Huber told the postwar investigators that he did not look into the pit, he was certain that it held the bodies of the 23 prisoners.

Another group of prisoners was executed at Bron the following Monday, August 21. This time the killers were members of the French Milice, according to French workmen who were inadvertant witnesses of the massacre. The mass graves at Bron were not discovered by officials until after the liberation of Lyon, when a total of 109 decomposing bodies were found in five spots around the airfield. Most were Jews, all those who were left in the barracks at Montluc after the August 11 convoy that carried some 650 French Jews to another kind of death in the Auschwitz and Ravensbruck concentration camps.

One of the few surviving witnesses to the departure of this convoy from Montluc is Dr. Alice Van Steenberghe, a Resistance member who was arrested in August 1944 and interrogated five times by Barbie. On August 11, she relates, ten Jewish women who had been in her cell were removed and assembled in the courtyard preparatory to being brought to the railroad station. "From the peephole of my cell I could see the corridor and the courtyard of Montluc," Steenberghe said in May 1983 during a court reconstruction of the 1944 deportation. "There the women were all put in a group. That's when I saw Barbie pass in the corridor. He was speaking with a member of his staff."

The last of the Jewish prisoners had been killed at Bron. It was now the turn of the Resistance prisoners in the main building at Montluc, where some 850 remained. On Sunday morning, August 20, following the first two days of butchery at Bron, a group of Barbie's Gestapo staff and fascist French aides assembled at the Place Bellecour headquarters and left in convoy for Fort Montluc. Among them was a French collaborator named Max Payot, who told postwar investigators the story of the day's events.

At Montluc the Gestapo assembled some 120 Resistance prisoners in the courtyard and bound their hands behind their backs with twine. The prisoners were attached together in pairs and loaded into two buses, one of which was marked as belonging to the French national police. The convoy left the military prison and proceeded to the Fort de Côte-Lorette, an unused military installation in the town of Saint-Genis-Laval, a suburb to the southwest of Lyon.

Payot told the investigators: "Upon arrival at the fort, the two buses entered the enclosure where there was an abandoned house, which the Germans inspected. Once that was finished, the prisoners were taken out two by two from the buses and led to the first floor of the house, where they were summarily executed with two machine gun bullets, usually in the back of the neck."

Payot said he was placed on guard outside, at a corner of the house, but he was accused by the Germans of shirking. They ordered him into the kitchen of the house, where he accompanied the prisoners from the ground floor up to the room where they were being slaughtered. "At this point," Payot testified, "the prisoners were obliged to climb up on the pile formed by the accumulation of the bodies of their own companions. Blood flowed through the ceiling and I could distinctly hear the victims falling as they were executed.

"The assassinations continued next on the ground floor, where about half the victims were in the same room in a pile of bodies five feet high. Sometimes the Germans had to climb on the bodies of their victims to finish off those who were still moving. The bodies were soaked in gasoline and incendiaries placed; the Germans had brought along phosphorus to activate the combustion, as well as explosives." Then the house was set on fire.

"I will add that during the fire we found, at the south side of the house, one of the victims who had accidentally been spared. She came to the window and begged mercy of her executioners. They responded with shots fired in her direction. At that point, hit by bullets and under the effect of the heat, her face froze in a horrible vision. The temperature rising, her face melted like wax.

"I also learned that two of the victims had jumped from a window of the same room, on the north side, and were shot on the ground. Two of the butchers took the bodies and threw them into the furnace of the ground floor. Their work accomplished, most of the Germans and the French had their clothes soiled by the blood and brains of their victims. The convoy returned to Lyon and the Wehrmacht soldiers were left to dynamite the remains of the house."

Among those executed at Saint-Genis Laval that day was the Abbé Boursier, a Catholic priest arrested in May 1944 when a radio transmission post, along with grenades, machine guns and pistols with silencers was found in his monastery. The raid was carried out by the Milice in cooperation with Francis André's PPF.

Barbie accorded no special considerations to members of religious orders who were involved in Resistance activities. Years later he was to recall a similar raid on a Lyon convent, in which Sten machine guns and ammunition were seized. His arrest of a number of nuns from the religious community led to a confrontation with Cardinal Gerlier.

"We showed him the arsenal found in the convent, and we argued," Barbie later recalled. "The cardinal harshly attacked the methods we used against the guerrillas, forgetting the barbarous crimes of the guerrillas against the German soldiers. We argued a long time, he, his secretary and I. We could not reach agreement.

Barbie continued, "The sisters of the convent were arrested. I don't remember if we executed the, but I think we did.... Yes. Now I remember. They were executed."

By August 21 the death toll from Montluc had risen to nearly 600, including the 109 shot at Bron, the estimated 120 massacred at Saint-Genis-Laval and some 350 murdered throughout the Rhône countryside in the preceding weeks. Scores of bodies had also been found floating in the Rhône and Saône rivers, most the victims of tortures and summary executions, usually by a bullet to the back of the neck.

That Klaus Barbie ordered the savage massacre at Saint-Genis-Laval has been asserted by a number of sources, among them his French collaborators. One was a man named Jean Baptiste Seta, who was interrogated in August 1945 by postwar investigators attempting to reconstruct the chronicle of the Gestapo chief's bloody last days in Lyon. Seta told the French officials that he had been detained at Montluc for apparent misbehavior while working with the Germans, and was called into the Montluc courtyard on the day before the massacre at Saint-Genis-Laval.

Barbie was there along with Bartelmus and others, but the prisoners were sent back to their cells. The next morning, at 6:00 A.M., the Germans again brought out the prisoners, but since Seta was still due to go before a German military tribunal, he was sent back to his cell by Bartelmus. Barbie, Seta said, was again present in the courtyard.

Seta was not witness to the actual execution of the prisoners, but he later heard the Nazis speak about the operation. "When the Germans left Fort Montluc on August 24 they took me with them as a prisoner. That is to say, the Gestapo itself came to get me to leave in the direction of Dijon. On the trip I heard conversations about the execution of Saint-Genis-Laval, and at that point, through a French agent, that the French and Germans had taken part in the massacre." Seta added, "I have no precise details about the other executions and those who carried them out, however, as I have indicated, it was Barbie who ordered and led these operations."

Francis André, Barbie's closest collaborator among the French, also implicated Barbie. After the war, during his own interrogation prior to his trial, condemnation and execution by firing squad,

André said that Barbie "certainly ordered, if not led, the executions at Saint-Genis-Laval and many others in the Lyon region." In a deposition to postwar French authorities, André characterized his German colleague as *"colereux, sanglant,"* angry and bloody.

Ω

Unlike the massacre of Bron, the murders at Saint-Genis-Laval became public knowledge almost immediately. One of the first to inspect the burned and dynamited ruins of the house was Cardinal Gerlier, who was informed of the atrocity by a subordinate within the archbishopric of Lyon. Outraged, Gerlier first went to lodge a protest with the military commander of Lyon, Colonel Von Fersen. Gerlier next went to the Hotel Terminus to personally deliver his letter of protest to Knab, Barbie's direct superior.

"I am 64 years old, *monsieur le commandeur,*" Gerlier wrote, "I fought in the war of 1914 and have seen in the course of my life many horrible sights, but I have never seen any which so revolted me as that which I witnessed only a short time ago." Gerlier concluded, "I do not hesitate to declare to those who are responsible for this that they are forever dishonored in the eyes of humanity." But Knab was apparently unmoved; nine more *résistants* were executed in the Gestapo headquarters in Place Bellecour on August 23.

The atrocities carried out that summer as Allied armies advanced on Lyon set in motion one of the final dramas of the German occupation of the city. It had become apparent to Resistance leaders, Gerlier and others that they would have to move quickly to prevent a final massacre of the 700 prisoners remaining in Montluc.

The Lyon-area Resistance sent a letter to the Germans via the Red Cross, the Swedish consul and the departmental prefect, putting Knab on notice. "We hold 720 Germans prisoner in the Haute Savoie. Tell Knab, commander of the police, that their lives depend on those of the patriots incarcerated at Montluc." This was sent before the Resistance learned of the killings at Saint-Genis-Laval; it was quickly followed by another informing Knab that 80 of the German prisoners had been executed in reprisal.

Gerlier and a Monsignor Rouche went back to Von Fersen to plead with him, and he promised to intervene on behalf of the prisoners in Montluc. But the Resistance had already put a plan into motion to protect their men and women. A Groupe Franc led by a German-speaking Alsatian named Koenig took up positions along the streets leading out of Montluc, ready to halt any vehicles attempting to remove prisoners from the fort. At 6:00 P.M. on August 24, a Resistance lieutenant named Nunninger sent two German-speaking Alsatians from his group, Sigrist and Diethhelm, equipped with false papers, to talk with the commandant of Montluc, a man named Boesche, who was already in negotiations with Gerlier.

Boesche told the two Resistance envoys that he was prepared to abandon the fort to the French, but only if he and his staff were allowed to retreat without opposition. The German commander told them he would leave Montluc at 7:30 P.M. and that the keys would be given to the ranking French prisoner. But the deadline came and went with the Germans still holding the prison. The Resistance men waiting outside the fort began to worry; they decided to effect a ruse to draw Boesche out of Montluc.

Koenig, the French commander, went to Boesche's home nearby in the Cours Gambetta, where a phone line was connected directly with the prison. Koenig picked up the phone and rang Boesche. When the prison warden answered, he shouted into the line in impeccable German:

"Commandant Kraemer here! I have an urgent order to give to you in person, but I cannot come because there are armored vehicles coming up the Cours Gambetta. You will leave immediately in the direction of Mâcon. All the others have already left Lyon. I alone have stayed to give you this important order. Heil Hitler!" At 9:30 P.M. Boesche and his guard staff abandoned the prison and joined the German retreat, entrusting the prison's keys to General Chevalier of the Resistance forces.

The prisoners were freed and assembled in the courtyard, joining in singing the Marseillaise. They were then led to a nearby monastery and convent, where the men and women were washed, clothed, fed and had their wounds treated. The following morning Gerlier came to the monastery and said a mass of thanksgiving in the garden. The ordeal of Montluc was over for the few who had survived. Thereafter the prison held French collaborators arrested upon the Liberation of Lyon by Allied forces on September 3.

Ω

In those last days of the war the Germans and their French collaborators were already preparing for the general retreat. Francis André told his postwar interrogators that on August 19, Knab called him in and told him to draw up a list of those members of his group of PPF collaborators who wanted to leave with the German Army. But André felt that he and his men were sufficiently numerous, and well-armed, to make their own way back toward Germany. Although they ran into *maquis* opposition along the way, many PPF men did make it to Germany or Italy at the end of the war. But most were arrested by Allied forces and sent back to Lyon to face charges of war crimes and treason. André, like many of these, died in front of a firing squad after the treason trials conducted in Lyon in the immediate postwar era.

Years later Barbie was to claim that he and his commando were assigned to the west of France after the Allied landing at Normandy in June 1944, participating in actions around the towns of Caen and Falaise. But there is little evidence to suggest that he ever left the Lyon region during that last brutal summer of occupation.

In one respect, Barbie's story of the war's end in France does coincide with the statements given by his associates to postwar interrogators. The main German force left Lyon in the last week of August, but rear guard actions continued for days as the Germans sent their own troops and French collaborators back to the main battle zone to slow up the Allied advance with sabotage and harrassing actions.

Barbie and his commando were assigned the mission of capturing General Henri Giraud, who was leading the French army approaching Lyon from the southwest. "Around noon on August 28," Barbie recalled, "a few kilometers before reaching Lyon, we were surprised by a guerrilla attack. With the first assault, a spray of machine gun fire hit two of my men and our driver, barely grazing me. The fight lasted more than two hours. It ended when the fragments of a mortar shell wounded me in the face, lacerating my mouth, severely wounding me in the left foot and leg. We left the dead, took the survivors and got on the road toward Lyon, which was 15 minutes behind the front." The skirmish took place in Limonest, about 10 kilometers north of Lyon, where, according to Barbie's associates, the commando's retreat was made possible by the arrival of a single Panzer tank.

The group brought Barbie and the other wounded to the German military hospital in Lyon, where Barbie was operated upon. Soon after he was sent back to Germany, to a hospital in Baden-Baden where, in November 1944, he was promoted to Hauptsturmführer, or captain. He was then sent to a hospital in Halberstadt, where he remained until the middle of February 1945, when he was again able to walk, although with difficulty.

Barbie was incorporated into a combat unit and was involved in heavy fighting around Essen, 25 miles to the southwest in the industrial Ruhr Valley. "On the first of April the Allied forces closed in around the valley. They captured us in a circle of about two kilometers diameter, more or less, and fired at us with everything they had. We were obliterated. At one point I saw that there were just five of us companions together, and I said, 'I'm not going to surrender; who's coming with me?' Together we reached the highway to Solingen. From soldiers we passed into the status of fugitives."

Barbie got off the highway, which was controlled by the Allies, and hid in the brush, where he encountered other German soldiers in the same circumstances. On April 18, a few weeks before Germany's official surrender, Barbie buried his arms and began his long flight from justice. "From an officer of the SS," he recalled, "I transformed myself into a beggar. I knew that, as an SS officer I would never be treated as a common prisoner-of-war. The Allies had already announced this, and I was in possession of many secrets."

It was these secrets which ensured Barbie's survival in the new power structure that would emerge in Europe after the defeat of the Nazi Reich.

VIII

CIC AGENT "BECKER"

T HE INEVITABLE DEFEAT OF THE NAZIS CAME IN MAY 1945, as the Red Army closed in on the burning city of Berlin and the Allies drove south into Bavaria to crush the last pockets of Nazi resistance. In these last months Barbie had been stationed in northwest Germany but now, like thousands of other wanted SS officers, he went underground, seeking to disappear into the great mass of displaced Germans.

Authorities were only beginning to make a full assessment of the atrocities Barbie had committed in Lyon during his tenure, yet his name already figured in 239th place on the first war criminal list established by the United Nations. Barbie knew that if he were arrested and handed over to the French, he would receive swift and summary justice.

Obscurity and anonymity were Barbie's only sure allies in the chaotic months after the defeat. To be in public circulation meant identity checks, questions, close scrutiny and probably arrest. Barbie later described that crucial period of hiding, one in which he set up a factory for false papers to protect himself and other SS men. "Finally," he recounted, "I took refuge in a village called Classonnette where I had to work hard. I dug the fields, I delivered wood, I cleaned stables. Six months later, I got to know a young carpenter and we set up a secret organization to forge documents. It was designed to protect members of the SS who were in the same situation as me. I managed to forge nearly 300 false documents."

Barbie was now employing the tactics used by the French Resistance members he had once pursued. After his period of hiding, Barbie—now calling himself Heinz Mertens—ventured forth and dabbled in the black market in Bavaria, selling coffee and cigarettes in Munich and nearby Buchloe. In the winter of 1945, the first after the war, he was jailed in Darmstadt in the American Zone of Occupation, about twenty miles south of Frankfurt. Unrecognized, he was released in two weeks and made his way south to Marburg, between the U.S. Zone cities of Frankfurt and Kassel. There he obtained an introduction to a family named Schmidt and rented a room in their home on Barfusserstrasse under the alias of Klaus Becker.

He told the Schmidts that he had just been released from a prisoner-of-war camp and had come from Kassel to study law at the University of Marburg. Barbie lived with the Schmidts until August 1946, when he told them he was moving to Düsseldorf to be with his mother. But "Becker" was to pass through Marburg on several occasions over the next year, each time spending a night or two with the Schmidts.

Barbie traveled frequently, keeping in touch with associates in the SS who had developed an underground network for their survival. In early February 1946 Barbie took the train to Hamburg in the British Zone, where he contacted a woman named Ellen Kuhn, who had been a secretary for the SS in Paris. Fräulein Kuhn offered to put him in touch with someone who could provide him with false army discharge papers, the document necessary for normal civilian life in postwar Germany. She had a friend, Jonny, a former SS officer, who in turn knew a German named Alexander Winter with good connections in the Hamburg municipal administration. Winter could set Barbie up with papers; Ellen Kuhn agreed to bring the two men together.

The following evening at 8:00 P.M., Barbie went to a cafe near the Sternschanze streetcar station and was directed to a corner table occupied by three men and two women, all of whom seemed very drunk. Barbie introduced himself as Becker. Winter rose and greeted him with the salutation, "Heil, Moscow." Barbie was further put off when after a few minutes of conversation, the group began to sing the Communist Internationale. When he asked Winter to explain, he was told they wanted to conceal their status as former Nazis. Somewhat disconcerted, Barbie nonetheless made an appointment to see Winter.

They met the next day, and Winter began to probe Barbie's political convictions. Convinced of his Nazi sympathies, Winter invited Barbie to join a clandestine organization of former SS and intelligence men. Winter boasted about the extensive spy network he was assembling and explained that he intended to sell intelligence to the British and the Americans as well as to the Soviets, with whom he had already established contact. Barbie declined the offer because he was not interested in working for the Russians.

Throughout 1946 Barbie developed his contacts in the SS underworld, but he was also involved in the black market, dealing in jewels and counterfeit documents in Hamburg. He also allegedly had been involved in a jewel robbery in Kassel, in which he and his accomplice posed as policemen. During this period, Kassel was one of Barbie's main bases; it was there that he set up a home for his wife and daughter, and that his second child, Klaus Georg Barbie, was born on December 11, 1946.

In the summer of 1946, Barbie finally came to the attention of the Americans administering the zone. On August 28 he was arrested by the U.S. Counter Intelligence Corps when one of Barbie's ex-Nazi acquaintances informed on him, but on the way to CIC headquarters Barbie escaped by simply jumping out of the jeep. A CIC report later revealed that Barbie had been in custody only fifteen minutes before he leapt from the vehicle and fled through the streets of Marburg as four shots were fired after him.

Three months later Barbie had another encounter with the Allied occupation forces, when he was fooled by a British agent posing as an ex-Nazi. This happened on another trip to Hamburg while Barbie was in the company of a friend, Karl Schaefer, and another man named Rolf Wilkening. Barbie was going to help the two men obtain false identity papers through Ellen Kuhn. They arrived in Hamburg on November 10, 1946, but Fräulein Kuhn refused to house Barbie. He then called on another acquaintance, Heinz Cloede, who had introduced himself to Barbie as a former Nazi official. That evening, Cloede told Barbie that he wanted him to meet another SS associate in the Nazi underground.

On November 12, Barbie and his two traveling companions went to the Café Larrange in downtown Hamburg at 5:00 P.M. A short time later Cloede came in with his SS contact, Acker, then left after introducing him. The four men went to another restaurant, where Acker bragged about his activities in the SS underground and dropped the names of former secret policemen whom Barbie knew. Acker boasted of having blown up a French occupation army installation near Stuttgart.

Barbie noticed that Acker seemed nervous; he was continually turning around in his seat and at one point got up to make a phone call. Barbie and his friends later recalled having seen a British officer in the company of three women take a table near theirs. When Barbie noticed the same group on a streetcar later in the evening he initially passed it off as a coincidence, but eventually realized he had been under surveillance.

That evening, in the Hamburg railroad station, the British arrested Barbie, Schaefer and Wilkening. Barbie at first thought it was an error, but it soon became obvious that either Cloede or Acker, or both, had betrayed him. One of the British agents referred to Barbie's August escape from the CIC, saying, "Well, my dear friend, we are not Americans. You are not going to run away from us."

The three former Nazis were taken to a British Field Secret Service office in Hamburg, where they were strip-searched and locked in basement cells. Though Barbie was in one cell and his two friends were in another, they could talk back and forth. On November 14, two days after their arrest, the prisoners, aided by Nazi friends on the outside, obtained a flashlight and an iron bar.

That night the building was guarded by a single soldier who appeared to be thoroughly intimidated by his prisoners. Each time he approached their cells he drew his pistol, and he refused to escort them to the latrine. Around midnight the Nazi prisoners attempted their break. They could hear the guard playing his flute. He was so absorbed by his music that he failed to hear them breaking the padlocks with the iron bar. As all other routes out of the basement were blocked, they carefully walked past the flute-playing guard while his back was turned. Barbie was later to comment: "I didn't even need to kill him."

Entering another room on the ground floor, they jumped to the street outside. The fugitives remained in the Hamburg area until November 19, when Barbie obtained false discharge papers and the three men were able to travel south back to the American sector.

Ironically, just a month after escaping from a British jail, Barbie received his first offer to join the British intelligence service. The offer was made through a German, Emil F. Hoffmann, who was already in British employ. Barbie first met Hoffmann in August 1946, when Hoffmann explained that he had served as a Nazi diplomat and later as a member of an SS propaganda detachment. After the war Hoffmann had been a prisoner, but he was released through the intervention of a friend, Markus, who had defected to the Allies before the end of the war. He had recruited Hoffmann, who specialized in communist and subversive activities, into his network of German informants for the British.

When Barbie visited Hoffmann, the informant complained that he was having difficulties with the British, who insisted that he was not producing enough information. He needed help, he told Barbie. Could he work for him as a sub-informant? Barbie declined the offer, explaining that any connection with the British would be too risky. Barbie was now increasingly a fugitive from the Allies. Only the month before he had narrowly escaped a U.S. Counter Intelligence Corps dragnet, cast at 2:00 A.M. on February 23, 1947. It had brought in 70 ex-Nazis who had been organizing an underground, right-wing movement. The American CIC had first become aware of this group in May 1946 and had infiltrated a German-speaking American agent posing as a Swiss Nazi.

The underground Nazi group styled itself after the Freikorps, a paramilitary organization started in Germany after the First World War. According to CIC documents, the leaders of the group realized that direct resistance would be futile. Instead, they had developed a plan of cooperation with the Americans and British. These former Nazis, some of whom had held high posts in the Third Reich, hoped the Allies would place them in key government positions to assure a stable, firmly anti-communist, postwar Germany. "Fantastic as this idea may seem, it made sense to these people and they believed that the British and American authorities would accept it," one CIC officer reported. "They then decided to make the supreme effort. At the risk of certain imprisonment if their plan failed, they sent five of their leaders to make contact with the authorities, reveal their identity as fugitives and make their proposition."

The Americans and the British played along with the ex-Nazis, obtaining names and details in preparation for a "swoop operation" in which the entire network would be arrested in a single night. One name that appeared regularly on their list was Klaus Barbie's. He was thought to be the leader of a section "responsible for the procurement of supplies for the organization and the establishment of an intelligence network throughout the British and American zones." The members of his unit were said to be former German intelligence officers.

Barbie appeared as a sinister figure in the sketchy CIC intelligence reports: "relatively large head, slightly bald, gray cold eyes, thin lips, stocky build, big toe missing...a dangerous conspirator." One of the CIC's informants said Barbie came to a meeting with two bodyguards, one of whom produced a .635 caliber pistol. This same source told the CIC that Barbie "planned three murders in Marburg."

For all this focus on Barbie, when the "swoop" operation finally went into effect on the rainy morning of February 23, Klaus Barbie—alias Klaus Becker, alias Heinz Mertens, alias Ernst Holzer —was not among those seized. The CIC later learned that Barbie had been at the home of a man in Kassel but had escaped through a bathroom window.

Fifty of the Nazis were captured that night and twenty more were subsequently arrested. When the operation was over, the CIC boasted: "This was the last large organized group of Nazis to be formed in the western zone of Germany. It was completely broken up, its activities were publicized and its story now serves as a reminder to the German people of the futility of nationalistic action outside the scope of the existing democratic processes now in operation in Germany."

But Klaus Barbie was still at large, seemingly too elusive for Allied agents to trap. The American Counter Intelligence Corps was now receiving reports of his movements through a German informant named Walter, whom Barbie had taken into his confidence. Following the mass arrests of his colleagues, Barbie had moved to the Munich area in the southern province of Bavaria. The CIC agent handling Walter recommended that "since Barbie is a high priority on the target list of Selection Board, his possible return to visit [Walter should] be closely watched...so that he will be available for arrest if deemed necessary."

CIC recognition of Barbie proved to be the turning point in his postwar life. While some CIC agents were seeking his arrest—not for war crimes but for his participation in the Nazi underground—other CIC agents were considering using his obvious talents as a counterespionage agent. CIC documents indicate that Barbie himself was then trying to sound out the CIC about joining them as an intelligence informant. Some CIC agents thought it was a reasonable idea. The agent tracking Barbie in the Munich area reported that he "has indicated...that he would not be unwilling to collaborate," adding that Barbie would be a good candidate for the penetration of a suspected Soviet courier ring in Bavaria.

"Barbie has expressed his willingness to undertake this task," the agent stated. "It is felt that the use of Barbie would serve a two-fold purpose: keep him under surveillance and utilize a man of some experience to penetrate this center." But at CIC Headquarters in Frankfurt, the proposal was turned down. Orders were issued that Barbie should be arrested "as quickly as feasible."

Meanwhile in Munich, Barbie was examining a number of options, including working for the American agency that had ordered him arrested. He had contemplated working with Hoffmann, but Barbie then heard of a more interesting possibility. Friends had told him of a former Abwehr captain, Petersen, who was employed by the Americans as an intelligence agent in Memmingen, 80 miles southwest of Munich. After receiving a personal description of Petersen, Barbie realized his good fortune. The man was actually Kurt Merk, an Abwehr officer who had been stationed in Dijon during the war and who was a close friend of Barbie's.

On March 22 Barbie traveled to Memmingen. At noon, according to his instructions, he sought Merk out at the Weinsigel Café, but Merk was not there. Barbie returned to Memmingen on March 28, and by chance ran into Merk in the train station, where the former Nazi was waiting for one of his sub-agents. The two men scheduled a meeting for 8:00 P.M. at Merk's office on the Kaiser Promenade, where they talked for several hours. Merk instructed Barbie to come back on April 17, promising that he might have good news for him.

Over the next few weeks Barbie traveled extensively, continuing to develop other leads, but as the 17th approached he headed back to Memmingen with his wife, who frequently accompanied him on these trips. He met again with Merk, who told him to find a room and come back to the office the next day at 6:00 P.M. To his satisfaction, when he returned the next evening he was met not only by Merk, but by American CIC agent Robert S. Taylor, who interviewed Barbie and immediately offered him a job as a CIC sub-agent or informant. Barbie accepted at once, and was instructed to take a room at the Bahnhof Hotel until further notice.

A week later Taylor informed Barbie that his superior in Munich, Colonel Dale Garvey, commander of the CIC's Region IV, had approved of the arrangement on the condition that Barbie "break off any connections he may have with illegal SS elements and Selection Board personalities," the latter a reference to the group of former Nazis arrested by the CIC.

Although Barbie was still a fugitive from the CIC in other parts of Germany, Taylor indicated apparent satisfaction with his new recruit. He described Barbie in one report as "an honest man, both intellectually and personally, absolutely without nerves or fear. He is strongly anti-communist and a Nazi idealist who believes that he and his beliefs were betrayed by the Nazis in power."

Within a month, Barbie had apparently consolidated his position with Taylor. When Region IV in Munich received a query from the Frankfurt CIC Headquarters on material informants had provided, Taylor was obliged to report that the source of the information had not been Merk, as had originally been stated, but Barbie. Taylor requested that Barbie "be allowed to retain his freedom as long as he works for this agent," adding, "it is felt that his value as an informant infinitely outweighs any use he may have in prison."

Ω

The organization that Klaus Barbie joined in the spring of 1947, the 970th Counter Intelligence Corps Detachment, was the principal instrument of the U.S. Army's European Command for the investigation and suppression of activities that could threaten American control within its zone of occupied Germany. The Americans were concerned that remnants of the Nazi regime might attempt to organize clandestinely and try to subvert the introduction of democracy in West Germany. The CIC was charged with blocking such espionage, sabotage and subversion, mainly, as the CIC stated, by preventing "the reorganization of ex-enemy intelligence services, security and secret police and paramilitary organizations."

It is ironic that within two years of the German defeat the CIC was recruiting former members of the Gestapo and the Abwehr to serve its aims. But to the Allied occupiers it seemed the expedient course, and the use of former German intelligence officers proved not to be inconsistent with U.S. policy after the war. A prime example was General Reinhard Gehlen, the German Army's senior intelligence officer on Soviet matters. As the defeat approached, Gehlen resolved to hand his extensive files and his agent networks in the Soviet Union over to the Americans. He smuggled truckloads of files out of Berlin south to the mountains of Bavaria, and buried his intelligence hoard in various locations near the town of Miesbach. A short time later Gehlen and his men surrendered to the American Seventh Army.

In June 1945, Gehlen met with Major General William J. Donovan, chief of the Office of Strategic Services, and OSS European chief Alan Dulles in Washington, D.C. At that conference Gehlen struck the following bargain: he would supply the U.S. with his intelligence resources—including agents on the ground in Russia—but he wished to keep his German intelligence unit largely intact and independent. The Americans agreed and out of this pact emerged the Gehlen Organization, which proved an excellent source of East Bloc intelligence in the immediate postwar years. In

April 1956 Gehlen became the first head of the Bundesnachrich-
tensdienst, West Germany's intelligence service.

There was, however, a moral difference between employing a
man like Gehlen and dealing with Barbie. Gehlen was never implicated in atrocities and was involved in military intelligence operations accepted as normal wartime conduct. Almost forty years after
the war, Gene Bramel, then a young American CIC officer assigned
to work with Barbie, explained the American attitude: "They say,
'Why did you use Nazis?' That is a stupid question. It would have
been impossible for us to operate in southern Germany without
using Nazis. We were Americans. I spoke pretty good German, but
by the time I got through ordering dinner they would have suspected I was American. And who knew Germany better than
anyone else? Who were the most organized? Who were the most
anti-communist? Former Nazis. Not to use them would mean
complete emasculation. And we used them, the French used them,
the British used them, and the Russians used them."

Region IV of the 970th CIC Detachment, one of twelve subdi-
visions of the intelligence service covering the American Zone and
the U.S. sector of divided Berlin, found Barbie to be a very effective
operative. He quickly assumed an important position as Merk's
second-in-command in a network of some 50 CIC informants
throughout Germany and extending into Eastern Europe.

Barbie's job within "Buro Petersen," as the network was called,
was described by one CIC official as "establishing a long-range
penetration of French intelligence installations in the French
Zone," which they feared was infiltrated by communist operatives.
By the autumn of 1947, the same officer reported that the work
was "beginning to show consistently excellent results." From their
American employers the German agents received a total of between 7,000 and 15,000 Reichsmarks a month, or about $700 to
$1,500. Part of the payment was made in the form of cigarettes and
food. Barbie himself received 500 Reichsmarks a month, or about
$50, not an inconsiderable sum in those difficult times.

Taylor was replaced in the early summer of 1947 by U.S. agent
Camille Hajdu. Although Hajdu criticized the relationship between
Taylor and Merk as being overly friendly and trimmed the network
down to about 15 informants, he shared Taylor's view that Buro

Petersen was valuable. Hajdu reported that Barbie "has so far demonstrated exceedingly successful results." It was clear that Barbie and Merk had made themselves an important part of the Region IV apparatus; in fact, the information they provided came to represent between 70 and 90 percent of what was sent up the line by Region IV of the CIC.

But Barbie's status as a former Gestapo officer did not go entirely unnoticed by American higher-ups in the intelligence organization. On October 17 the Region IV commander, Lieutenant Colonel Garvey, brought it to the attention of CIC Headquarters that Barbie had been listed as a target of Operation Selection Board the previous February, and asked "what disposition should be made" of him. On October 29, the chief operations officer of the 970th CIC, Major Earl Browning, directed Region IV to arrest Barbie and send him to the European Command Intelligence Center at Oberursel, near Frankfurt, for "detailed interrogation."

From his Frankfurt office, Browning oversaw the activities of about 800 American agents and their numerous informants. Browning had taken part in the Allied drive across Europe and was among the shocked U.S. soldiers who liberated the Dachau concentration camp in 1945. Transferred back to the States in September 1945, Browning returned to Germany early in 1946 to take command of a CIC regional office in Bremen, and in 1947 was promoted to the top Frankfurt CIC post. One of his first administrative moves was to attempt to control the CIC informant system by creating a central approval mechanism. As a result, Browning says today, Barbie's name came before him.

"When Barbie's name was submitted for approval as an informant, I recalled that when I had been a regional commander we had received a directive to arrest him on sight," remembers Browning, now a retired U.S. Army colonel living in Arlington, Virginia. "He was a fugitive, and his wartime rank and record would have made him an automatic arrestee. So I ordered his arrest."

Browning's account is confirmed by James Ratliffe, then Browning's second-in-command, a semiretired publishing executive in Cincinnati, Ohio. "Our chief dislike of the Barbie situation was that he was a captain in the Gestapo and therefore an automatic arrestee," says Ratliffe. "We had to pick up all Gestapo agents, under orders from the top command of the whole theater, and a Gestapo agent of Barbie's rank was quite high." Ratliffe stresses that in intelligence organizations, the powers exercised by an officer are generally far out of proportion to what his rank would suggest. "I remind you that Eichmann, who was hanged by the Israelis, was only a major," he says. "It was simply impossible in my opinion, to allow a Gestapo captain not only to run loose but to be used as an American informant."

The recent U.S. Justice Department investigation of that post-war period suggests that Barbie's war record in Lyon was not, as claimed, the stimulus that prompted Browning to order Barbie's arrest. The decision was based on pragmatic, not moral, considerations. In his 1983 U.S. Justice Department report, "Klaus Barbie and the United States Government," Allan A. Ryan, Jr., Special Assistant to the Assistant U.S. Attorney General, contends: "Although CIC's 'Central Personalities Index' card had identified Barbie as head of the Gestapo in Lyon, there was no evident concern over Barbie's Gestapo background or any of his wartime activities. Nothing in Browning's arrest order or his detailed interrogation instructions to ECIC [Oberursel interrogation center] showed any interest in the Gestapo connection; indeed, there was no reference to it. Browning's concern was in gaining information not about Barbie himself, but about Barbie's former associates in the SS network."

Whatever Browning's motives, his decision to arrest Barbie displeased Region IV of the CIC, which wanted to protect Barbie, who was now using the name "Becker" on a regular basis. Hajdu attempted to persuade CIC Headquarters to block the arrest and permit Barbie to remain under his control for a "voluntary" inter-rogation to be conducted by Region IV agents. In his report of November 21, 1947, Hajdu wrote that Barbie had "extensive con-nections with high-level former German intelligence circles" and had been providing rich intelligence material, particularly on French activities in Germany.

Hajdu's direct superior, Lieutenant Colonel Ellington Golden, who had by then replaced Garvey, concurred with this pro-Barbie analysis. He stated that Barbie should receive "some type of preferential treatment" in the interrogation process. Moreover he wanted an assurance that Barbie could return to his work in Region IV following the questioning.

Browning rejected this proposal and ordered that Barbie be transferred immediately to the Oberursel interrogation center. But at the same time, Browning seemed to be persuaded by Region IV's opinion of Barbie's value. In his order of December 1, 1947, Browning omitted mention of Barbie's Gestapo past and noted that CIC records indicated Barbie "has in the past engaged in subversive activities," an apparent reference to his prominent role in the postwar SS underground. However, Browning concluded, these activities were "not of the nature to demand his imprisonment."

In his Justice Department report of 1983, Ryan concludes that Barbie's Gestapo past was of little concern to the CIC. "This apparent disinterest in Barbie's Gestapo background apparently reflected the attitude in CIC that, by 1947, former Gestapo agents were no longer considered the 'security threat' that had made them targets for arrest immediately after the war. By the time of Barbie's transfer to ECIC in December 1947, the Allied authorities had thoroughly obliterated any remnants of the Nazi regime."

Ω

The entire orientation of U.S. intelligence and counterintelligence in occupied Germany had undergone a profound shift in the two years since the war had ended. If Barbie, in the first days after the Nazi defeat, had not escaped twice, once from the Americans and once from the British, he undoubtedly would have been delivered up to the French for trial and execution. Moral outrage at the Nazi death camps was at a high point, and war crimes were a major concern of the Allied powers as they began to remake Germany.

But within two years American preoccupations had undergone a 180-degree change, moving from one end of the political spectrum to the other. The deeds of the Nazis seemed more remote, and the specter of Nazism had been eclipsed by that of communism. The U.S. government was now increasingly worried that the Soviet Union intended to spread its influence across Western Europe. Using an ex-Gestapo agent to serve U.S. purposes seemed a small compromise.

The use of former Gestapo agents by the CIC had become

common enough by the late 1940s for headquarters to clarify the terms on which these people could be employed. A June 1949 circular noted that there was "a certain amount of confusion" on the matter, while adding that "U.S. authorities have not relaxed for one minute their moral rejection of War Criminals." The memorandum stated that "it is the policy of this headquarters to discourage the use of Gestapo personnel," but added that their employment for certain uses, such as contacting sources, were allowable. But, the memo stressed: "A major project involving a long period of time... is to be discouraged."

Considering the employment of Barbie and other former Nazis by the CIC for three years in infiltrating the German Communist party, the following passage is significant: "Under no circumstances should the impression be given that the CIC is putting the Gestapo back in business. Proposals will undoubtedly be made by Gestapo personnel indicating their desire to set up nets or effect penetration of the KPD (German Communist Party) for CIC. This should be politely listened to, but in no way endorsed or supported."

Ω

The CIC was quick to adapt to the new American view. Colonel Earl Browning says that as early as 1946 he was organizing surveillance of communists in the Bremen area. Though the circumstances were somewhat humorous, Browning believes he was instrumental in focusing attention on communist activities in the American Zone.

"When I came to Bremen around the end of March, first of April 1946, I found that our city office was sharing its space with the Communist party," Browning recalls. "They were working together with the CIC to hunt down the Nazis and they had just moved into our office. I put a stop to that. In the process, I discovered that we had been using some of them to inform on the communists themselves."

Browning applied for permission from the central CIC in Frankfurt to mount a full-scale operation against the communists, and finally received permission to maintain surveillance on the party. The communists, he says, "were agitating politically to gain influence and prestige and to take over the government and gain control over other organizations. As far as I know, this was the first time that the CIC began penetration of the Communist party, but it became a standard operation after that and was approved for other regions."

By 1950, when CIC agent Gene Bramel arrived in Germany and was assigned to the Augsburg group controlling Barbie, the process was even further advanced. "We didn't give a good doodly-damn about Nazism," says Bramel, today a retired federal narcotics agent living near Dayton, Ohio. "It was dead. They were at our feet. But we were threatened with communism. It was the age of McCarthy. Don't forget the Korean War had started, with Russian and Chinese weapons. We were personally threatened with communism. A lot of it was bullshit, but we were very young men and we were indoctrinated with the words 'national security.' We had to perform, even if we didn't want to."

Along with this shift in political perception, another, related, change was taking place: the rehabilitation of the Germans in the eyes of American soldiers. Veterans such as Browning who had seen Nazi atrocities first-hand maintained reservations about the Germans. But the new recruits who had not fought in the war were less inclined to judge the German people harshly. "If you look back at surveys conducted among the troops in Germany in 1945 and 1946, after the end of the war," Browning says, "we found to our dismay that they liked the Germans better than they did the French or the English. The Germans went out of their way to be friendly, and as a defeated enemy they fawned on the Americans, trying to get as much sympathy and help as they could." The fresh recruits, Browning adds, "hadn't had the wartime experience. They hadn't seen what the Gestapo had done or how they operated. There was a general feeling of friendship and liking for the Germans in general, and this included some of the Nazis and Gestapo types as well."

A calculating former Gestapo agent like Barbie realized that the Americans were quite naive and had short political memories. Playing on weakness was second nature to Barbie. "Barbie was super-correct," says Bramel, who occasionally dealt with him as a handler. "He was low-key and extremely courteous. When you spoke with him he would listen intently. He was very proper and he was very interested in anything you had to say."

Bramel recounts an anecdote that suggests how Barbie shrewdly played on the interests of his America handlers. "There was one time I was sitting in a beer garden, waiting for somebody I was supposed to meet, and I saw another agent come in with Barbie. The agent saw me and waved me over. So I picked up my glass of beer and went over. And the most fascinating thing—do you know what they were talking about? Baseball. Barbie wanted baseball explained to him and he was very interested in trying to understand it."

Bramel considered Barbie a man of extremely cynical nature. "I never saw him smile," says the former CIC officer. "He had a very thin mouth and he kept it rather shut, not much in a stern way, but he kept it rather immobile. There is an old saying that in intelligence there is no such thing as morality or ethics, there is only expediency. That is an absolute description of Barbie. If he could turn me into someone and gain by it, he'd do it. He wasn't an emotional man, not at all."

Ω

Browning's order to arrest Becker-Barbie was finally put into effect on December 12, 1947. CIC Lieutenant Dick Lavoie brought Barbie to the interrogation center in Oberursel, near Frankfurt, where he remained incarcerated until the following May. Although it would seem natural to probe Barbie's Gestapo past, this part of his life was never thoroughly investigated by the U.S. Army interrogators. A chronology of his career with the Nazis was established, but Barbie glossed over the Lyon period with a series of lies: he claimed that he had spent most of the war in SS headquarters in Paris and later in Italy. He also said he had spent the summer of 1944 on the Normandy front. The interrogators also missed the fact that Barbie was officially a war criminal, both in the United Nations list of 1944 and in CROWCASS, the Central Registry of War Criminals and Security Suspects, where he was listed as being wanted for murder.

During Barbie's six months in jail, the Oberursel interrogators focused on his postwar activities during 1945-47, particularly with the SS underground and his knowledge of German agents working with competing Allied intelligence services. Barbie was also questioned about his activities with the Region IV CIC office, indicating that CIC Headquarters was worried about what was happening at the Munich regional level.

The interrogators reached the following conclusion about Barbie's motives in working for the Americans: "Although Barbie claims to be anti-communist, it is felt that the main reason for his great efforts and endeavors to work for the Western Allies is based on a desire to obtain his personal freedom. Barbie falls under the automatic arrest category, and his present employment offers him personal freedom, the liberty to be with his family, a decent wage, an apartment, and security."

The interrogators also supported the CIC argument for the continuation of Barbie's employment. "Because of Barbie's activities with Region IV during 1947, it is not deemed advisable to intern him for his affiliation with the Waffen SS [the interrogators also failed to correctly identify the SS branch in which Barbie served]. His knowledge as to the mission of CIC, its agents, sub-agents, funds, etc. is too great." Barbie was close to his goal: he had already attained a certain threshhold of security with his thorough knowledge of American CIC operations. By imprisoning him, or releasing him, the CIC would risk his releasing information or his falling into the hands of a Soviet or competing Allied intelligence service, which would want information on the CIC.

While Barbie was in prison, the position of Merk, the man who had brought him to the Americans, had deteriorated. In February 1948 CIC Headquarters had been informed that Merk was wanted by the French for war crimes allegedly committed in Stuttgart. Hajdu was growing dissatisfied with Merk's output and suggested that he be let go. Hajdu's superiors in Region IV were also complaining about Merk; he had, they said, overstepped his authority in running agents in the French Zone and in sending an informant to Berlin without authorization. The Region IV officials would later realize that the Merk network had been compromised by other intelligence services. In spite of these objections, after Barbie's release from Oberursel on May 10, 1947, the Merk network was given a new lease and relocated from Kempten, 70 miles southwest of Munich near the Austrian border, to Augsburg, 50 miles west of the Bavarian capital. Barbie was clearly marked as someone who offer the U.S. counterintelligence services far more than the average German informant.

This was the impression of Erhard Dabringhaus, then a 31-year-old CIC civilian agent who was ordered to take a three-quarter-ton truck from Augsburg, where he was stationed, to the town of Memmingen, for a special assignment. "I remember this one outstandingly," says Dabringhaus, today a professor of language and literature at Wayne State University in Detroit, Michigan, "because I learned during the time I was working with him that he was wanted by the French." In Memmingen, Dabringhaus was ordered to drive further south to Kempten, where he picked up Barbie, Merk and Andrée Rivez, the daughter of a French police official and the mistress who had stayed with Merk after his days in France.

Dabringhaus installed the trio in one of the CIC safe houses reserved for such contingencies at 10 Mozartstrasse, on a tree-lined suburban street in Augsburg. Merk and Rivez took the first floor and Barbie occupied the second floor; his wife and children remained in Trier with his mother. Thus began a six-month relationship in which Dabringhaus as a CIC handler maintained close contact with Barbie and Merk, whom he describes an an elite intelligence team.

Dabringhaus, who had been born in Essen, Germany, and emigrated with his parents to the U.S. in 1930 while in his early teens, was fluent in German. It was his job to translate Barbie's weekly reports into English. "For six months I lived with Barbie," says Dabringhaus. "I gave him an office, I gave him a house. He reported to my office every morning. He was totally free, he had all the passports and identification he needed. Periodically, we'd talk to him to try to debrief him, but he was really running the show. He and Merk had a secretary and everything. It was a big operation." The network's office was connected to a municipal swimming pool building, which had the advantage that both Germans and Americans could enter without arousing curiosity.

One of Dabringhaus's responsibilities was to pay Barbie. His recent description of the form this took would unleash speculation about whether the CIC was the only intelligence agency running Barbie. "I got the money from higher headquarters," Dabringhaus recalls. "I happened to get one envelope open and at one time I saw 1,700 American dollars in cash. Barbie insisted on the greenbacks because he didn't want to change the scrip on the black market. He claimed he had so many informants in the field and he had to keep them alive. That's why he asked for that kind of money."

Others in the CIC question whether Barbie would have been paid such large sums in American dollars. Browning says all CIC informants at that time were being paid in goods from Army post exchanges, rather than in any form of currency, since the German mark's value was dropping rapidly due to inflation. "This was considered a very economical way to get information, because the cigarettes and coffee and chocolate didn't cost us very much at all, but they had quite a bit of value for the Germans," Browning recalls. "We paid all of our informants at that time in commodities from the PX. Dabringhaus's story about paying these people in greenbacks just doesn't ring true. We didn't have the greenbacks and I have no knowledge of greenbacks ever being used for paying anybody for anything."

The large cash payment, combined with the fact that Barbie was investigating areas that the CIC theoretically had no interest in, leads Browning to suspect that Barbie may possibly have been serving another agency besides the CIC. While Barbie and Merk were looking into French and Soviet activities outside the American Zone, Browning says "we did not have any positive intelligence responsibilities and were not interested in that kind of information." It was only in late 1948 that Washington began directing CIC to gather intelligence on Soviet bloc countries, and this was done largely through CIC informants among displaced persons.

But another U.S. intelligence branch, the Department of the Army Detachment, or DAD for short, was a bridge between the wartime Office of Strategic Services and the postwar Central Intelligence Agency. "We were separate organizations," Browning says of the CIC and DAD, "but we maintained liaison and we had friendly relations. There were no conflicts of jurisdiction. We were concerned with the security of the U.S. Zone against sabotage, espionage and subversion, the classic counterintelligence task. DAD was more concerned with making long-range contacts and developing sources of intelligence information from a long-range or special point of view."

Could Barbie have been an agent for DAD under the guise of working for the CIC? "That's possible," says Browning. "And the fact that Dabringhaus claims to have paid him in U.S. dollars—that kind of money in those amounts would have been available to the DAD detachment whereas it was certainly not available to the CIC. So that is a possibility."

Others disagree, among them Justice Department investigator Ryan. "There is no evidence," he states in his report, "on which one could reasonably conclude that Barbie had a relationship with any other U.S. government agency during this time." Ryan says there is no evidence in CIC or CIA files to suggest Barbie was employed by DAD, although a March 1948 CIC report does say that Region IV was passing some of the information Barbie had gathered along to the DAD.

Another theory is offered by a former Justice Department official, John Loftus, author of a book detailing how American intelligence agencies smuggled former Nazi war criminals into the U.S. after the war. Loftus was formerly a prosecutor in the Office of Special Investigations within the Justice Department. The branch, which was headed by Ryan until he was assigned the Barbie case, was set up under President Jimmy Carter to find and deport former war criminals living in the United States. Loftus believes that during those postwar years in Germany, Barbie was also in the employ of the Office of Policy Coordination, a State Department intelligence wing that ran agents under civililan, diplomatic and military cover. Ryan, however, denies the claim, stating: "This investigation has yielded no hint or suggestion, let alone evidence, however fragmentary, that OPC [Office of Policy Coordinator] had any knowledge of or involvement with Klaus Barbie."

Ω

By August 1947, Region IV officials had drawn up an ambitious list of areas to be investigated by the Merk net, concentrating on Soviet and communist-infiltrated French activities in the U.S. Zone. But according to Dabringhaus, Merk and Barbie were also running an extensive network of informants who provided information on Soviet activities in Yugoslavia, Bulgaria and Romania, as well as on communist activities in France, where, according to Dabringhaus,

Barbie still had numerous contacts among former fascist wartime collaborators.

One piece of information supplied by Barbie that Dabringhaus believes was evaluated as important by U.S. officials concerned a uranium mine near Aue, Germany, then being exploited by the Soviets. This touched on the Soviet development of the atom bomb, something that greatly concerned the U.S. government in the period before the American atomic monopoly was broken.

In late August, CIC Region IV officer Richard Lavoie, Dabringhaus's direct superior, officially asked CIC Headquarters for permission to operate the reorganized net. Lavoie called it "one of the most fruitful sources of information for Region IV." But in October CIC Headquarters told Region IV's commander that Merk's organization should be dissolved. It cited the problems arising from its undisciplined operation, as well as the fact that the network was carrying out missions that had nothing to do with the CIC's main work: counterintelligence.

During this period there was a continuous battle between Region IV and CIC Headquarters over whether to continue the Barbie-Merk network. Headquarters felt that dissolving the network would send its members directly into the arms of the French, British or even the Soviet secret services. They felt it would be disastrous if the Soviets were to obtain information on the inner workings of the CIC, but there was also the fear of embarrassment if it was learned that the CIC was employing a former Gestapo agent.

Joseph Vidal, a CIC special agent working in the Frankfurt headquarters, later expressed this concern in a memo. He wrote: "At that time the revelation of [Barbie's] connection to the CIC as an informant would have been a serious blow to the CIC's prestige in the eyes of the British. His continued employment then with CIC was based on his utility and the desire of CIC to obviate an embarrassing situation."

Some CIC agents, however, believed that the Merk net, except for Barbie, was a waste. "That was a ridiculous goddamn thing," says Eugene Kolb, now a retired U.S. Army intelligence colonel living in Maine who joined the Region IV office in 1949 and worked closely with Barbie. "That net was operated out of Munich by a bunch of people who didn't know which end was up. They extended their operations—what they thought were operations— into Romania, into France against the French intelligence service, the French government, all contrary to the projects which had been assigned to the CIC. They bought information like mad, most of which was ridiculous in the first place. When that net was thrown out, dissolved, the worthwhile elements of it, like Barbie, were retained."

Browning contradicts Kolb's memory, claiming that he does not recall worthwhile information being supplied, even by Barbie. "That was the objection we had to his use," Browning says. "We didn't feel that he was in a position to give really worthwhile information to counterbalance the stigma he carried as a Gestapo officer. As far as I know, I have no evidence that he was contributing worthwhile information. I'm sure there are people down in Munich or Augsburg who would make claims to the contrary, but I never saw any such kind of information coming into my office."

Ratliffe today believes Region IV's persistence in using Barbie as an informant stemmed from personnel problems in the Munich and Augsburg CIC offices. "They needed Barbie because they were incompetent," he says. "Any good secret police officer getting into that area of CIC would have been a winner in nothing flat, even if he had murdered 500 babies on the side." Ratliffe says CIC Headquarters became so frustrated with the total unresponsiveness of the Munich and Augsburg offices that an inspection raid was staged at one point in 1947, and the whole command structure was changed. "Being a professional Gestapo agent, Barbie was thoroughly conversant with command. As I understand it he had a very sharp authoritarian personality. Dealing with these dimwits who were supposed to be U.S. intelligence agents—is it any wonder they were suckers for Barbie?"

This view is confirmed by William Larned, who replaced Ratliffe in the summer of 1948 as Browning's second-in-command. Today an executive with a Greenwich, Connecticut, consulting firm, he remembers clearly the problems CIC had in developing qualified personnel. "Americans are not very good military occupiers," Larned says. "Because they don't like the job, they were not very good at it. In a war-torn, hungry populace with a lot of displaced persons, with chaos, confusion, and war crimes on everyone's mind, people hiding under pseudonyms, it was a difficult time for us. We were trying to do our job with only 800 agents throughout our zone of Germany, of whom most were 18-year-old draftees. With the war in Europe over, they were wondering what the hell they were doing there."

These young CIC recruits were cast into a world that had few common denominators with the life they had left behind. In occupied Germany, the old values and standards had either been destroyed or vastly altered by years of Nazism and war. One 1949 CIC report reflected this social upheaval through a discussion of the unique problems encountered in the use of the polygraph machine, or lie detector, in postwar Germany.

"It was found," the report stated, "that European nationals, or at least those whom agents of this detachment had been interrogating, were not [suitable] subjects for polygraph testing, for the reason that many of them had a complete lack of fear of detection and a conscious belief that their lying was justified. They apparently did not consider lying as morally wrong and appeared to experience little or no sense of guilt in their attempts to deceive." Because lying had become a normal survival reflex in postwar Germany there was no guilt attached to it for the machine to measure.

Larned sees the CIC's use of Barbie as a personnel expedient resorted to by a harried and inexperienced army of occupiers. "You've got to look at the use of Barbie in the context of the situation in the zone," he says. "All the good people had gone home, were screaming to get out. Some very fine intelligence operatives and agents were being replaced with 18-year-old draftees with a nine-week basic agent's course behind them. At the same time the missions assigned to the CIC in Germany were expanding. Tremendous pressure was being brought on Army Intelligence. So what happens? You recruit more informants and are less careful about them than you used to be. People who can contribute really valuable information, the Barbies of this world, become increasingly important and you tend to bend the rules."

THE COVER-UP

IF UTILIZING A FORMER GESTAPO AGENT WAS AN EXPEDIENT, sheltering a war criminal was a matter of another dimension. Thirty-five years later, as Ryan and his Justice Department staff investigated the CIC's use of Klaus Barbie, one central question would be asked over and over again: At what point did the U.S. intelligence officers learn of the brutal crimes Barbie had committed? When did they find out that the French government wanted him for his murders in Lyon?

The available evidence indicates that American awareness of Barbie's true history developed in stages. It took place in such a manner that the moral issues involved were not clearly framed until a point when—for reasons of security or prestige—the CIC concluded that it was no longer possible to turn Barbie over to the French for prosecution.

The U.S. interrogators at Oberursel and the CIC's headquarters staff may have failed to notice Barbie's name on two lists of war criminals, but when Erhard Dabringhaus began working with Bar-

bie in the summer of 1948, he soon learned what type of war
Barbie had fought. His main source of information was Merk, who
had been stationed in the same region of France and knew the
methods Barbie had employed in Lyon. "Merk told me that Barbie
was one of the worst interrogators that the German SD had over
there and that he killed a couple of hundred people at one time. He
told me Barbie's primary job was to penetrate the French Resistance, the underground, and that if he couldn't turn a guy around,
he would kill him after severe torture. He said he strung 200 of
them up by their thumbs in the basement of his headquarters. A
real nice guy."

Dabringhaus says he passed this information along to his superiors, but it did not change the official attitude. "They said, 'Take it
easy, we need him yet, he's still useful. After a while we'll turn him
over to the French, when his value is finished.' Under those conditions, I agreed to work with him."

The CIC's first contacts with the French came only a few days
after Barbie was released from Oberursel in May 1948. At this
point the French had not yet formally demanded Barbie's extradition as a war criminal. A military tribunal prosecuting war crimes
in Lyon had issued warrants for Barbie's arrest on August 31 and
September 12, 1945, but it was not until 1948 that the French
secret service learned of Barbie's whereabouts in the American
zone of Germany and contacted the CIC.

He was being sought by the French for his war crimes, but a
new urgency had been given to the search for Barbie. He was
wanted as a key witness in the upcoming trial of René Hardy, who
was facing charges of treason for allegedly betraying Jean Moulin
and other Resistance leaders to Barbie. In May 1948, when the
French learned that Barbie was in Bavaria, in American hands, a
team of interrogators was dispatched from Paris to Frankfurt to
question the Nazi.

The first confrontation between Barbie and French officials
took place on May 14 near the CIC headquarters in Frankfurt, at
the Farben Building, the former headquarters of the German chem-
ical cartel, I.G. Farben. The French delegation, which included
Louis Bibes, a top official of the Direction de la Surveillance du
Territoire, and another DST inspector named Charles Lehrmann,

was closely watched throughout the encounter by CIC special civilian agent John Willms. "I got a call to pick him up and take him over to the French to be interviewed and then to take him back to the people who delivered him," Willms recalls. His assignment was to make sure no harm came to Barbie during the interview, a real possibility given the fury of the French officials faced with a smirking Barbie.

"He was an arrogant bastard," says Willms, who recently retired after a long career in counterintelligence work, most of it spent in Germany, and who now lives in Pittsburg, California, south of San Francisco. "He taunted them and told them what a fantastic intelligence network he had in France. He felt very secure being in the custody of the Americans and he didn't pass any information along to them.

"They didn't touch him," reports Willms. "They came very close to him and banged the table, and slammed a few chairs down, but they didn't harm him. They asked me to turn him over to them, but I said I couldn't do that. Before the interview was over, they said, 'Why don't you let us take him out in the hall with us and shoot him, and we'll say he got shot trying to escape and it will eliminate the problem for all of us.' "

But Willms rejected the proposal and escorted Barbie away from the meeting. "I wasn't going to leave him. With the French attitude toward Barbie, I wasn't going to permit the French to be alone with him. My only task was to make sure no physical violence was used, so we wouldn't fall into the same category of brutality that Barbie was in." The French team saw Barbie again a few days later, on May 18, and a third time on July 16, but in each case the Americans placed heavy restrictions on French access to the prisoner. At times they even screened the questions the French wanted to ask Barbie.

During this same period Dabringhaus was also approached by the French. Dabringhaus now says that he received instructions not to cooperate with the French, "to tell them I didn't know the guy." He met twice with the French investigators, once in Augsburg and another time in Munich, locations Dabringhaus chose in order to disguise Barbie's true whereabouts. "They asked about Barbie," Dabringhaus remembers. "They told me who he was, but I played dumb and said that I didn't even know the name. I felt badly, even wanted to say, 'Come on, I know where he lives, let's go get him.' Then they elaborated a bit more of what I already knew. I felt nauseated. They had found several mass graves that they believed Barbie was responsible for. Since he was a killer of Frenchmen, I saw the urgency these people had in trying to get him. But I would have been court-martialed if I had done what they asked. They had to go home empty-handed."

Surprisingly, the French only seemed interested in Barbie for his knowledge of the Hardy case. Allan Ryan, who examined the transcripts of the French interviews with Barbie for the U.S. Justice Department, reported that the French officials "questioned Barbie only on the matter of his actions involving the French Resistance and did not raise the question of Barbie's own involvement in alleged war crimes." In a 1950 memo, CIC agent Vidal was to claim the same: "No mention was ever made [by the French] that Barbie was wanted as a war criminal. All requests up to that time on the part of the French... centered on Barbie as a material witness in the Hardy case."

Ryan makes the point that "by allowing French officials to have access to Barbie, CIC was taking a very great risk that its employment of Barbie would sooner or later become public, or at least widely known in the French government. But this risk did not appear to concern anyone." In other words, the fact that the CIC permitted the French access to Barbie suggests that there was not widespread suspicion among the Americans that Barbie was guilty of wartime atrocities. In Ryan's words, they felt "There was no reason to hide him from French eyes."

The French attempted to convince the Americans to deliver Barbie for the Hardy trial, but they were unsuccessful. In late 1948 a French-speaking Canadian, Lieutenant John Whiteway, a liaison officer for the French to the U.S. European Command, approached the CIC and asked if Barbie could be sent to Paris as a witness. But Vidal and other American agents argued against it. Vidal wrote that Barbie would probably be interrogated "in the usual French manner and forced to not only reveal information pertaining to the Hardy case but also to reveal information pertaining to his own activities with CIC and his connections in the French Zone."

It was not until May 14, 1949, CIC officials maintained, that they had their first clear idea that Barbie might be a war criminal. On that day, a story appeared in a Paris newspaper describing Barbie as a "torturer" who "burned his victims with an acetylene torch to make them confess during interrogations which lasted more than 48 hours." Other atrocities were listed in the article, which announced that Barbie was then living quietly as a businessman in Munich. That last fact was inaccurate, but the article was generally true, and it set off a wave of angry protest in France. Since Munich fell in the U.S. Zone of occupied Germany, two French Resistance organizations wrote to the U.S. ambassador in Paris, demanding Barbie's arrest.

The CIC reacted quickly. CIC Headquarters sent an order, signed by Larned, who had replaced Ratliffe under Browning. Stated Larned, "Although it was known to this headquarters that during the German occupation of France subject had performed several successful missions and had been responsible for the arrest of a number of French Resistance personnel, his actions from a professional point of view were interpreted by this headquarters as mere performance of his duty. It was not, however, known that such barbaric methods had been employed by subject to obtain confessions from his victims." Larned concluded, "This headquarters is inclined to believe there is some element of truth in the allegations."

If CIC Headquarters in Frankfurt now suspected that Barbie might be a war criminal, the CIC agents in Augsburg working with him were still unconvinced, and stood by the Gestapo agent. By then Eugene Kolb had become the top agent of the regional office in Bavaria. Reporting to headquarters, Kolb said that Barbie "had upon occasion admitted that he used duress during interrogations such as continued interrogations over a long period of time, in the middle of the night, etc., but has never implied or indicated that he used torture."

Kolb clearly was unconvinced of the charge of brutality against Barbie, pointing out that although the French had interrogated Barbie on numerous occasions, they had never previously sought him for war crimes. "Subject is intelligent and skillful enough to accomplish a successful interrogation by use of his head and conse-

quently did not require the use of his hands," he wrote his superiors. "This office consequently feels that while the charges against
subject may possibly be true they are probably not true."

The Americans Barbie was dealing with had already been
conditioned not to give credence to the French charges. Even today
Kolb is not totally convinced that Barbie was capable of committing the crimes he is accused of. "We generally agreed, as two
fellow professionals, that when you're interrogating someone, it's
skill and adroitness that count," says Kolb, who stayed in intelligence work until 1963, then, after some years as a teacher, retired
to Cape Elizabeth, Maine. "It's not in the character of the Barbie I
knew. He is a shrewd individual and I'm sure he hid a lot from us,
but that's just out of character. He's too skillful for that."

Kolb, who was born in Germany and immigrated to the U.S.
with his family at the age of 7, says other agents felt the same way
about Barbie. "Herb Bechtold, his major handling agent throughout this period, was a Jewish refugee whose family had fled Germany in the 1930s. If he had sensed that this guy was a war
criminal, he wouldn't have touched him. He would have come into
my office and refused to deal with him."

Kolb is skeptical of the allegations that Barbie persecuted the
Jews. Throughout his association with Barbie, Kolb says, this
aspect of the case was never raised. "All the time that we used
Barbie down there at the Augsburg level, there were never any
allegations, never any charges raised by the French or anybody
else, to our knowledge, of involvement in the roundup of Jews or
anything of that sort. If these charges were and are true, we did not
know about them."

As far as the CIC was concerned, the main issue was Barbie's
handling of his Resistance prisoners. In their eyes, at least initially,
this was a gray area. To them Barbie was a "fellow professional," as
Kolb says. They could see his alleged crimes in terms of his wartime
duties. Gene Bramel makes this point strongly. "I never knew the
specifics of what he was charged with, except that I heard he had
executed some of the underground," Bramel says. "In Germany, if
the Germans had been blowing up our trucks, blowing up our
ammunitions dumps and killing our soldiers, we would have executed some of them. We sure as hell would have shot them. So this

charge didn't mean anything to us."

But it was not simple incredulity or inertia that kept lower-level, and later, upper-level, CIC officials from responding to French demands that they turn over Barbie. By 1949 and 1950 Barbie had become one of the Augsburg region's most valued informants. He knew almost as much about the CIC's operations as its top officers, and in some areas, since he had been there longer than many, he knew more. He was particularly useful, says Bramel, in penetration of the German Communist party in Bavaria and of the French intelligence service and the French Communist party.

"He gave us information that completely emasculated the Communist party in southern Germany, or in our area, at least," says Bramel. "A situation arose where we had enough on the secretary of the Communist party in southern Germany that we could threaten to turn that over to his own people and they would have handed him his head. We were getting the minutes, copies of the minutes of every communist meeting." Bramel says this blackmail involved correspondence between the communist official and his wife, which detailed some bizarre sexual practices.

Bramel reveals that Barbie also provided information on the penetration of the French secret services by the communists, crucial information which finally persuaded the Americans that Barbie could not be released to the French. Moreover, Bramel alleges that Barbie was providing this information to the Department of the Army Detachment. "What saved Barbie originally, and what kept him saved," says Bramel, "was his information on the French Communist party and the infiltration of the Communist party into the Sûreté and French Intelligence."

Today, Kolb scoffs at the allegation that Barbie was working under deep cover for the DAD or CIA, but he does subscribe to the notion that handing Barbie over to the French would have seriously jeopardized the CIC's own security. "Barbie's value was primarily against the left, and primarily in recruiting sources," says Kolb. "He himself was not of any great value, except in that role. When we sought to protect Barbie and keep him away from the French, it was not because we wanted to keep his services. That was important, but given the loss-benefit, French pressure versus his services, that was relatively unimportant. What concerned us primarily was the identity of sources he recruited for us. We knew that some French agencies had been thoroughly penetrated by the KGB and other Communist party agencies functioning under Moscow. And we were deadly certain that if Barbie were to be handed over to the French, they would pump him dry on what he had done for us. Within a few hours, the information would be on its way to Moscow, and our sources would be blown. In the context of the postwar years, when kidnappings and disappearances were common occurrences, their lives would be at stake. This is what we sought to protect. Not Barbie. This is the key element."

Kolb was more inclined to suspect the accusers—those who charged Barbie with war crimes—than to modify his previous attitude of trust in the Nazi. "The charges in 1950 came in primarily from various organizations that called themselves the Veterans of the Resistance, the Veterans of the Jura, and there was no doubt in anybody's mind that these were left-wing organizations. In reading Headquarters' mind, I'm guessing that they were saying: 'These are left-wing groups, embroiled in a battle with the French government and figures within it. So we're on fairly safe ground in not handing him over.' The thinking was, 'This will probably simmer down over time, because the French government is probably reluctant to do anything about it.'" Ryan supports this last claim: "Even the French authorities, who knew from their interrogation that Barbie was under U.S. protection, made no demand on CIC for his return or a renewed 'interrogation.'"

A little over a year after France's first overture to the CIC in early 1950, Whiteway again approached the U.S. intelligence agency with the request that Barbie be sent to Paris to testify against Hardy. But again no mention was made of Barbie's war crimes. Whiteway initially guaranteed Barbie's safety in Paris and return to the U.S. Zone, but when the French government would not subscribe to these guarantees, the CIC refused to allow Barbie to testify. Whiteway then candidly informed the Americans that if Barbie showed up in Paris he would be arrested.

Meanwhile, Browning hoped the embarrassing Barbie controversy would disappear. In his own words, he wanted Barbie to "be dropped administratively as an informant but that relations with same be maintained as in the past until necessary action is dictated by the State Department and/or Department of the Army."

The CIC tried to put distance between itself and Barbie, but only through an administrative subterfuge. On January 27, 1950, Vidal, at Headquarters, instructed Region XII (formerly Region IV) to maintain contact with Barbie and to continue paying him so he would remain in the area. The CIC feared that if Barbie ceased to receive a salary or suspected that his position was jeopardized, he would join another intelligence service. As one Region XII official noted: "It is desired to add that subject is still under the impression that he is viewed by this office as a source, and is not aware of the fact that this office is only maintaining contact with him to keep track of him in the event French authorities desire to try him as a war criminal."

This essentially meant that nothing had changed: Barbie would continue to be protected by the CIC. As Ryan points out: "In short, what CIC Headquarters is saying to Region XII, in a somewhat roundabout way, is this: to prevent Barbie from discovering that he is no longer being used, you may continue to use him."

At the beginning of 1950 the American intelligence officials were desperately hoping that somehow the dilemma of Klaus Barbie would be resolved. They were encouraged by the fact that there was not yet any official French or U.S. government inquiry and they opted for a policy that Ryan would later describe as "studied neglect."

Ω

What the CIC did not know at the end of 1949 and the beginning of 1950 was that the Barbie affair was moving along several separate tracks. While they assumed the case was dying down, it was consistently gathering momentum. The contacts between French and American military intelligence establishments were only one part of the complex situation, and the inability of each to understand the overall situation would lead to the eventual U.S. cover-up. On the part of the U.S. intelligence establishment there was deception. On the part of the U.S. diplomatic and occupation government apparatus there was at least bureaucratic inertia and ignorance. On the French side there was a substantial measure of confusion and ineptness, and perhaps some deception. The final effect was to create first shelter and survival, then finally an avenue of escape, for Barbie.

In April 1949, shortly before the publication of the newspaper article that informed the CIC that Barbie was a war criminal, a group of Lyon Resistance members and Nazi victims wrote to the U.S. ambassador in Paris to demand that Barbie be extradited. They drew a detailed account of his atrocities in the Rhône-Alpes region. Following this, the French consulate in Munich wrote on June 7 to the U.S. Office of Military Government for Germany (OMGUS), asking for more information on the whereabouts of Barbie, indicating that he was wanted for war crimes.

Ryan explains that this branch of the French government seemed to be unaware that Barbie had already been interviewed by the French secret service in 1948. He also concludes that "it is virtually certain that no one in OMGUS knew that Barbie had been in the employ of CIC for more than two years. Nor is this fact surprising, given that military intelligence operations were not OMGUS's concern."

The letter from the French consulate in Munich did have the effect of prompting queries by the Public Safety Branch of OMGUS, its civil police authority. But instead of contacting the CIC, they went to the Munich police, who honestly replied that they could not locate Barbie. The American authorities, unaware that Barbie-Becker was living in a U.S.-paid apartment in Augsburg, forwarded this response to the French. On July 12, the French in Munich wrote directly to the Office of Military Government in Bavaria, stating that Barbie was a wanted war criminal and urging "all inquiries possible." When this initiative also proved unfruitful, the French consulate in Munich, on September 9, brought the matter to the attention of the French High Commission in Baden-Baden, the top authority of the French Zone of occupation.

The French occupation authorities had already been brought into the case. By the end of May 1949 the top French diplomatic official in Baden-Baden had sent a communiqué to his counterpart in the legal division on the subject. He asked Henri Lebegue, who besides being the leading justice official in Baden-Baden was the French High Commissioner, to contact the chief of the legal division of the U.S. High Commission to "tell him how anxious the French government is to have this person handed over." Baden-

Baden was now sure that Barbie was in the American Zone.

By this time the French suspected that they were dealing not only with a Nazi criminal in hiding, but with an American government that was protecting him. A French justice official in Baden-Baden wrote to the French commissioner for German and Austrian affairs on July 28, 1949, to say, "I have just learned from a semi-official source that Barbie is said to reside now in Kempten, Bavaria, in the U.S. Zone.... However, I must respectfully bring your attention to the fact that Barbie enjoys the protection of the American occupation authorities and that it is possible that these authorities will not facilitate the necessary investigation, thus preventing us from completing the required dossier of extradition."

That last phrase is important. The French labored for months, futilely, to obtain an exact address for Barbie to place on their petition for his arrest and extradition. The problem was rooted in the already-strained relations between the French and Americans over extradition issues. The major point of contention was the July 1947 announcement by U.S. Military Governor General Lucius D. Clay that all requests to the U.S. for the extradition of alleged war criminals from its zone had to be submitted by November 1 of that year. The supporting evidence for the petition was to be presented to the American authorities no later than December 31.

The French, like the other Allies, strongly protested this decision. One French official argued that "our lists of wanted war criminals include at least 20,000 names and increase every day as new names are added as a result of new discoveries." The French sought assurances that the U.S. would make exceptions to this ruling in the case of any war criminal they might request, but General Clay refused to grant such a blanket dispensation. Finally, France was forced to accept the decision along with more stringent requirements for documentation backing up each extradition demand.

The American action had been directed against the Iron Curtain countries but France became an inadvertent victim. One reason for the American decision was that U.S. officials believed the existing extradition agreements had been misused by Communist East Bloc countries to lay their hands on political dissenters living in the West. A May 1947 memo from the justice office of the U.S.

Military Government for Germany cited "bad faith" on the part of East European countries, recommending that a new policy be established for Yugoslavia, Poland, Czechoslovakia, Hungary, Italy and Austria. But in July 1947 the new policy was extended to cover any country seeking the extradition of war criminals, perhaps to avoid the appearance of political discrimination.

This new policy was to prove a paper hurdle for the French in their efforts to find and extradite Barbie. One of the new requirements was that the exact address of the war criminal had to be provided. The U.S. response would probably have been no different if this requirement had not existed, but it delayed the filing of a formal extradition request by France.

The failure of the French to file a timely extradition request was a severe setback in their efforts to retrieve Barbie. Frustrated, the French approached the U.S. State Department through their Washington embassy. In a formal note sent on November 7, the French ambassador explained that "despite repeated efforts" to obtain Barbie's arrest, "the American occupation authorities in Germany have not...proceeded to the arrest and rendition of this war criminal on whom the French authorities set a high price."

The State Department made inquiries with the U.S. High Commission for Germany (HICOG) but was told by the High Commission that not only was it ignorant of Barbie's whereabouts, but that it had no record of a request from the French for Barbie's surrender. The State Department told the French to go back to the U.S. High Commission.

It was technically true that no extradition request had been filed by the French government. The military examining magistrate in Lyon, a Captain Poignet, had sent an extradition request to the French High Commission in Baden-Baden on November 25, but it had stalled there, ostensibly because the French were still trying to obtain Barbie's address. The only address they had was 38 Schillerstrasse in Kempten, Bavaria, but Barbie-Becker had since moved to the U.S. safe house in Augsburg. It was not very far away, but it was distant enough to frustrate the French.

After this seeming rebuff from Washington, the French pushed ahead along more forceful lines. On March 2, 1950, in Baden-Baden, Lebegue wrote to the HICOG's Office of General Counsel to renew his appeal, explaining the Catch-22 regarding Barbie's address. "It is a fact that we did not request from you the extradition of Barbie. In order to...file such a request, I must be in possession of the certificate of residence which is indispensable for making up the record of extradition." Since Lebegue did not know where Barbie was, he said, "it was not possible to apply to the competent Public Safety Officer for this certificate [and] I was not in a position to file a regular request for extradition."

Ryan points out the American civil authorities were now as confused as the French. "Lebegue implied that this certificate could be quickly furnished by the Americans, since they obviously knew where Barbie was," Ryan states. "In fact, HICOG knew nothing of Barbie beyond what Lebegue had told them." The High Commissioner apparently was not privy to the intrigue going on in the CIC office in Bavaria.

The French letter had been sent to Elizabeth Lange, an attorney in the HICOG extradition department. She referred it to General Counsel Robert Bowie, who sent it to Assistant General Counsel John Bross, who gave it over to Lange's boss, Jonathan Rintels, director of HICOG's Administration of Justice Division. Then Rintels returned it to Lange, where it had begun. In this bureaucratic morass, the Barbie investigation had not advanced a single step. A copy also went to James L. McGraw, head of the Public Safety Division, who unwittingly denied that the Americans were shielding Barbie. "The inference of...the French authorities that Barbie is being granted refuge in the U.S. Zone is unjustified and unwarranted," he states. Rintels wrote back to Lebegue telling him that nothing had been turned up; more information was needed.

Ryan has concluded that HICOG was not stalling, and that it actually was ignorant of the truth all along. "All the evidence suggests that Rintels, bucking the request back to Lebegue, was acting in good faith. Klaus Barbie was just a name to Rintels and others at HICOG, albeit one against whom some French citizens had made some fairly serious charges. Nonetheless, it would be reasonable to assume that Rintels's letter struck Lebegue as curious and perhaps disingenuous. Lebegue knew that Barbie was in U.S. custody, and yet HICOG was asking Lebegue to provide specific information including his date and place of birth, as though Barbie were a common fugitive."

The Barbie case might have remained in this bureaucratic limbo indefinitely if not for the second treason trial of René Hardy, which got underway in Paris in the spring of 1950. On April 28 the depositions given by Barbie to the French in Frankfurt implicating Hardy as a collaborator were entered into evidence. Hardy's attorney, Maurice Garçon, charged that it was "an outrage to French justice" to use the testimony of a man who "took pleasure in torturing French patriots." But the incident also focused on the fact that Barbie was in the hands of U.S. authorities and was being protected, a situation Garçon characterized as "scandalous."

The U.S. European Command (EUCOM) based in Heidelberg in western Germany now became the object of French press inquiries. On May 3 EUCOM advised CIC Commander Colonel David Erskine that "French newspapers are making a large splash stating that Barbie is guilty of war crimes and is being held by the Americans for security reasons." Vidal, who had become a top CIC operations officer, was the one to respond to EUCOM and Erskine, though he did not provide the same explanation about Barbie in each case.

To EUCOM Vidal wrote that Barbie had worked for the CIC only from May 1947 until May 1949, and he rejected the war crimes accusations against Barbie as "a malicious distortion of fact." But to Erskine he said that "CIC sees no reason for denying the French the extradition of Barbie." The CIC now knew that l'affaire Barbie was potentially explosive. On May 4, 1950, Colonel Erskine met with four of his top officers, including Vidal. It was at this meeting that an important decision was made. According to Vidal's note, the group agreed "that Barbie should not be placed in the hands of the French." Vidal also noted that two EUCOM officers were in agreement with this decision. At the middle bureaucratic level, the U.S. had decided to keep Barbie and face the consequences, which were thirty-three years in coming.

The events at the Hardy trial created an official furor over Barbie, and the American High Command received a cable from the U.S. Embassy in Paris demanding an explanation. At first HICOG maintained that the French charges were "unjustified and unwarranted," but apparently even the U.S. diplomats in Paris were unpersuaded. They beseeched HICOG to release the "real facts." This last cable was sent on May 3, and within hours HICOG made an about-face, informing Paris that "our statement regarding presence [of Barbie] in the U.S. Zone may possibly be inaccurate or incomplete." HICOG asked the embassy to hold all further releases, in effect, to stall, until it could clear up the situation.

At HICOG, public safety chief McGraw was now qualifying his denial that Barbie was now in the U.S. Zone. The denial, he hedged, was "accurate insofar as any official information is available to this headquarters." Ryan interprets this to mean that HICOG had finally received "unofficial information" that Barbie had found refuge with the Americans and conjectures that EUCOM had passed the unpleasant information along to the High Commission. This still leaves open the question whether HICOG knew Barbie was still in the hands of the CIC. Ryan believes they did not. "On balance...the evidence compels the conclusion that HICOG did not know on May 3—and in fact never knew—that Barbie's relationship with CIC continued past April 28, 1950."

This does not mean that the U.S. High Commission for Germany was being perfectly candid with the French. On the evening of May 5, 1950, HICOG sent a cable to Paris instructing the embassy to do nothing until HICOG's political affairs director, James Riddleberger, could get there. Riddleberger was in Paris over the weekend of May 6-7; on Monday the 8th the U.S. embassy sent a cable to the State Department in Washington, to say, "Barbier [sic] case has highly embarrassing possibilities to put it mildly." The embassy recommended that State limit its statements to the "line set forth" by HICOG on May 5—that the Barbie case was under study by the U.S. headquarters in Germany.

But French outrage did not die down in May as the American embassy in Paris had hoped. One member of the French Senate suggested that Rintels's letter to Lebegue of April 25 gave less than "the impression of perfect uprightness," adding that one should never make use of assassins. In Washington, the French embassy sent another coldly worded note to the State Department on May 5, urging that Barbie be handed over. A worried EUCOM director of intelligence, Brigadier General Robert K. Taylor, wrote to Colonel Erskine, "It is highly probable that this case may develop into something very embarrassing for us. Therefore, we should be prepared to answer any inquiry." U.S. officials in Washington, Paris, Heidelberg, Frankfurt, Stuttgart and Augsburg finally had to come to terms with the Barbie case. All of them, to one degree or another, chose to cover up the U.S. involvement.

In Paris the reaction was mostly bewilderment. "The problem," one American diplomat wrote to HICOG, "is what to do about the apparently widespread French belief that Barbier [sic] not only was employed by us in the past, but continues to be employed by us at present, and that we are blocking his extradition. We should appreciate your assistance in dealing with what promises to become a constant and convenient source of anti-American propaganda." HICOG, which now knew that Barbie had at least been in U.S. employ at one time, was saying nothing to the French other than that the matter was "under study."

The Americans were not moving toward extradition, but some believe that, despite the verbal outbursts, the French were equally reluctant to see Barbie handed over to Paris. Barbie, they felt, was a potential source of embarrassment to some highly placed French officials who had been members of the Resistance and might have compromised their colleagues under the pain, or threat, of torture. This would explain why the French had never filed formal extradition papers and had used the absence of a specific address for Barbie as an excuse.

"According to this theory," Ryan writes, "the actual surrender of Barbie would pose an acute embarrassment to the French because...Barbie could and would reveal the names of French collaborators, some of whom had risen to prominence in postwar France...often on the strength of their Resistance credentials." Using this line of argument, one State Department official wrote that "the Department might well decide...that the whole business [might] blow over."

But whether the surmise about the French was correct or not, the controversy did not die down. June 16, 1950, was a critical point in the evolution of the U.S. cover-up. On that day the director of HICOG's intelligence division, Benjamin Shute, met in Heidelberg with Brigadier General Robert Taylor and Major Wilson, then the CIC operations chief. According to his own memo on the meeting, Shute was told by the two Army intelligence officers that

Barbie's employment ended on May 24, 1949, and "has not been employed by them since that time." They also told Shute that the CIC "has not been in touch with him since late April 1950 and does not know his present whereabouts."

Obviously, none of this was true. As Ryan bluntly concludes, "these representations by CIC and EUCOM were false." He leaves open the possibility that General Taylor did not know of this deception, but reminds us that "it is likely that, given the prominence of the Barbie matter and Taylor's responsibilities, he had been fully briefed by CIC. Moreover, it was General Taylor who had written to CIC's commanding officer on May 12 that the Barbie case may prove to be 'very embarrassing' and that 'we should be prepared to answer any inquiry.'"

During the summer, the pressure began to mount on the CIC and its parent organization, EUCOM. The State Department and the High Commission had come to the conclusion that Barbie would have to be turned over to the French if he were found. In fact, Barbie was still living well in Augsburg, Bavaria, on the CIC payroll. HICOG began to move through the paperwork for extradition, and on August 21 sent the CIC a request for "extradition clearance" for Barbie, a move that alarmed the CIC. CIC chief Erskine reminded EUCOM on August 30 that a mutual CIC-EUCOM decision "not to place Barbie in the hands of the French" had already been made and asked EUCOM to provide more "details concerning the circumstances surrounding this extradition request."

Erskine spoke with a Lieutenant Colonel W. L. Hardwich in the EUCOM Intelligence Division on September 9. The latter officer later cabled CIC: "It is proposed that this Division notify HICOG that it has no objection to the extradition of Barbie. Further propose that HICOG be notified informally that Barbie is no longer under control of any agency of this Division." It seemed as if the CIC was giving up its Nazi informant, but in reality nothing was to happen. As Ryan points out, "A comprehensive memo on Barbie's CIC history written at CIC Headquarters three months later makes no mention of any change in Barbie's status; in fact, it states 'Region XII is still harboring ... supporting ... and utilizing' Barbie, 'acting properly under orders of this headquarters ...'" Ryan concludes that at this point the CIC was simply lying to the American command higher-ups. "Having misrepresented Barbie's status once to HICOG, CIC appears to have found it expedient to do so again."

As of November 1950 the Public Safety Division of HICOG was no longer actively looking for Barbie. In January 1951 the French at Baden-Baden again contacted HICOG to inquire as to the progress of the investigation. They were told by Mrs. Lange that "continuous efforts to locate Barbie are being made," but in reality, as far as HICOG was concerned, the Barbie case was dead. More than that, the CIC and EUCOM were already at work to ensure that Barbie would be put far beyond the reach of either American officials at HICOG or the French. The U.S. cover-up the Butcher of Lyon was about to enter the last stage.

Ω

By December 1950 Klaus Barbie had become a major problem not only for the CIC but for the entire U.S. European Command as well. One briefing memo prepared for the CIC's commander stated, "It is deemed important that this organization immediately disassociate itself with Barbie." As for Barbie, the same CIC officer noted that he was "living in constant fear of being apprehended by the French." Simultaneously, the German civil authorities were now actively seeking Barbie in connection with the 1946 Kassel jewel robbery.

The CIC was now faced with two alternatives, one as unsavory as the other. In a review of the Barbie situation, a top CIC officer recognized that if Barbie were extradited to the French, the CIC would be implicated. "In order to vindicate himself, Barbie will point out that he has served CIC faithfully against communism for the past several years," the review states. "This unit has probably used the services of a war criminal and protected such person from legal authority."

The other possibility was simply to cut Barbie loose, an option favored by this officer, who added that Barbie was "a professional intelligence man who is very capable and qualified to take care of himself—unless this organization persists in remaining his guardian angel." But releasing Barbie into the German population carried the risk that he might be picked up by law enforcement authorities or another intelligence agency.

A third alternative was at least briefly considered by some of the Augsburg CIC officers. That was to eliminate Barbie by killing him, an option that former intelligence agent Gene Bramel claims went far enough even for U.S. agents to consider drawing straws to determine who would carry it out.

"If worse came to worst, the one who drew the small straw would take him up to the *Autobahn* and shoot him," says Bramel. "Drive him up the *Autobahn* at night. Pull off in a parking place. Shoot him. Push him out. Come back.

"We didn't want to," Bramel explains, "but we knew we would have to shoot him rather than let the French get him."

Kolb has since questioned Bramel's account, calling his story "rubbish." He adds: "That's the kind of talk you might hear among a bunch of sergeants in a *Bierstube* over their tenth beer."

But there was a more realistic option, one which the beleaguered CIC finally chose. It was to get Barbie out of Germany, and preferably out of Europe. The answer was "The Ratline," a clandestine emigration route passing through Austria and Italy. It would remove Barbie from Europe and the scenes of his crimes to faraway South America, an environment that was friendly to runaway Nazi criminals.

The Ratline was a "service" of the 430th CIC Detachment, a U.S. counterintelligence agency operating in Austria and a sister organization to the 970th, which had now been renamed the 66th CIC Detachment. Based in the divided city of Vienna, the 430th had in 1947 been looking for a means to discreetly resettle defectors or informants from East Bloc countries—which it referred to euphemistically as "visitors"—outside Europe.

In the summer of 1947 officers of the 430th entered into negotiations with Father Krunoslav Dragonovic, a Roman Catholic priest of Croatian origin based at a Rome seminary for young Croat candidates for the priesthood. For all of his religious status, Dragonovic's single virtue was that he offered the Americans a solution to their relocation problem. Operations officer Paul E. Lyon noted in a 1950 report that Dragonovic had "developed several clandestine evacuation channels to the various South American countries for various types of European refugees." On the other hand, Dragonovic was "known and recorded as a Fascist, war criminal, etc.," whose "contacts with South American diplomats of a similar class are not generally approved by the U.S. State Department."

Dragonovic established his Ratline to help other Croats who during World War II had been involved in the "Independent State of Croatia," a puppet nation established by Hitler and Mussolini in 1941. By exploiting the existing antipathies between Yugoslavia's Croats and the Serbian majority, the Nazis managed to install Ante Pavelic at the head of this state, whose capital was located in Zagreb. This illegitimate government slaughtered several hundred thousand Serbs and some 30,000 Jews between 1941 and its downfall in April 1945. When the communist partisan leader Josip Broz Tito came to power after the war, the Croats implicated in the wartime atrocities fled. Pavelic himself was said to have emigrated to South America with the assistance of Father Dragonovic, whose escape routes were believed to still be in active use by the Croatian war criminals when the 430th contracted with the priest. The 430th obviously wished to keep its involvement with Dragonovic secret.

The 430th's use of Dragonovic was, like the 66th's use of Barbie, a moral compromise seen as a necessary expedient. Ryan suspects that in exchange for Ratline favors the CIC may also have helped Croatian war criminals escape from Europe. In a 1948 memo, a CIC agent explained that "the agreement consists of simple mutual assistance, i.e., these agents assist persons of interest to Father Dragonovic to leave Germany, and, in turn, Father Dragonovic will assist these agents in obtaining the necessary visas to Argentina, South America, for persons of interest to this command." The price established for Ratline transport, including safe houses and hotels, was $1,000 to $1,400 per person.

When the 66th CIC learned about this system it resolved to export its greatest problem, Klaus Barbie. On December 11, 1950, Lieutenant John Hobbins, a technical specialist with the 66th CIC, traveled to Salzburg, Austria, to meet with officers of the 430th. An American officer named Neagoy, who was with the 430th CIC in Salzburg, was responsible for supervision of the Ratline. He agreed to come to Germany to interview the candidate—Klaus Barbie, alias Klaus Becker.

The plan was for Neagoy to transmit Barbie's personal details to Dragonovic, who would invent a new alias for Barbie-Becker. Using this assumed name, the 66th CIC would obtain documents from the Allied High Commission for the Barbie family to travel to Italy in the company of a 430th CIC agent. Barbie, his wife and children would then board ship for South America, never, it was hoped, to be seen again by the CIC.

"Upon embarkation," Hobbins reported back to the 66th CIC, "the emigrant is given $50 in greenbacks. He is given no further assurances and is strictly on his own. From the beginning of the processing, the 430th tries to create an atmosphere which leads the emigrant to believe that he is being treated with great consideration; that everything within reason is being done to provide for his welfare; that he is entitled to nothing further and has no right to ask or expect further assistance after boarding ship."

On February 12, 1951, the name of "Klaus Altmann" appeared in U.S. files, in a cable from the 66th CIC Headquarters to Region IV in Munich. This was one of Barbie's infrequently used aliases in the SS underground. In another cable, CIC Headquarters told the Munich office: "Following represents information regarding difficult disposal case, Klaus Altmann, that can be passed on to Uncle Sugar representative Combined Travel Board, Munich. Representative should be told subject is of extreme interest to Uncle Sugar Intelligence and is traveling on highly sensitive task." The Combined Travel Board issued "Altmann" a temporary travel document numbered 0121454, and a second document for Barbie's wife and two children.

Acting at the request of the United States, the Italian consulate in Munich issued Barbie a travel document to pass through Italy; the Combined Travel Board papers included a visa for Austria. Neagoy and another CIC agent, Jack Gay, came to Augsburg, Bavaria, and on March 9, after a hasty debriefing of the ex-Nazi and a rushed visit by his mother, left with Barbie and his family for Salzburg. Two days later they continued on to Genoa, where they arrived on March 12, where Barbie was placed in the hands of Father Dragonovic. The priest, who had already obtained a Red Cross travel permit for the family, accompanied "Altmann" to the Bolivian consulate in Genoa on March 16.

With a new name, a new birthdate of October 25, 1915, and a new birthplace in Kronstadt, Germany (a nonexistent town), and the occupation of "mechanic," Barbie obtained the immigrant visas necessary for himself and his family, with Dragonovic acting as his sponsor. Next the Barbies went to the International Commission of the Red Cross in Genoa, where they used the Bolivian immigrant visas to apply for temporary travel documents. Barbie also presented the Allied High Commission document and Dragonovic signed the application in support of the Red Cross documents, which were issued the same day. Argentine transit visas were obtained later that week, and passage was booked.

On March 23, Barbie, his wife and two children left Genoa on the Italian vessel *Corrientes*, bound for Buenos Aires, with an estimated date of arrival of April 10, 1951. Neagoy and Gay filled out a report describing the passage as "without incident." At the beginning of April, with the "Altmanns" safely at sea, CIC Headquarters congratulated all involved in the operation for the way in which "the final disposal of an extremely sensitive individual" was carried out. "This case," an officer in CIC Headquarters wrote, "is considered closed."

$$\Omega$$

"Justice delayed is justice denied," concluded the U.S. Justice Department's Allan A. Ryan. As a result of his inquiry, the U.S. government, in a virtually unprecedented move, apologized formally to the French government for having hidden Klaus Barbie in the years 1947-1951, then spiriting him away to Bolivia. But the Barbie case carries far deeper implications than a simple obstruction of justice. It suggests that some highly-placed Americans lost their moral bearings in the political maelstrom of postwar Europe and stained the victory the U.S. had achieved in defeating men such as Klaus Barbie.

In summing up the actions and judgments of the U.S. intelligence officials involved in sheltering Barbie and helping him to escape justice, Ryan weighs a number of competing considerations. He condemns what took place, stating that, "for the United States Government to have collaborated in any way with former Gestapo officers was, at the least, a grave misjudgment that, however unwittingly, betrayed those who had died fighting Nazism or fallen innocent victim to it."

But Ryan simultaneously acknowledges the pragmatic needs of the CIC officers who took part in the Barbie cover-up. "The job of understanding and countering Communist influence was there, it was legitimate and important, and it had to be done. If a Klaus Barbie was available and effective and loyal and reliable—and those who worked with him found him to be all of those—his employment was in the best interests of the United States at the time."

Ryan points out, too, that "Klaus Barbie is far more notorious today than he ever was, except in Lyon, during or immediately after the war.... Whatever his crimes, he has never been in the same category as Adolph Eichmann, Heinrich Himmler, Reinhard Heydrich or other SS leaders."

One point of view is "visceral," Ryan says; the other is "pragmatic." But each, he maintains, is "compelling.... Each has a genuine and indisputable strength.

"For that reason," he adds, "I cannot conclude that those who made the decision to employ and rely on Klaus Barbie ought now to be vilified for the decision. Any one of us, had we been there, might have made the opposite decision. But one must recognize that those who did in fact have to make a decision made a defensible one, even if it was not the only defensible one." Ryan also points out that all the other nations that emerged victorious from the Second World War—France included—made use of former Nazis to further their respective national interests.

The moral failure of the American officers was greatest, Ryan says, when they continued to hide Barbie after it had become known that he was a war criminal. "Responsible officials of the Army interfered with the lawful and proper administration of justice," says the Justice Department official. "They knowingly obstructed the bona fide efforts of the office of the U.S. High Commissioner for Germany to carry out its lawful obligation to effect the extradition of war criminals." Sending Barbie through the Ratline was an extension of that same misconduct, Ryan concludes. However, under U.S. criminal code, any case against those involved has long since lost its legal validity. Only the moral burden remains.

ALIAS ALTMANN

KLAUS BARBIE, ALIAS KLAUS ALTMANN HANSEN, AND HIS family arrived in the city of La Paz on April 23, 1951. The "Altmanns" had docked in Argentina, but within a few weeks had boarded a train for the Bolivian capitol, a long journey aboard a crowded, slow train that traveled through pampas, jungle, high plain and Andes passes. Buenos Aires was the sophisticated model of a Europeanized South American capital, but in La Paz the Altmanns found just a thin layer of urbanity over an ageless peasant-Indian society.

At 13,000 feet above sea level, La Paz lay in the bottom of a colossal bowl scoured out of the hardened altiplano soil by the Choqueyapu River. In the near distance loomed the snow-glazed peaks of Mount Illimani in the Western Cordillera of the Andes. A business district sat in the bottom of the La Paz crater, while stucco settlements peopled by native *campesinos* climbed the sides in a confusion of earthy pastels. Other peasants flocked in daily from the surrounding altiplano to sell crops and handcrafts on the city's steep sidewalks or in the market district surrounding the Spanish colonial church in the Plaza San Francisco.

Bolivia was a world distant from the busy European centers the Altmanns had fled, but Klaus Altmann had already had indications that he could make a place for himself in this backward Andean country. The Altmanns had spent a night in Santa Cruz, in the southeast of Bolivia, during their trip from Argentina; there the ex-Nazi came across something that gave him an immediate sense of belonging. "When I arrived in Bolivia," he later was to recall, "one of the first sights I saw was a Falange Socialista march down the streets of Santa Cruz, with brown uniforms and leather belts and Nazi armbands. I decided that when I had an opportunity I would do what I could to help a party that had the same philosophy as I."

The Falange Socialista Boliviana was only one manifestation of a strong fascist undercurrent in Bolivia's political life, a phenomenon strongly influenced by the sizeable German colony implanted in the country since the 1920s. The postwar wave of immigrants, which included the Altmanns, was the latest of those that had built the German population up to several thousand. It was numerically small relative to the larger Bolivian population, but highly influential both politically and economically.

Despite its political independence wrested from Spain a century and a half before, Bolivia was still essentially a colonial society. The *latifundistas*, the large landowners of Spanish descent, dominated the agricultural sector of the economy. The country's rich tin mines were tightly held by a three-family oligarchy known as the *rosca*. The German immigrants had carved out their own niche, specializing mainly in the import and export business. Their acumen quickly gave them sufficient economic power to exert a strong influence on the country's politics.

But Altmann was a newcomer. He had to start at the bottom, which meant striking out into the forests of the Yungas valley north of La Paz, where there were opportunities in the timber industry. "As I remember," says one La Paz German who met Altmann in those early days, "he was manufacturing wooden cases in the Yungas." Altmann went into business with a German Jew named Ludwig Kappauner, who managed a Jewish agricultural settlement near Coroico, from which Altmann purchased wood products.

Doing business with people he had persecuted and murdered did not trouble Altmann; in fact, it was a useful cover for his new identity. "He made friends with Kappauner," the German business-man says, "and it seemed he hadn't done anything against Jews and was a friend of Jews. It was very important for him to assume a new face."

Altmann then moved his activities to La Paz, where he estab-lished another wood business with a German named Gutmann. The firm exported the quinine-bearing hearts of quinquina trees to German pharmaceutical firms for processing into antimalarial drugs. But the partnership did not thrive. "He had economic diffi-culties with Mr. Gutmann, who died soon after," says this German informant.

The Altmann family established itself in respectably middle-class circumstances, renting a stucco house at 991 Calle Manzane-da, high on the side of the La Paz bowl atop the steep, cobbled Calle Yanacocha, which mounted straight up from the center of the business district. The steepness of the grade meant that the front of the main floor was ten feet above the street, with a square, four-paneled bay window facing outward to the city far below. Alt-mann's children, Ute Maria and Klaus Georg, who were 9 and 4, respectively when they arrived in Bolivia, attended classes in a school established by the German colony, the Deutsche Schule Mariscal Braun. "It was a good home," observed one La Paz German.

Altmann was becoming a recognized figure in the tight Ger-man colony. The initial impression he made was positive; he seemed to have all the requisite virtues of a good German—intelli-gence, diligence, good grooming and a bit of culture. People also recognized another, less positive facet of his character. "At first he seemed very modest," says the German businessman. "But when he drank he became different. In his drunkenness he spoke of his life before, the things he did in France, in Lyon, and how he enjoyed torturing people. He was very proud of this." The German informant adds, "He never denied that he was an SS official. Contrary to all the prominent Nazis who said, 'We only followed orders,' he was proud, and said, 'Yes, I did this.'"

"When he was here in the German clubs, he didn't make a secret of what he had done," adds another German resident of La Paz. "When he drank he would sing the old songs. If he had been quiet and acted as a normal citizen nobody would ever have known of him here. This was as far away as he could get." But as suspicions stirred in the La Paz German community, some began to question Altmann's background. "It was known that Altmann was not his real name," says the businessman. "Instead we called him Alias Altmann."

Raised eyebrows evolved into open ostracism following a series of unpleasant incidents in the late 1950s at the German Club of La Paz, a focus of German social life in Bolivia. "I can't remember what the occasion was," says the German businessman, "but there was a reception at the German Club, with a lot of members and invited people present. The pastor of the German Lutheran Church said, 'It is impossible for me to be under the same roof as a murderer.' Then Altmann's wife got up and said, 'Who is a murderer here? You can't say that!' It was an awful event."

Relations between Altmann and mainstream German society became intolerably strained around 1960 when, in the course of a reception at the German Club for a West German diplomatic official, Altmann drunkenly threw a Nazi salute. "Heil, Hitler," he shouted at the diplomat. As punishment, he was barred from the club. A West German embassy official in La Paz confirms the story. "When he made a fuss several times, the German Club said he had gone too far and excluded him."

Barbie's expulsion was not a reflection of strident anti-Nazism among the German La Paz community; it was more a question of bad manners than bad politics. The Bolivian German community was fundamentally conservative and prior to the war it had been strongly pro-Nazi. Swastikas hung in the local German school and a sign outside the German Club stated: "Dogs and Jews not admitted." The tone was moderated in the postwar era, but even in the 1960s local German Jews were still excluded from the club.

Although Altmann eventually found himself out of favor with both the main German organizations and the German Jewish community, which formed a separate group, he was not isolated from the powerful German trading families of La Paz. Political circumstances also favored Altmann. The conservative establishment found itself threatened by a wave of populism, which crested on April 9, 1952, when Bolivian revolutionaries overthrew the *latifundistas* and the *rosca*. Working class rebels armed with German Mausers, led by the leftist political leader Hernan Siles Zuazo, forced the surrender of the Bolivian Army on April 11. The exiled leader of the Nationalist Revolutionary Movement, or MNR, Victor Paz Estenssoro, flew in from Buenos Aires to claim the presidency and the Palacio Quemado.

The MNR and its ally, the Bolivian Workers Center, the national trade union confederation known as COB, set about reducing the strength of the army, which had previously maintained the power of the country's elite. By 1957 the armed forces were reduced to only 7,000 men, most of whom bore not rifles but shovels as they marched to public works projects and into the fields. This process drew a counter-reaction from the right, and the new populist government soon found itself faced with a bitter opponent in the right wing groups led by the Falange, the storm troopers who had so impressed Altmann on his arrival.

But the leftist revolution had not totally remade Bolivia; in the context of what was to follow, it was simply the first of numerous assertions of organized labor against the right-wing military circles. The military had been absorbed bodily into the revolution, but its soul was never committed. By the early 1960s, under Paz's second presidency following a four-year Siles term, the military rapidly recovered strength with the help of the U.S. In November 1964, two Bolivian generals staged a bloodless coup and Paz was again exiled.

The coup—executed by Bolivian Air Force General Rene Barrientos Ortuno, who became president, and General Alfredo Ovando Candia, commander of the army—was solidly backed by the German communities in La Paz, Cochabamba and Santa Cruz. It also created a major opportunity for Altmann. The new military regime wanted weapons, and the former Nazi had by this time developed the necessary contacts to supply them.

During the fifties, Altmann established close links with former Nazis in the two neighboring countries of Paraguay and Peru, to which he frequently traveled. Austrian Nazi-hunter Simon Wiesenthal says that Barbie was involved in the Kameradenwerk organization, which he described as a mutual aid group made up of former Nazis in South America, Germany and Austria. These ex-Nazis, he says, maintained contact with police officials in several South American countries to assure their safety. Simultaneously, they had cultivated sources in the West German embassies in these nations in order to learn of impending extradition requests.

The terms Kameradenwerk and ODESSA are frequently used interchangably by sources in Bolivia, but Wiesenthal believes that ODESSA, the group formed after the war by SS alumni, was inactive after 1953. Kameradenwerk continued to operate through the 1960s, but he questions how effective it was thereafter, mainly because of the advanced age of most of its members.

But in Bolivia, Barbie continued to make use of the contacts he established through this network, and he collected intelligence from neighboring countries in the Southern Cone that was useful to the Bolivian government. On several occasions, Altmann was seen in La Paz with Hans Ulrich Rudel, a former Luftwaffe colonel and a celebrated flying ace of World War II who was reputed to hold a central position in the Kameradenwerk organization. Rudel, who flew 2,350 missions on both fronts despite the loss of one leg, became one of Hitler's favorite soldiers. In Peru, Altmann had also developed close relations with Friedrich Schwend, a former SS colonel who attained a certain notoriety during the war for his role in Operation Bernhard, the failed Nazi attempt to cripple the British economy by flooding the world with counterfeit five pound notes.

But Rudel was a key figure for Altmann. He faced no charges of war crimes, yet as a stalwart Nazi had chosen to go into a partial exile in Argentina and later in Paraguay, where he maintained strong connections with President Alfredo Stroessner, Paraguay's dictator. Rudel's prowess as a combat pilot gave him access to military circles in Europe and South America. One member of the La Paz German colony recalls meeting Altmann at the El Alto Airport outside the city in the company of Rudel. "I knew who Rudel was, of course," he confided over coffee in the Club de La Paz. "We chatted for a few minutes. He told me that not long before he had flown in one of the latest model American jets."

Rudel also operated an import-export company based in Asuncion, Paraguay, that did business throughout the Southern Cone: Argentina, Chile, Peru, and Bolivia. Since his wartime record was clean, Rudel could also transact business deals in Europe, particularly in Germany and Austria.

Altmann's links with the financially and politically powerful Bolivian German colony qualified him to serve as part of the South American Nazi network. Says a German writer in Cochabamba: "After the war, a lot of Nazi money stayed in South America. Altmann plugged into it." This melange of fascist politics, financial leverage and old-fashioned cronyism was to move Altmann into the highest Bolivian military ranks, where he became involved in the lucrative arms deals of the local Nazis and their South American friends. Barbie's vehicle was the Transmaritima Bolivia, the shipping line of the landlocked nation.

The Republic of Bolivia boasted an impressive number of admirals for a country deprived of access to the Pacific Ocean for nearly a century. These naval officers were on hand in December 1967 when President Barrientos ceremonially snipped a tricolored ribbon in the form of an elongated Bolivian flag for the official opening of the home office of Transmaritima Boliviana. Waiters filled the champagne glasses of the assembled Bolivians elite—ministers, subministers, generals, colonels, captains, as well as diplomats and military attachés from neighboring countries—who were there to celebrate the establishment of Bolivia's bid for a commercial presence on the world's oceans.

Conspicuously absent were representatives from Chile. It was not a lapse of protocol but the product of a feud between Bolivia and its western neighbor that dated from 1883, when the War of the Pacific was concluded. Bolivian texts are clear that Chile had been the aggressor in that conflict; it began in 1879 and concluded with the defeat of the allied Bolivian and Peruvian forces and Chile's annexation of every inch of Bolivia's Pacific coastline.

"Bolivia reclame su mar" had been the rallying call of the nation ever since. Aristocrats in the reading room of the Club de La Paz still fumed over the national insult when Bolivian President Victor Paz Estenssoro had asked Chilean leader Carlos Ibanez del Campo for a port on the Pacific, and Ibanez had answered: "What do you

want a port for, if you haven't got an ocean?"

Transmaritima was the creation of Gaston Velasco, for whom the shipping line was not only a step toward the recovery of lost Bolivian honor, but a personal triumph. He and other Bolivians had developed the idea of a shipping line for their country, forming the ad hoc organization Accion Maritima Boliviana. If Bolivia could not retrieve its coastline, they reasoned, it could maintain a presence on the high seas. Velasco's father, Theobaldo, had fought in la Guerra de la Pacifica, and throughout his life as a politician and businessman Theobaldo's son had never tempered his inherited hatred of Chile. With great satisfaction Velasco watched President Barrientos ask the guests for their attention.

"He said he had found a man who was going to buy a ship for Bolivia," recalls Velasco, a courtly man in his late seventies who has been involved in Bolivian politics all his life. "He said this man was a businessman and a marine engineer, an expert in all things concerning ships. Then he introduced Klaus Altmann to the crowd —to the country, in fact, since all the Bolivian press was there." Altmann, who had no naval experience at all, was named general manager of the new shipping firm.

Velasco, who had never met Altmann before, was impressed as he chatted with the short, balding German. "I had the best impression of him," Velasco explained when interviewed in his home in La Paz. "He was a first-class gentleman, very friendly and well-spoken." Moreover, says Velasco, "he came with nothing less than the personal recommendation of the president."

As Transmaritima's first manager, Altmann had free access to the $450,000 that had been deposited in the Banco Central de Bolivia following a national fund-raising campaign knows as La Crusada del Mar. It had been initiated by the Barrientos government at the behest of Accion Maritima. The slogan *un barco por Bolivia* stirred enormous popular enthusiasm, and contributions poured in from all levels of Bolivian society. By September 1967 the requisite $300,000 for the down-payment on a cargo ship had been met and exceeded, and on December 15 of that year, a government decree brought Transmaritima Boliviana, S.A. into existence. The Bolivian government held a 51 percent interest in this mixed company, while the balance was distributed among a group of private, and anonymous, investors.

Initially, it seemed Barrientos had made a good selection of a general manager, for Altmann produced fast results. In September 1968, Velasco learned that the cargo ship *Birk*, operated by Transmaritima Boliviana, had arrived in the Chilean port of Arica. He regretted that he could not meet the ship personally at the dock, but that was impossible since Chile had declared Gaston Velasco *persona non grata*. Still, Bolivia now had its ocean-going vessel.

Altmann soon procured more ships to sail under Bolivian national colors. After the *Birk* came the *Angolakust*, the *Argolis*, the *Argonautis* and others, until Transmaritima was finally operating a fleet of seventeen leased vessels. Some were pleased but Velasco was beginning to question Altmann's activities. "The Banco Central, on the orders of the president, gave him all the money to buy a ship," says Velasco. "But instead, Altmann rented ships."

Transmaritima was acquiring dimensions Accion Maritima had never anticipated. Altmann opened offices in Valparaiso, Chile; Colon, Panama; Anvers, Belgium; and Hamburg, West Germany. When Velasco visited the Transmaritima offices in Colon, a port at the eastern end of the Panama Canal, he was surprised by the luxury: a carpeted suite with an impressive bronze plaque outside the door. Velasco was also troubled by Altmann's staff. "Nobody knew who was working for him. They were all Germans, friends of his or members of his family," says Velasco. Barbie's son, Klaus Georg Altmann, then in his mid-twenties, was managing the company's Hamburg office.

Altmann was able to operate without official scrutiny, for he had the backing of the most influential people in Bolivia. "He was now a very important person here in Bolivia," says Velasco, thumbing through files of old documents and albums of press clippings about Transmaritima Boliviana. "Altmann used to travel all the time, to every part of the world," Velasco recalls. "No one looked into what he was doing."

According to U.S. immigrations records Altmann stopped in Miami and New Orleans several times in the period 1969-70, but his bodyguard, Alvaro de Castro, maintains that he also visited Galveston, San Francisco and Atlanta. His work also brought him to a number of European cities, including Hamburg, Madrid,

Vienna and, as he was later to claim, to Paris, where in the Panthéon he laid a wreath on the memorial to Jean Moulin, the Resistance leader he had tortured to death.

Most of the cargoes shipped by Transmaritima were routine: tin from Bolivian mines, wood from the country's forests, sugar, coffee and other agricultural products. In return, Transmaritima brought back grains and industrial products from other nations, particularly from Germany. But in addition to traditional commercial activity, Altmann coordinated the shipment to Bolivia and other South American countries of substantial quantities of arms. Some of the arms shipments for Bolivia were legal but other of Altmann's weapons transactions violated international law and were carried out in secrecy.

One of Altmann's most secretive weapons deals involved the purchase of arms for the state of Israel in 1967. Altmann, either out of perversity, or for added protective coloration, had first been involved in business with Bolivian Jews and was now helping to secure arms for Israel. The project was backed by a group of high Bolivian military officials who stood to gain immense profits by acting as middlemen in the Israeli arms deal. "Barbie participated in various arms transactions that Barrientos had with the Israelis," says the current Bolivian subminister of the interior, Gustavo Sanchez.

The deal might never have become public had it not been for a series of assassinations in Bolivia. Early on the morning of March 14, 1970, a package was delivered to the La Paz home of Bolivia's most powerful publisher, Alfredo Alexander Jordan, owner of the two La Paz dailies *Hoy* and *Ultima Hora*. The messenger who brought the package to the door said it was urgent and had come from the Israeli embassy. The houseman brought it to the bedroom of Alexander and his wife Martha, and ten minutes later a powerful explosion tore through the home on the Avenida 6 de Agosto, instantly killing Alexander and his wife.

Bolivian President Alfredo Ovando, the general who succeeded Barrientos after the latter's death in 1969, expressed shock at the brutal bombing, but according to the Alexander family, officials in the Ministry of the Interior made only a perfunctory investigation of the bombing. For a year, the case was unsolved, until a German,

Gert Richard Heber, came to the medical offices of one of Alexander's sons, Dr. Luis Alexander Dupleich. He said he knew why the publisher had been slain: It was believed he had learned of the Israeli arms deal.

Heber explained that he worked as an intelligence agent for the Bolivian Ministry of the Interior. But prior to that he had worked for the West German secret service under the guise of an Opel technician for the Gundlach import house in La Paz. The family confirmed his connection with the Interior Ministry, but there was no way to establish the truth of the deposition Heber gave before nine witnesses in the offices of the newspaper *Hoy* on March 12, 1971. Much of it seemed to provide a rational explanation for the series of murders that followed what Bolivians call "the Israeli arms deal."

General Barrientos was the prime mover of the transaction and stood to profit the most by it, Heber said. He was to be paid $5 million commission by the Israelis on an intended $50 million sale. In 1967 Barrientos traveled to Switzerland with a Bolivian *campesino* leader, ostensibly for reasons of health. Actually, Heber said, the trip was made "to verify the progress of the transaction. It was in Switzerland that the Israelis, for whom the arms were destined, were to deposit the initial 25 percent payment of the total amount."

Secrecy was vital, for the arms sale was a violation of the arms embargo imposed on the Middle East by the major world powers following the Six Day War of 1967. The Israelis sought to circumvent the embargo by using the Bolivians as go-betweens. The consignment consisted of small arms: machine guns, automatic pistols and revolvers, all of 9 millimeter caliber. Most were of Belgian manufacture but some originated in Spain. The arms were to be shipped in three stages over a period of twelve months. The first shipment left Belgium, crossed France to Spain and was eventually transported to Israel in March of 1968, presumably aboard a ship leased by Altmann for Transmaritima Boliviana. After the first delivery, the Israelis and the Bolivians realized that the CIA and other Western intelligence services had become aware of the transaction, and the remaining shipments were cancelled.

Heber did not specify the involvement of Altmann or Transmaritima in his deposition to *Hoy* journalists, but the German's role involvement has been asserted by several Bolivians, including Interior subminister Sanchez.

Although the Israeli arms deal promised large profits for everyone, the regular activity of Transmaritima Boliviana was not profitable. In fact, by 1971 the company would become bankrupt. But before this took place, Velasco and the other critics of Barbie's management had an opportunity to examine the affairs of the shipping line. It came about by chance on March 23, 1970, the 91st anniversary of the beginning of the War of the Pacific.

When the Transmaritima ship *Birk* put into port in Valparaiso, Chile, the story was covered by the Chilean newspaper *El Mercurio*. Thirteen years later, Velasco's eyes burned as he held the clipping in his hand, railing at Klaus Altmann's perfidy. "He humiliated us, the Bolivian people!" said Velasco. "Altmann was lying to the Bolivian people!"

He read the clipping aloud: "A German flag displayed over its stern, the merchant ship Birk arrived in Valparaiso yesterday after calling at Arica. Since its arrival in Valparaiso, the merchant ship has provoked all sorts of comments due to the fact that it is rented by a country that has no coast.

"The ship's smokestacks bear the colors of the Bolivian flag. Its crew, however, includes not a single Bolivian, but has numerous Germans, six Spaniards and one non-national. Paradoxically, the ship rented by Bolivia, according to its manifests, is carrying material for the Chilean Army: 40.5 tons of explosives."

Transmaritima Boliviana collapsed in the spring of 1971 with debts of between $800,000 and $1 million and eight lawsuits lodged against it in the Hamburg and Panama courts. Even though Accion Maritima demanded an investigation of the loss of $450,000 in initial capital, Altmann was never called to account. The military were protecting Barbie; an examination of the shipping line's books would be too revealing. The records were placed in the inaccessible archives of the Fuerza Navala, Bolivia's river and lake-patrolling navy, and no more was heard about the case.

Ω

Altmann decided to remove himself from the heated Bolivian scene, and in October 1971 Klaus Altmann-Barbie moved to Lima,

Peru, where life proved to be as comfortable as it had been in Bolivia. Altmann turned 58 that October, but the rhythm of his existence was not that of a man graciously sliding into retirement. He woke every morning at 6:00 A.M. in the house he had purchased from an Argentinian journalist in the wealthy suburb of Chaclacayo. At 6:30 A.M., he began his exercises in the interior garden of the house. Fifteen minutes later he was in his pool, swimming for a quarter of an hour before taking breakfast shortly after 7:00 A.M. with his wife, Regina.

Barbie was planning other projects in the marine shipping business. For a time, he had business relations with such Lima shipping concerns as the Consortio Naviero Peruana and North Suite, hoping to put together a shipping group that would operate in a parallel manner to the Grupo Andino, the Common Market of the Andes. But when the project failed to materialize he turned to his old friend, ex-Nazi Friedrich Schwend. Altmann's home was only a short distance from the fence-enclosed chicken farm operated by Schwend and used as a cover for a range of illegal activities. A career swindler in the Third Reich, Schwend had developed his contacts in Peru with the police, Peruvian intelligence and the criminal underworld. His main business was illegal currency exchanges, but Schwend reportedly worked closely with the police denouncing his clients after changing their Peruvian *soles* into dollars. For an additional payment, he then arranged to have the charges dropped by the police.

Altmann-Barbie and Schwend shared the same political orientation; both were unreconstructed Nazis. Shortly before his arrival in Lima, Altmann had written Schwend about the military coup of August 21 that had put General Hugo Banzer Suarez into power. "The new government is anti-communist. Those people in Bonn and Berlin should follow the example of Bolivia to know how to deal with the reds," Barbie wrote. "The only way to talk to them is with a machine gun. It's a language they never fail to understand."

Schwend was a key figure in the Nazi network of the Southern Cone. In June 1973 Peruvian police raided his home while searching for evidence in a murder case and found documents on postwar Nazi activities in a concealed basement storeroom. Altmann had worked with Schwend on arms deals as early as the mid-1960s, when the two men sold weapons to Peruvian leftist groups before informing on them to the Peruvian secret police. They also collaborated in freelance intelligence work, keeping exiled Bolivian leader Victor Paz Estenssoro under surveillance in Lima for the security apparatus of the new president, General Barrientos.

Barbie and Schwend allegedly were partners in various currency swindles. In September 1972, after an investigation by Judge Luis Carnero Checa, Altmann-Barbie was officially charged with violating Peruvian currency exchange laws in collaboration with Schwend. The former Nazi was also charged with tax evasion by the Peruvian judge, who subsequently moved for Altmann-Barbie's extradition to Peru from Bolivia, a demand that was ultimately turned down.

Ω

After almost thirty years of secrecy and two decades of life under an alias in South America, Altmann's past suddenly came to public attention. On January 19, 1972, the Paris newspaper *l'Aurore* ran an article and a set of photographs of Klaus Barbie, war criminal, alongside those of Klaus Altmann, Bolivian businessman. The headline was unequivocal: "Former Nazi Klaus Barbie Has Just Taken Refuge in Peru After a Long Stay in Bolivia — Is France Going to Demand Him?"

The French newspaper revelation reached Lima on January 20, 1972. The next day Altmann himself denied he was Barbie. "My legitimate name is Klaus Altmann Hansen," he told a reporter for Agence France Presse. "I have never changed my name and the only thing I can say is that I was a member of the German Army and held the rank of lieutenant in an assault commando. I am not that ex-Gestapo chief in Lyon. I am a former soldier and nothing more. Now I am a manager for Transmaritima Boliviana. The important thing for me is peace for me and my children."

Under questioning by local authorities, Altmann and Schwend denied that Altmann and Barbie were one and the same. Schwend, who had given Altmann shelter within his *rancho*, stated that Altmann could not be Barbie because he, Schwend, knew where the real Barbie was. "We were prisoners of war together and I'm sure he's in Egypt. The last time I heard from him was seven years ago, when he sent me a card. He's not the Altmann who's in Lima.

There's been a mistake."

From France came a steady stream of accusations, together with documentation provided by Beate Klarsfeld, the Nazi hunter who had tracked Altmann-Barbie to Lima. West German authorities were also categorically stating that Altmann was Barbie. "We have numerous reasons to believe it is him," said a prosecutor in Munich. An anthropologist at a Munich university, who had made a scientific comparison of photos of Altmann and Barbie, added: "If he is not Barbie, he is his brother. But we know that Barbie has no brother."

On January 24 Altmann was interrogated for several hours at the Peruvian Ministry of the Interior, where he again denied any connection with Barbie. Altmann immediately hired a bodyguard and, faced with the possibility of an extradition request from France, stopped the next day at the Bolivian embassy in Lima to assure himself a clear line of retreat.

Altmann knew almost nothing about the woman who was relentlessly pursuing him. But Beate Klarsfeld had not disguised her intention; she had come to Lima for an open confrontation with Barbie. Beate Klarsfeld landed at the Jorge Chavez Airport late on the evening of January 28 and the following day gave interviews to every newspaper in the city. By then, however, Altmann was driving east at the wheel of his Volkswagen, accompanied by two of Schwend's bodyguards. At noon he crossed the Rio Desaquadero back into Bolivian territory and was taken into custody by police authorities. He was home, where he had strong allies, but for the first time since Allied troops had marched into Lyon in 1944, Klaus Barbie knew that he faced a fight for his life.

The image of the Nazi hunter has been shaped in the public consciousness by the Vienna-based Simon Wiesenthal, an aging survivor of the death camps obsessed with his biblical pursuit of justice and vengeance. But the woman who had tracked Altmann to La Paz was cast in an entirely different mold. A German Protestant whose father had served in the Wehrmacht, Beate Klarsfeld had, in her twenties, decided that her generation shared the collective guilt for the Holocaust. She assumed the mission of atoning for the sins of her elders by bringing those most responsible to justice.

Beate Klarsfeld was strongly influenced in this resolve by her husband, Serge, who she met in Paris in 1960. As a child Serge, who is Jewish, had huddled behind a false wall in the Nice apartment of his family as his father, Arno, was dragged away by the Gestapo and sent to his death at Auschwitz. Today Beate credits Serge with having sharpened her consciousness of the moral burden she and other Germans bear. The couple has become one of the most formidable teams involved in the research of the Nazi deportation and murder of Jews in France and the prosecution of those responsible.

Beate Klarsfeld first attained public recognition through a symbolically violent act: In 1968 she publicly slapped the face of Kurt-Georg Kiesinger, the West German chancellor, shouting, "Nazi! Nazi!" Kiesinger had held a top propaganda post in Hitler's foreign ministry. Later, in the early 1970s, the Klarsfelds launched an effort to close a loophole in a 1954 French-German treaty which had prevented Nazis who had committed war crimes in France from being judged for their crimes. In connection with this effort, the Klarsfelds attempted to kidnap Kurt Lischka, a former SS Sturmbannführer with the Paris SD who had played a major role in the deportation of French Jews.

The Klarsfelds were the most vocal supporters of a new judicial treaty ratified by the West German parliament in 1975, which allowed for the prosecution in German courts of Lischka and several other former Nazis who had committed war crimes in occupied France. In 1980 Lischka was convicted by a Cologne court and received a ten-year sentence; Ernst Heinrichsohn and Herbert Hagen, who also ordered and administered deportations, received six- and twelve-year sentences in that same proceeding.

The Barbie case came to Beate's attention quite by chance. In July 1971, while she was doing research in the Contemporary Jewish Documentation Center in the old Marais section of Paris, someone pointed out a court action recently taken in Munich. A prosecutor in that city had dismissed a case brought against Barbie in 1960 by a German association of Nazi victims. Beate and Serge decided that the Barbie case, aside from whatever crimes he might have committed, was important because of its legal ramifications.

The Munich prosecutor had dropped the case, in part because he felt there was no evidence that Barbie was aware of what awaited the Jews he was deporting from France. The Klarsfelds felt this reasoning was patently false, and that it set a dangerous precedent. "We were afraid at the time, because it was just before the ratification of the treaty," said Beate Klarsfeld as she sat behind her desk in offices she shares with her husband on the Rue de la Boétie in Paris. "Once the treaty was signed and the German courts took responsibility for German Nazi criminals like Barbie, Lischka, Hagen and Heinrichsohn, who were tried in absentia by French courts, it could have become a decision, a precedent for the other trials that would have opened."

Beate launched a press campaign, beginning in Lyon, where the newspaper *Le Progrès* headlined the story: "German Prosecutor Drops Charges Against Klaus Barbie, Chief of Lyon Gestapo and Torturer of Jean Moulin." The national wire service Agence France Presse and the Paris daily *Le Monde* picked up the story, providing French public support of Klarsfeld when she went to Munich that September with a Lyon delegation to press for the reopening of the Barbie case. Beate was armed with information provided her by the former UGIF official who recalled hearing the story of Barbie's statement: "Shot or deported, there's no difference."

In Munich, Public Prosecutor Manfred Ludolph, under pressure, agreed to reopen the case if Klarsfeld could provide a first-hand witness to Barbie's alleged statement. When she located former Lyon UGIF official Raymond Geissmann and brought his affidavit to Munich on October 1, Ludolph immediately reinstated the charges concerning Barbie's alleged role in the deportation of Jews from France to the East.

Ludolph also provided Klarsfeld with her first lead as to the whereabouts of Klaus Barbie. He handed her two photographs of the Nazi. One dated from the war era, while the other showed a similar looking man, though much older, seated at a conference table with a group of businessmen. The group photograph, Ludolph told her, had been taken in La Paz, Bolivia, in 1968.

Ω

In pursuit of Barbie, Beate Klarsfeld arrived in La Paz on January 30, 1972, but not without some anxiety. "You know," says Klarsfeld, today a handsome woman in her mid-forties who speaks softly but with an underlying tone of firmness, "I arrived there all alone. I didn't know anyone. Not a single soul. The journalists all came around, attracted by the news, the sensation, but at night I was totally alone." Despite this she had little fear of being attacked by supporters of Barbie. "At that point I was already well enough known publicly, so that if Barbie got someone to kill me, he himself would have problems, since it would have been clear that he organized it."

With her Klarsfeld carried the incontrovertible evidence that Klaus Altmann was in fact Klaus Barbie. A Munich anthropologist had, on the request of prosecutor Ludolph, confirmed his identity through an anthropometric study. One telling feature was the unusual shape of his ears. Klarsfeld had also brought with her documentary evidence of Altmann-Barbie's crimes, particularly the deportation of the children of Izieu and the death of Jean Moulin.

"In the newspapers there," she recalls about her Bolivian trip, "his name was already written as 'Altmann-Barbie.'" She had successfully accomplished part of her mission: to inform the Bolivian public of Barbie's true identity and to recruit the assistance of the mass media. "There were certainly services that knew Altmann was Barbie ," she says, "but the average person didn't know anything about him."

But she found official resistance to her revelations about Barbie. Beate obtained an interview with a Bolivian immigration minister who warned her she could have problems if she continued to make public statements about Altmann-Barbie. The threat was clarified soon after when a Bolivian secret police officer told her she could be expelled from the country if she kept up her activities. Klarsfeld was not surprised at the threat, but she obtained one significant official result before she was actually forced out of Bolivia on February 3: The French ambassador in Bolivia requested the extradition of Altmann-Barbie.

La cazadora de nazis, the Nazi hunter, had left Bolivia, but for the first time in over twenty years Barbie was alarmed about his future. His cover had been destroyed and he now feared becoming the target of a revenge assassination or of an Eichmann-style kidnapping. For his safety, Altmann-Barbie arranged for his own arrest at the beginning of February 1972, and was incarcerated in the Panoptico prison on the Plaza San Pedro.

He was jailed on an old charge, predating even his involvement in Transmaritima. In the early 1960s Altmann had run an export business, Empresa Madereira Santa Rosa, which mainly handled wood shipments. He had agreed to ship 30 tons of sugar for a national industry called the Corporacion Boliviano de Fomenta and was paid in advance. But instead of performing as promised, Altmann sold the sugar at below-market prices and kept the proceeds. The 55,000-peso debt was a convenient pretext that provided Barbie with the asylum of San Pedro prison until February 12, when the threat had momentarily subsided. Altmann-Barbie paid his debt and was released. It is ironic that the same ploy which protected him in 1972 facilitated his expulsion and arrest by the French in 1983.

Twelve days later, an undaunted Beate Klarsfeld arrived back in La Paz, determined to press the Bolivian and French governments by keeping Altmann-Barbie's name in the public eye. This time she brought along someone whose presence in La Paz was in itself an indictment against Barbie: one of his most abused personal victims, Itta Halaunbrenner, then 68. Together, Beate and Itta chained themselves to benches on the Prado in front of Altmann-Barbie's office, and Mrs. Halaunbrenner later filed suit against Barbie in the Bolivian court system for the murder of her husband and children. Again, Klarsfeld was ejected from Bolivia, this time more forcefully, but as she was escorted onto a plane at El Alto, she knew that she had launched a process that would deny Altmann peace of mind for the rest of his life. "I did it because it had to be done," she says now. "I was driven by the inaction of others. Something was needed to set it in motion."

Meanwhile a diplomatic farce had begun between French President George Pompidou and Bolivian leader Banzer. Their falsely cordial exchanges of letters yielded only the strong suggestion that Banzer would not consider allowing Altmann to be returned to France.

On February 11, Pompidou wrote to Banzer, "Time erases many things, but not all. Also, the French people cannot accept, lest the idea of justice be tarnished, that crimes and sacrifices be forgotten indifferently. I do not doubt your noble country, and I am confident in a rapid decision by the Bolivian government which, in spite of the tricks employed by a vile man, will allow justice to exercise its rights."

Banzer responded on February 24: "You are right not to doubt the nobility of my country, whose history shows a clear moral tradition. My government, above all, is trying to keep high the reputation of respect for the laws and procedures that inspire and direct out legal system. Based on these concepts I can assure you, *Monsieur le Président*, that Bolivian magistrates, called by the law to look into this matter, will pronouce the last and just word." The truth hidden within this veiled rebuff was amplified by Banzer's secretary. "There is no reason to move to extradite Klaus Altmann," the functionary told reporters.

Ω

By July 1972, in the middle of the Bolivian winter, Barbie was again seen freely strolling the streets of La Paz. But now he wore dark glasses and was accompanied by an armed plainclothes policeman. But the former Nazi's tranquility was disturbed once again that year when, at 11:30 A.M. on July 17, he was accosted by two men accompanied by a photographer who presented themselves as journalists. One was a writer from the French weekly *Paris Match*, but the other was former Resistance leader René Hardy, whom Barbie had accused as the betrayer of Jean Moulin in a lengthy interview that had appeared that spring in a Parisian daily. Barbie, with a Bolivian soldier at his side, appeared not to recognize Hardy. He agreed to an interview later that day at his office, but when Hardy arrived at 3:00 P.M. he found his way blocked by agents of the Bolivian police. Hardy returned to Paris without the confrontation that he had hoped for.

French hopes were raised when Barbie was again jailed by the Bolivians, on March 2, 1973. Earlier that day, Barbie had been called before the Superior Court of La Paz, which wanted to establish his true identity. The life history he detailed was remarkably similar to that of Klaus Barbie; he even granted that at one point he had used the name Klaus Barbie, but he coyly avoided ever admitting that he *was* Klaus Barbie. It was a defense based on a palpable fiction:

Question: Are you the person who under the name of Klaus Altmann or Klaus Barbie was the chief of the SS in Lyon and who is also the same person who has been judged by the Military Tribune of Lyon?

Answer: That's a difficult question to answer...because I am not aware of the Lyon trial. I was never asked or called, nor had any news. I admit having used this name during the war, as well as various others, but I can't answer the last question.

Question: To what do you attribute the extraordinary similarity in your personal description, in your dates of identity, in the names of your family members, in the dates of birth and many other dates, between two persons called Altmann and Barbie?

Answer: These points which you have just made have appeared in numerous publications, and for me it is just a matter of pure coincidence, because you have, for example, I don't know how many Klauses—it's a very common name—and it's a nice trap for me.

Despite his evasive answers, Altmann-Barbie found himself once more behind the bars of the San Pedro prison, awaiting the final determination of the Bolivian Supreme Court on the French extradition request. For the next 241 days, he stayed in the gilded cage of San Pedro, where he could receive daily visits from his wife and friends and watch television in the carpeted cells of his wealthy convict neighbors. On October 29, 1973, after almost eight months of confinement, Barbie was released, telling reporters: "I feel very happy. I have confidence in Bolivian justice."

His freedom was only provisional, but Barbie's faith in Bolivian justice was not misplaced. He spent a few days in the German Clinic of La Paz for treatment of a mild cardiac condition, then moved his residence to the more temperate climate of Cocha-bamba, 235 miles to the southeast. During this time, the Supreme Court was in deliberation. The decision came on December 11, 1973: Klaus Altmann, a naturalized Bolivian citizen, could not be extradited. No treaty existed between France and Bolivia providing for such an action. Besides, said the court, the statute of limitations had ruled out prosecution for any crimes Altmann-Barbie might have committed during the war.

It was a wonderful Christmas present, Barbie told reporters who asked his reaction. Unmasked and cornered, the 60-year-old former Nazi's influence had served him well. Though he would maintain bodyguards from then on, Barbie could resume his life as the discreet manipulator and friend of dictators, secure in his Bolivian redoubt.

XI

THE ADVISOR

W HEN KLAUS ALTMANN WAS SIGHTED IN ASUNCION, Paraguay, late in 1973, it was erroneously concluded in both Paris and La Paz that the Nazi had fled Bolivia after his unmasking as Klaus Barbie. But as he accurately told a reporter in Asuncion, he had gone to Paraguay only for a few days of business. By early 1974, Barbie was firmly settled in Cochabamba, Bolivia. "At no time have I left this country," he told a reporter, claiming that any contrary statements were the work of an "international conspiracy."

Now that his true identity had been revealed, Altmann-Barbie feared that he would become the victim of an assassination plot or a carefully planned kidnapping. His uneasy state of mind was reflected in the precautions he took in arranging an interview with the Cochabamba correspondent for the La Paz daily *Hoy*.

Journalist Freddy Espinoza recalls that Barbie refused to receive him at home, instead making an appointment to meet Espinoza in a deserted garage on a downtown street. "I went into the garage and I saw nothing," Espinoza relates. "Then the door shut behind me and I was in total darkness. When the light came on Altmann was standing there, behind the door." The startled journalist asked Barbie to explain the melodramatic introduction, and was told: "I am being pursued by an international group of communists."

Barbie-Altmann's concerns were not entirely unwarranted, if misdirected. In April 1974 someone did come to La Paz with the intention of assassinating him, but it was not part of a political plot. It was a killing planned in retribution for the Jewish lives Barbie had taken. Michel Goldberg, a Frenchman working for a U. S. corporation in Caracas, Venezuela, had decided to execute Barbie. Goldberg's motive was simple: he wanted revenge. His father, Joseph Goldberg, had been arrested by Barbie's Gestapo in February 1943 in the raid on the Lyon UGIF and deported to Auschwitz, where he was murdered. When Goldberg learned that Barbie's extradition had been blocked by the Bolivian Supreme Court, he decided he would personally deliver justice to Barbie.

At a cafe table on the Boulevard de Montparnasse in Paris, Goldberg recalled his thoughts at the time. "If there's no other way of getting the son of a bitch, I will," Goldberg, a trim man in his mid-forties, explained. "It was a way out of the problems that Barbie and the likes of him had created for me. Killing him or someone like him was the only way out." Goldberg made a preliminary trip to La Paz in the beginning of 1974 and returned in April, equipped with two .38 caliber handguns, intending to carry out the deed.

He located Barbie in La Paz through a North African Jew who had lived there for many years. In La Paz, Goldberg presented himself as a journalist and one morning shook Barbie's hand in the Club La Paz cafe. They sat down to talk. Barbie, Goldberg says, struck him as "a well-adjusted European in South America," with the air of an "old man with financial problems, basically in retirement. La Paz was his Miami Beach."

Goldberg engaged Barbie in journalistic probing and at one point asked the former Nazi about the arrest and deportation of the Izieu orphans. "That wasn't me," Barbie told him. "It was Eichmann. I was responsible for the struggle against the Resistance—in other words, against communism. The anti-Jewish struggle was the work of special commandos who hardly saluted me on arrival and departure."

When the subject of Jean Moulin arose, Barbie bragged: "By arresting Jean Moulin, I changed the course of history. Jean Moulin, de Gaulle's man in France, was so intelligent that had he lived it would have been he and not de Gaulle who would have presided over the destiny of France after our departure. France would probably have become communist."

A few days later, Goldberg had decided upon his execution plan. Wearing a poncho to conceal the snub-nosed revolver in his hand, he positioned himself outside the entrace to the Daiquiri, a La Paz restaurant that Barbie frequented at lunchtime. On the Prado bench, Goldberg saw Barbie approach with another man, and the pair stopped to chat directly in front of Goldberg. His grip tightened on the revolver, but Goldberg found himself unable to squeeze the trigger.

It was not the legal consequences that held him back, Goldberg says today. Nor was it the fear of being murdered afterwards. It came, he states, from a realization that killing Barbie would be to condone the very methods Barbie had used. Goldberg later wrote, "What does a quick death mean to a purveyor of slow death? What is death to a man who has worn the uniform with skull and crossbones? No, justice will never be done." Goldberg concluded that a better punishment for Barbie was the "eternal flicker of anxiety...living always to look over one's shoulder."

Nearly a decade later, in Paris, Goldberg explains that it was within himself that he found reasons not to kill Barbie. "Elie Wiesel once wrote that every murder is a suicide and every suicide is a murder. I pondered that phrase in La Paz."

Ω

Because of the threat of such revenge-seekers, Barbie and the Bolivian government took extra precautions to ensure that the ex-Nazi did not present a vulnerable target. "From the time of the Banzer government on," says a La Paz German, "he was never alone in the street. There were always people from the *policia* with him." Gaston Velasco is one who remembers how closely Barbie was guarded by Bolivian officialdom. One day a friend of Velasco's accosted Barbie on the street in La Paz over a long-standing debt. "It appeared that Barbie was walking alone, but as soon as this man took him by the lapels, three men appeared and grabbed him," Velasco relates. In addition to police protection, Barbie hired Alvaro de Castro as his personal bodyguard and aide.

Cochabamba proved to be an even safer sanctuary for Barbie than La Paz. He quickly established close relations with the army's Seventh Division and with the Departamento de Orden Politico, which was attached to the division. Little happened in this town of less than 150,000 inhabitants that the DOP was not aware of, and one of the agency's concerns soon became the security of the resident Nazi. "The DOP agents knew Altmann was in Cochabamba," says an informant. "He was intimately connected with them as an advisor."

Cochabamba, 135 miles southeast of La Paz over the Eastern Cordillera of the Andes, offers a dramatic change from the rarified air and cold nights of the altiplano capital. The difference is not only physical, in the distinctly Spanish colonial architecture and palm trees that replace high rise banks and apartment buildings, but is also found in its much slower pace. La Paz is a busy political and business capital, while Cochabamba, sprawled lazily beneath low, reddish-brown hills and spilling out into adjacent high-plains valleys, is a provincial market town that rivals La Paz only in its production of aggressive political climbers.

In many ways, Cochabamba was a more favorable base of operations for Barbie. It was far from the spotlight of international reporting and distant from the political dangers of La Paz, where allegiances shifted rapidly. Yet Cochabamba was only a 40-minute flight from the capital; Barbie still had convenient access to the Palacio Quemado and the Ministry of the Interior. From Cochabamba one could also connect with flights to Paraguay, Brazil and Argentina via Santa Cruz, some 200 miles further east. Cochabamba was also preferable from the standpoint of health. The altitude of La Paz had placed an undue strain on Barbie's heart, requiring a brief hospitalization after his release from the San Pedro prison in October 1973.

Good relations with the Seventh Division were essential for Barbie. The authority of the military commander of a Bolivian provincial garrison—and Cochabamba's was the largest in the nation—was unchallengeable on a local level. It was equally important for Barbie to cultivate his relations with the Bolivian intelligence services, which included the army's Segundo Seccion and the DOP. If he were to continue receiving protection from the Banzer regime against his enemies, foreign and domestic, Barbie would have to continually prove his usefulness.

Barbie made connections in Cochabamba with a number of right-wing groups, in particular with the Legion Boliviana Social Nacionalista, a paramilitary formation that served as a lower-level instrument of political control for the Banzer government. The Legion included people who were also members of the Falange Socialista Boliviana, the group that had so inspired Barbie upon his arrival in Bolivia. The revelation by Klarsfield that he was Klaus Barbie, ex-Nazi and hunted war criminal, did not damage his status. Instead it seemed to heighten Altmann's prestige in this extremist milieu.

During his first year in Cochabamba, Barbie was not deeply involved in advising the Banzer regime on internal security matters. Drawing upon his Nazi contacts throughout the Southern Cone, he first set about establishing an external intelligence network. The trip to Paraguay, where Rudel was based, was part of Barbie's strategy to reconstruct his power base in Bolivia. He could also call upon several other Nazi expatriates: Walter Rauff, a former SS officer responsible for the use of mobile gas chambers to kill Jews, was living in Chile. Schwend was in jail in Peru on fraud charges, but Barbie had other contacts in that country to call upon in his continual search for useable intelligence information.

By 1975 Barbie was collecting and transmitting information on communist and left-wing activities throughout the region to the Bolivian Ministry of the Interior, whose intelligence service was intimately linked to the Segundo Seccion of the army. "His role at that point was to provide information on the movements of the communists in surrounding countries," says a former Banzer official, who adds that Barbie received much of his information through ODESSA, a reference to a worldwide organization of former Nazis.

Another party in La Paz, the American CIA, was involved in a similar quest for information, but American officials deny that the CIA worked with Barbie after he was dropped by the Counter Intelligence Corps. Allan Ryan's Justice Department report categorically denies that Barbie worked for the CIA in South America. The report is probably accurate in that Barbie never met or spoke with the CIA, but some observers in La Paz believe that the CIA connection was made indirectly through the Bolivian government.

American journalist Peter McFarren, now a correspondent for the Associated Press in La Paz, has been following Altmann-Barbie's activities for years. McFarren interviewed a former high official in the Ministry of the Interior who reportedly served as a CIA conduit for information received from Barbie. "It was a high functionary of the Bolivian Interior Ministry," says McFarren. "Barbie would meet with this guy on a regular basis, giving him information, particularly on leftist and communist activities, not just in Bolivia, but in the whole Southern Cone. It was key information in terms of trying to control Southern Cone leftists and covered activities in Brazil, Argentina, Paraguay, Chile, Peru, including information links in Germany and Austria. Barbie was not paid for it; he volunteered the information. Barbie was receiving money from abroad from the ODESSA-type network of ex-Nazis.

"This information was given to the Ministry of the Interior, and passed on to a CIA contact at the American embassy," McFarren adds. "He gave them regular reports on what Barbie was feeding them. The embassy then told the Interior official that they checked out the information and that it was accurate. They wanted to have more of it. They knew the source was Barbie. He's absolutely certain of that."

Ω

Serge Klarsfeld has produced additional information that Barbie may then have had some relation with the CIA. Following Barbie's return to France in 1983, Klarsfeld released copies of a document from the files of the Direction de la Sécurité Militaire, an intelligence division of the French Ministry of Defense. The 1963 memo concerned the disposition of several leading SS figures in Lyon during the war. It explained that Barbie was in La Paz, adding that he had "a cover occupation in the service of the American and German intelligence services," expressly mentioning the CIA and the Bundesnachrichtendienst, the West German intelligence agency.

American Justice Department investigator Allan Ryan, however, rejects this theory. He examined CIA files and concludes that, "at no time from the end of World War II to the present time has the Central Intelligence Agency had any relationship with Klaus Barbie." Further, Ryan states that "there is no indication that Barbie ever reported to the CIA, was employed or paid by that agency, or was notified, directly or indirectly, of matters that the CIA wished to gather information on. Interviews of CIA officials were consistenct with this fact." He adds that a 1965 CIA internal memorandum based on a review of files stated that Barbie had been used by the CIC until 1951 and that there was "no current operational interest in subject."

There was, however, a proposal by U.S. Army intelligence in 1965 to "reactivate" Barbie as an agent in Bolivia. The Army had sought the names of potential agents for South American operations from personnel of the Office of the Assistant Chief of Staff for Intelligence. Someone in that agency worked in the CIC with Barbie in Germany and suggested the ex-Nazi might be used. The Army contacted the CIA to request information and also asked a military attaché at the La Paz embassy to "discreetly attempt" to determine Altmann's status. A report came back that he was operating a "carpenter shop" or "lumber yard." The proposal stalled until 1967, when the Army intelligence branch sent another request for information to the CIA prior to "re-establishing contact with subject for purposes of an assessment of his present capabilities."

On April 5, 1967, CIA and Army personnel held a meeting to discuss the matter. Ryan's report states that a resulting CIA memo "indicates that they discouraged the Army's interest in reactivating Barbie." Adds Ryan: "According to the memo, the CIA respresentatives told the Army delegation that the allegations of war crimes against Barbie required serious consideration in light of the fact that he was still being sought by German authorities, since exposure of CIC's role in evacuating Barbie would have serious consequences, especially if there was current use of Barbie." Ryan goes on to state that the CIA advised the Army it would have to demonstrate that Barbie could provide "unique information of significant importance under secure operational conditions" before it would approve reactivation. In April 1968 the Army sent a letter to the CIA, saying that the proposal to re-hire Barbie as an agent had been "terminated."

Ryan also contradicts McFarren's description of the relationship between Barbie, the Bolivian Ministry of the Interior and the U.S. embassy contact. The Justice Department investigator reports that he spoke with the Bolivian official and was told that although information supplied by Barbie did go to an embassy official, "the information was unsolicited and... the U.S. government representative did not relay any information or desires through the Bolivian official intended for Barbie."

Thus, concludes Ryan, "this incident does not demonstrate a relationship between Barbie and the United States government."

Ω

But Barbie did maintain a close relationship with the Bolivian government. During the first years of the Banzer regime, which began in 1971, the Bolivian security forces initiated a concerted campaign to wipe out the last traces of the leftist revolutionary movement that had begun in the 1960s with the Che Guevera insurgency. His guerrilla force had been whittled down to a handful of men by the time he was killed on October 9, 1967 by forces of the Barrientos government working in conjunction with the CIA and anti-Castro Cuban exiles.

After Guevera was killed, the Bolivian revolutionary impulse reappeared in the form of the Ejercito de Liberacion Nacional, the National Liberation Army. The ELN's ranks were made up mainly of young, radicalized Christian Democrats, highly educated but inexperienced revolutionaries who were massacred by the Bolivian Army under the Ovando government within months of their appearance in 1970.

When Banzer seized power he began to repress the left-wing student, political and labor groups that had been allowed to flourish during the regime of the exiled General Juan Jose Torres, who held power from 1969 to 1971. "Urban guerrillas were still raging," stated Eudoro Galindo, the executive head of Banzer's current political party, Accion Democratico Nacional, when interviewed at

ADN headquarters in La Paz. Galindo asserts that Banzer was acting to prevent the "Vietnamization of Latin America." He acknowledges that the Banzer government pursued leftist groups, but believes it was necessary. "Bolivian society had all rights to defend itself. The war was fought on the terms the guerrillas proposed—dirty war."

The Banzer coup was solidly backed by the wealthy Bolivian German colony which numbers only about 4,000 but which controls about thirty percent of the nation's private industry. The German magazine *Stern* reported that the Banzer putsch of August 21, 1971, had been financed largely by Bolivian Germans.

Though spokesman Galindo denies that Altmann ever held any formal commission in the Banzer government, he concedes that the ex-Nazi had been active in an informal way. "Altmann approached Banzer's security organizations at different times and provided some types of information," he says. "It was more an informal type of thing. But that he was paid, or was a regular functionary, I insist categorically that there wasn't any such thing."

It was after 1975, most Bolivian sources say, that Altmann-Barbie undertook an active role in the campaign of political repression, advising the Banzer security services in a broad range of matters. "He was supposed to be a counselor in military matters and arms buying," says a La Paz woman with numerous left contacts. "He's identified with training torture groups. Torture in Bolivia only started to get efficient during the Banzer period. People were startled at the sophistication of the torture used on political prisoners."

Gustavo Sanchez, the current Bolivian subminister of interior, argues that Altmann-Barbie introduced foreign elements into the Bolivian security organizations, though he admits there are no witnesses to Barbie's participation in torture sessions. Still he believes Barbie was involved. "No," Sanchez stated when interviewed in his ministry office, "just as there are no witnesses to the murder of Moulin. Barbie didn't take part personally, just as he didn't use weapons himself against the prisoners in Lyon—he just ordered. So we can't expect to find documents or photographs showing Barbie executing Bolivians.

"It was Barbie who directed the repression in this country, against the people," he insists. "He won't admit it, but he was the leader, the brains. In Bolivia we never had as great a tradition of cruelty with prisoners. We didn't have a mentality as sick and as corrupt as Altmann's. We Bolivians settled our differences with bullets, but we didn't martyrize each other!"

Sanchez says that Barbie, along with Argentinian advisors, had a strong impact on the brutal methods of the now-deposed Garcia regime. Some believe he personally participated in executions and tortures. "Barbie has a very organized mind, as he showed us in the Second World War," says Sanchez. "He naturally used these methods, along with those who participated in the second part of the repression in the Garcia Meza coup, when there were trainers, teachers and active members of the Argentinian armed forces."

There is also evidence that during this period Barbie returned to his prior role as an arms merchant. "He handled all of Banzer's security needs—Smith and Wesson revolvers, bulletproof vests, mostly light stuff," one La Paz arms dealer told the *Miami Herald*. Barbie's arms deals reportedly included the purchase of 50,000 rounds of .38-caliber bullets and a quantity of Ingram submachine guns, a standard weapon used by criminals in the cocaine trade. In Europe, Barbie lined up Israeli-made Uzi and Galil submachine guns from West Germany.

Nazi hunter Simon Wiesenthal believes that Barbie's arms purchases on behalf of the Banzer regime went beyond the "light stuff." Wiesenthal charged in September 1980 that the semi-nationalized Austrian industrial concern Steyr-Daimler-Puch sold 100 Kuirassier tanks to Bolivia. Barbie, Wiesenthal says, took a leading role in this transaction. Steyr-Daimler-Puch has denied these charges, stating that it never had relations with the ex-Nazi.

"Austria has sold tanks to Bolivia," Wiesenthal added in a recent interview. "And the man who handled it was Barbie." Wiesenthal believes that Rudel, before his death in 1982, may have provided the contact for Barbie with European arms manufacturers. "Rudel was the representative of a number of German firms for heavy industry, and they were interested in exports," Wiesenthal adds. Barbie, he says, was in a position to help members of the Bolivian military make money on such arms transactions through kickbacks and other illegal practices. The military, Wiesenthal says, could be "sure that Barbie would keep silent, because his safety was in their hands."

Ω

Throughout the course of the Banzer regime, which was in power for seven years until July 1978, Barbie continued to cultivate his government connections as well as attend to his own private business interests in the Cochabamba and Santa Cruz regions. He returned to the wood export business, establishing a company in Santa Cruz that was managed by his son, Klaus Georg. Barbie also reputedly acted as the broker in one business deal on behalf of Banzer, involving the purchase of an interest in the Buenos Aires franchise for a major American soft drink manufacturer. According to La Paz sources, Barbie was a key figure in the sale to the pension fund of the Bolivian Army of what proved to be a useless sulphuric acid plant in the southern mining town of Potosi.

The Banzer regime had been particularly good to ex-Nazi Barbie. He was settled in a secure new home in the Calacala neighborhood of Cochabamba. His physical safety was guaranteed by the government, his business interests were multiplying, his political position was stronger than it had been before his identity had been revealed. Altmann—as he continued to call himself—demanded and expected to receive a certain amount of deference. He was Don Klaus, a man who could chat with local police officials in the Café Restaurant Continental over coffee, picking up the bill as befitted a man of some estate. He was, above all, respected.

But some in Cochabamba detested him for what he was and had done. "My voice is only hate," says Gustavo Stier, 82, an Austrian-born Jew who came to Bolivia after the 1938 Anschluss that merged his country with the Third Reich. "I have nothing to say in favor of him." Stier might have emigrated to the United States, but he was told that he would have to wait eight years for a visa. "I'm very grateful to Bolivia," says the neatly dressed old man whose thin white hair is carefully combed back. "If not for Bolivia I wouldn't be alive."

Stier has since traveled back to Europe, but has refused to set foot in either Austria or Germany. "I am one of the people who doesn't go there anymore, not to Vienna, not to Germany. They killed all my people—brother, sister, mother..." Tears showed beneath his white eyebrows as he explained. "I was never very religious, but I was building the synagogue in Bolivia, like a monument for my people. When I go in the synagogue, it is like the tomb of my people."

Each morning Stier remembers those who perished by picking a half-dozen miniature purple violets from his garden. The flowers lay wilted in the buttonhole of his jacket as he talked in a Cochabamba hotel coffee shop, casualties of the midday heat. But they would soon be replaced by fresh ones.

Stier had an encounter with Barbie in the Café Restaurant Continental on the Plaza Principal, where the police *prefectura* faces the cathedral across a square filled with flowers and palm trees. The Continental is Cochabamba's equivalent of the Confiteria Club de La Paz, but with white and pink semitropical stucco walls. A Pepsi advertisement covers an entire wall of the back dining room. Mornings, in the cafe's front room, customers eat *saltenas*, spicy filled pastries, and drink strong, muddy coffee beneath a rotating ceiling fan.

"Every morning I am in the cafe with friends," Stier says. "One day Altmann and his wife came in. I said to my friend, 'You know him?' My friend was afraid, and says, 'He can hear us.'

"'You are afraid of this assassin?' I asked. Altmann was sitting there and not facing me, but his wife heard all I was saying. A little later a lady, the wife of a doctor I know very well, came in. I was trembling when I showed him to her. This is the Lyon murderer!'

"He was sitting there, eating the morning *saltena*, without looking at me. When he put on his hat to go, he looked at me. My friends said, 'What are you doing? He can kill you!'"

The confrontation between the two came another day. Recalls Stier, "I was going to the post office with my friend, to pick up my mail. In front of the post office was Altmann. He was afraid to go in. He was sending his bodyguard in for the letters. I pointed across the street and told my friend, 'You know him?'"

Angered, Barbie crossed the street, shouting at Stier in German, *"Wissen Sie nicht, dass man nicht mit dem Finger auf einen Menschen zeigt?"* Don't you know enough not to point with your finger at people?

Stier replied, *"Aber auf so einen Bluthund wie Sie kann man zeigen!"*
But that is how one points at a bloodhound like you!

Barbie was furious. His bodyguard had now arrived, but he did
not understand German and was confused by the exchange.

"Ich könnte Ihnen ins Gesicht schlagen!" Barbie shouted. *I could slap
you in the face!*

Stier, enraged by the sight of the Nazi before him, reached deep
into his well of hatred. *"Sie geben keine Nackenschüsse mehr?"* *Aren't
you shooting people in the back of the neck anymore?*

Barbie stalked off. From that day on, he avoided Stier, looking
away whenever the old man walked past his table in the Continental. Stier still trembles with rage when he tells the story. "In the
Bible there is a very important sentence," he says. " 'May his name
be forgotten.' "

Ω

In Bolivian politics those who rise through the mechanism of
the *coup d'etat* fall in much the same way. In July 1978, Barbie's
friend and protector, Hugo Banzer, who had overthrown the prior
regime, found himself outmaneuvered by army General Juan Pereda. Banzer's grip on power had been weakening as he faced not
only insistent popular demand for democratization, but dissatisfac-
tion within the officer corps. Banzer called elections in June 1978,
but the results were discarded due to claims of widespread fraud.
The following month Pereda, supported by the Santa Cruz garrison
that had once been Banzer's, staged his coup.

The overthrow of Banzer ushered in a two-year period of great
instability in Bolivia, one that was to create a major opening for
Klaus Barbie, intelligence *asesor*. Pereda's administration was
shortlived; from the time he was deposed in November 1978 until
the summer of 1980, there were four Bolivian regimes and constant violence between the irreconcilable left and right wings. As
the crisis deepened in early 1980, attention shifted to the commander of the army, General Luis Garcia Meza. La Paz veterans of
Bolivian upheavals wondered when Garcia would exercise the
traditional option of the country's military commander in such
times.

The answer came at dawn, July 17, with an uprising in the
northern outpost of Trinidad; within hours the Cochabamba and

Santa Cruz garrisons of the Bolivian Army had thrown their support behind Garcia Meza. There was bloody opposition to the new regime for weeks, particularly in the mining towns where workers fought with bullets and dynamite, but Garcia Meza had taken the centers of force that first day, which meant he had taken Bolivia.

What was unique about the Garcia coup was that it had been carried out in large part by paramilitary commandos rather than by regular army units. In La Paz the paramilitaries, clad in civilian clothes, used 50 ambulances to transport their prisoners to the city stadium where they were held for days, except if they were removed to be shot. Paramilitaries also carried out the bloody assault on the La Paz offices of the labor headquarters of the Central Obrera Boliviana. By mid-afternoon on July 17 the Palacio Quemado, COB and the university had fallen; thousands were under arrest by the new regime.

In Santa Cruz, 350 miles southeast of La Paz, the takeover was virtually immediate, carried out with the support of conservative German business interests that dominated the city. When the shooting stopped in Santa Cruz, nine men dressed in camouflage fatigues assembled for a group photograph, machine guns nestled in their arms, bandoliers of bullets slung over their shoulders. "We took the picture just as a joke," explains Jacques Leclerc, one of those who appears in the photo, and who has now been jailed by the Bolivian government. They called themselves *Los Novios de la Muerte*, or the Fiances of Death, after a song of the Spanish Foreign Legion, and had become the masters of Santa Cruz.

Someone was missing from the group portrait taken that day in Santa Cruz. It was Altmann-Barbie, the man who had played a key role in linking up the group with the Garcia forces. Barbie preferred to remain in the background, secure in his new role as an *eminence grise* of the Garcia Meza regime. The Novios had first established ties with Klaus Barbie and the army's security section, headed by Colonel Luis Arce Gomez in 1979. Arce Gomez had been a major figure in Bolivian security since the days of Ovando; from 1978 onwards he was one of the chiefs in the army's intelligence branch. Arce formed an alliance with army commander General Luis Garcia Meza, and began to lay the groundwork for the 1980 coup.

Interior subminister Gustavo Sanchez confirms Barbie's connection with Arce Gomez and the creation of the paramilitary forces. "Barbie was a friend of Arce Gomez during the formation of the paramilitary groups," says Sanchez. "He was the one who organized them; he was the planner. Once Barbie was linked with Arce Gomez, the brain of this organization was no longer Arce Gomez, but Barbie."

It was logical that Arce should call upon Altmann-Barbie to coordinate his network of paramilitary commandos. Barbie had close links to the German colony in La Paz, which was providing financial support for the Garcia coup. He also knew the arrangement of political groups—left and right—in the Cochabamba-Santa Cruz region, and was already in regular contact with the La Paz intelligence community.

After the successful Garcia coup in 1980 Barbie stepped up his travels between Cochabamba, Santa Cruz and La Paz, overseeing the job of consolidating Garcia's power, collecting information, reporting back to Arce Gomez in La Paz. Barbie also took a hand in coordinating the political repression in the capital, where he had an office in the Ministry of the Interior. Says one European diplomat, "We have some rather precise accounts of his presence at Miraflores and other military headquarters." Catholic priests who went to see prisoners at the SES torture center on the Calle Hermanos Manchego in La Paz also reported seeing him there.

Barbie, the Novios and the new Garcia regime came together for the first time in early 1980 in Santa Cruz, a southeastern outpost of civilization tenuously linked to the rest of Bolivia as a fiefdom of the local military garrison. The cultural differences between La Paz and Cochabamba are exaggerated in Santa Cruz, where the raw strains of a postcolonial Spanish and Indian heritage have flowered in the tropical lowlands. In the late 1970s Santa Cruz was experiencing another of the economic surges that had made it the fastest growing component of the Bolivian economy. This expansion was no longer propelled by the U.S. development grants that had poured into the region in the 1960s. It was fueled by the coca plant that Bolivian peasants and miners had chewed for centuries to allay the pangs of hunger or ease the burden of labor. But now, when processed into cocaine paste, it could be sold at an astronomical price to the Colombian reprocessors, who controlled the distribution of refined cocaine powder as it moved north to the United States.

Barbie has also been accused of participating in this lucrative cocaine trade, not as a dealer but as the organizer of paramilitary groups originally created to protect the smuggling routes. There have been many allegations that the illegal cocaine traffic in Bolivia grew enormously during the Banzer regime. One European diplomat in La Paz believes that Barbie helped to organize control of the trade in the eastern region of Santa Cruz. "People in the east had the problem of protecting their investment, their business, the plantations, the landing strips," says this diplomat. "Barbie had the necessary experience."

The Novios, who were now working with Altmann-Barbie, helped train other paramilitary outfits for the 1980 coup by Garcia Meza. "One day," a former Novio told an Italian reporter, "we were visited by Klaus Altmann, advisor to the Ministry of the Interior. He told us, 'The time has come. We must bring down this government before Bolivia becomes a big Cuba. With other foreign comrades, we are forming a security corps.'

"We began to cover trade union demonstrations, identify our adversaries, follow and punish subversives. We worked well," he says. "We had a private prison for torture. 'We must kill all the communists,' Barbie told us. And our commander said, 'You can count on us. We're ready for anything.'"

Ω

But despite the efforts of Barbie and the paramilitaries, the Garcia Meza regime soon became unraveled as the result of widespread corruption and economic dislocation caused by government neglect. There was also outside pressure, particularly from America. In an attempt to curb the greatly increased cocaine traffic to the U.S., the American government, which had temporarily withdrawn its ambassador following the coup in 1980, put increased pressure on the Bolivian government.

Garcia Meza was ousted in the summer of 1981, and after two short-lived interim governments, Siles Zuazo took office in October 1982 pledging to move against Altmann-Barbie. But despite the obvious threat represented by the new left-liberal government,

Barbie doggedly stayed on in Bolivia, convinced that Siles, who had given citizenship to "Altmann" in 1957, would not deport him.

Another reason for his inertia was the illness of his wife, who was to die two months after Siles came to power. Expressing loyalty to another person, one of the few decent acts of Barbie's life, was to keep him in La Paz. It was the first time in decades that he did not scrupulously plan for his own survival.

Meanwhile, the Klarsfelds were setting in motion the diplomatic initiative that, after Barbie's arrest on January 25, 1983, by the new Bolivian government, resulted in his deportation to France to await trial for the torture and murder of thousands of Frenchmen.

THE ACCUSED

B ARBIE IS NOW ISOLATED IN A HIGH-SECURITY WING OF THE Saint-Joseph Prison in Lyon, located on the Quai Perrache over-looking the Rhône River, living in a two-cell suite linked by the corridor where he takes his exercise. He spends his days reading the local press and German newspapers and preparing his defense. The only visitors he is allowed are his lawyer, his daughter and the French court officials who are readying his prosecution. To prevent a suicide attempt he is observed around the clock, and each night his cot is shifted between the two cells he inhabits in order to make the calculations of any would-be assassin more difficult. It was for reasons of security that he was transferred from Montluc, the scene of his own crimes, to Saint-Joseph, a more modern facility.

Barbie stands accused of "crimes against humanity," a special category created by the International Military Tribunal at the end of World War II to deal with the unprecedented atrocities of the Third Reich. The bill of particulars issued against him in February 1983 after his forced return to France lists eight specific charges, all of which concern his acts of violence against civilians, particularly against the Jews of Lyon. These include the "liquidation of the Lyon committee of the Union Générale des Israélites de France" as the result of the February 9, 1943, Gestapo raid on UGIF offices in the Rue St. Catherine; the massacres of Jewish prisoners at Bron and Saint-Genis-Laval; the deportation to death camps of Jewish children arrested at Izieu in April 1944; the deportation of some 650 Jews and Resistance prisoners in a rail convoy sent from Lyon to German concentration camps in August 1944; the execution of 40 Jews in the period of 1943 to 1944; and various other arrests, tortures and killings.

Barbie will *not* be tried, however, for the tortures and executions he inflicted on members of the French Resistance during the occupation. Those crimes of war were dealt with by two military tribunals that heard his case after the war. Both military courts sentenced him to death *in absentia*, once on April 29, 1952, and again on November 25, 1954, but that ultimate penalty cannot be carried out. Under French law, no sentence can be executed if more than twenty years have elapsed since it was pronounced. The statute of limitations also prevents Barbie from being tried for any "ordinary" crimes he committed that were not judged in the immediate postwar era. Nor does Barbie risk execution if he is convicted of the crimes against humanity with which he now stands charged. The death penalty was abolished in France after the Socialist government of President François Mitterrand came to power in May 1981.

The case against Barbie is being prepared by the same Lyon magistrate who issued the arrest warrant served at the airport in Cayenne, French Guyana, on February 5, 1983. Judge Christian Riss of the Tribunal de Grande Instance, located in the Palais de Justice overlooking the Saône River in Lyon, is responsible for investigating the entire case in a procedure called *l'instruction*. He must interview Barbie and those witnesses who will testify against him when the actual trial begins, as well as research the documentary evidence in the case.

The *instruction* is carried out in secrecy. Only those directly involved—the judge, the accused, lawyers for the defendant and those for the civil parties who will press their own claims within the structure of the criminal proceeding—have access to the *dossier d'instruction*. Barbie himself, like any other defendant in a French criminal case, may not communicate directly with anyone but his counsel and members of his family. He regularly sees his lawyer, Jacques Vergès of Paris, and his daughter, Ute Regina Messner, who lives in the small mountain town of Kufstein in the Tyrol province of Austria.

Barbie's trial will take place in Lyon in the criminal chamber of the Cour d'Assizes, France's superior court, before a jury of twelve persons. It will be presided over by a panel of three magistrates, one of whom holds the title of "president." According to Barbie's attorney, the panel of judges exerts a "great moral authority" over the jury, but the vote of the jury will be final. Eight votes are required to obtain a conviction; the accused can be acquitted with only five votes in his favor. Both the defense and the prosecution will have the right to challenge jurors in the initial phase of the trial, much as in the U.S. system of jury selection.

Says Judge Riss: "He is a prisoner like all other prisoners." But Barbie is obviously no ordinary prisoner and his case no routine matter of jurisprudence. From the moment Barbie landed in France and was escorted into the military prison of Fort Montluc, his trial promised to be one of the most significant in postwar France, a country for which Barbie is a symbol not only of wartime oppression but of national shame.

Ω

The capture of the former Gestapo chief of Lyon initially seemed a matter of delayed justice. "Klaus Barbie Will Be Judged at Lyon for Memory," a Parisian daily wrote following his incarceration at Montluc. Many who had been tortured by Barbie have expressed their deep satisfaction at his arrest. "I felt a very strong emotion," recalls Raymond Aubrac. Lise Lesèvre adds, "I was very happy, of course, though it came rather late. It was a mixed feeling, obviously, a feeling of joy that was immediately offset by regret that it came so late."

The sentiments on a national level were similar. "In taking the decision to have Klaus Barbie arrested, the French government was not impelled by any spirit of vengeance," commented French Prime Minister Pierre Mauroy. "It had simply two concerns: to permit justice to be carried out and to be faithful to the memory of those hours of sorrow and struggle through which France saved her honor."

Gaston Defferre, who had met with Jean Moulin the morning the Resistance hero was arrested by Barbie forty years ago, and who was the interior minister of Socialist France at the time of Barbie's arrest, stated: "Barbie was condemned *in absentia*. It is proper now that he be judged in person and that the families of those he arrested and tortured be able to make their voices heard."

But following the personal and national exhilaration after Barbie's arrest, second thoughts surfaced. "Barbie: The Demons Exhumed," one newspaper headlined the week after. Another put it more candidly: "Behind Barbie, the Specter of the Traitor."

After sober contemplation, it was becoming apparent that an examination of Barbie's Gestapo career in Lyon would also resurrect the divisions that afflicted wartime France and uncover actions of some Frenchmen that the nation would prefer not to acknowledge. "At heart, the Barbie affair is like a family that finds a closet full of skeletons," said Philippe Viannay, a former member of the French Resistance and a prominent figure in French journalism. "Barbie is going to bring all that back up. His trial is going to resurrect the France of 1944."

Some warned that reopening the wounds of wartime France would be a destructive, fruitless exercise that would serve no one but the accused Nazi criminal. "What I hope is that my country will not tear itself apart one more time," says Simone Veil, a former Jewish deportee and today a prominent member of the European Parliament, president of its judicial commission. "To reopen this kind of old dossier today is to lose sight of the true target. We can count on Barbie to try to turn the debate and bring the dirty laundry of the French collaboration out of the closet. That would be the best way to help his defense."

Mme. Veil criticized the emphasis the French press had placed on the question of whether Barbie's testimony would finally resolve the mystery of who had betrayed Jean Moulin. That is not the point of his prosecution, Veil stressed. "What I hope, in fact, is that my country will learn, with respect for the memory of the dead, the political lesson of Nazism. If this trial allows us to analyze more deeply the Hitlerian phenomenon, then it will be very useful."

But the trial of Klaus Barbie may reveal less about Nazi Germany than it does about Vichy France, particularly if defense lawyer Jacques Vergès has his way. "The trial of Klaus Barbie, if it is ever held, will be like a mirror that I will hold up to French society to show it to itself as it is," says Vergès. "Not only today, but since the 1930s, the attitude of the French nation faced with Nazism—at once fascinated and repelled."

Ω

Jacques Vergès is not a man to shun controversy. During the turbulent years of the Algerian War, this blunt-spoken and incisive criminal defense attorney was the attorney for the FLN, the National Liberation Front that led the fight for Algerian Independence. As soon as he took the Barbie case in May 1983, Vergès made it clear that he would spare no effort, nor the sensibilities of other Frenchmen, to obtain the acquittal of his client, however improbable such a verdict might seem.

Barbie's first attorney had been Alain de la Servette, the president of the Lyon bar, who undertook the case in his capacity as a public defender—a traditional role in France, where local bar associations assure the defense of the indigent. But de la Servette came under pressure from such groups as the League Against Racism and Anti-Semitism (LICRA) and was threatened with death if he defended Barbie. When de la Servette was joined by another Lyon lawyer who was a Jesuit priest, the local Catholic authorities intervened. "The Bishop of Lyon violently criticized Father Boyer," says Vergès, "in a communiqué that in my opinion was a *communiqué de Tartuffe*, in which he said that as a lawyer Father Boyer was free, but that as a Jesuit who belonged to the Church he was compromising the Church." When Vergès entered the case de la Servette removed himself.

As Barbie's new attorney, Vergès immediately filed a motion with Judge Riss for the Nazi's release, a move that provoked general outrage and a demonstration at the gates of Barbie's prison. Vergès argued that Barbie's expulsion from Bolivia and subsequent arrest by French authorities in Cayenne, French Guyana, were irregular and illegal. Riss rejected this motion, as did a Lyon court of appeals, but Vergès has continued to appeal the decision, promising to carry it to the European Court of Human Rights in the Hague, Holland. Vergès alleges that Barbie's expulsion from Bolivia was actually a "disguised extradition" in which France played a directing role. He also alleges that the French government made a one-million franc payoff to Bolivian officials to bring about Barbie's expulsion.

It is unlikely that any legal argument, however persuasive, could bring a French court to grant Barbie freedom. In rejecting Vergès's request, Riss maintained that the expulsion and arrest of Barbie was entirely legal, and that Barbie's life would be endangered if he were released.

Defense attorney Vergès argues energetically that, as ironical as it seems, France must release a twice-condemned Nazi killer to maintain its own principles of judicial fairness. "For legal reasons Barbie should be a free man," says Vergès, who insists that the expulsion of Barbie from Bolivia involved a fraud. "The Bolivian government pretended that Barbie was no longer a Bolivian citizen, that he was never a Bolivian citizen, because he had obtained his nationality by fraud. However, this is false, because in 1974 there was a decree by the Supreme Court saying that Barbie or Altmann were the two names of the same person, and that person had acquired Bolivian citizenship. The Supreme Court had already refuted the argument Siles Zuazo later used."

The position of the French court is that the Bolivian legal status does not concern France since Barbie was arrested on French soil after this procedure—legal or otherwise—had taken place. But Vergès rejects this argument, claiming that because France was heavily involved in Bolivia's decision to expel Barbie—not at the border of his choice but to French territory—that the legality of the subsequent French arrest was tainted.

A compactly built man with jet black hair, a Mediterranean complexion and an incisively intellectual manner, Vergès has taken the offensive in a case that nevertheless seems destined for only one verdict. In his office on the Rue Notre Dame des Champs in the Montparnasse neighborhood of Paris, Vergès maintains that an aura of "political show-business" has surrounded *l'affair Barbie*. The French establishment, he insists, "wants to see an Eichmann Trial, Part II."

To his attorney, Barbie is thus the victim of France's need to exorcise the pain of the German occupation and to find a scapegoat for the shame of wartime collaboration. "They have painted Barbie as a monster to cover up the treason of French officials during World War II," Vergès maintains, even insisting that Barbie's crimes have been grossly distorted. "They have made an SS captain of 30, which was his age back them, the devil—the most visible symbol of the German occupation of France."

Across the city, seated in his office on the Rue de la Boétie a short walk from the Champs Elysées, Serge Klarsfeld expressed agreement with the proposition that Barbie has become a highly symbolic figure. The difference in their viewpoints is that Klarsfeld, one of Vergès's chief adversaries in the case, believes that Barbie deserves the distinction. "He is a prototype of the Gestapo agent," says Klarsfeld. "He is a symbol of the Gestapo officer corps. France was terrorized by the Gestapo, and in every region of France there was a Barbie. If Barbie is known, finally, it is due to the sum of the suffering that he inflicted upon Lyon.

"If you are going to pursue someone like Barbie as we did," Klarsfeld adds, "there has to be a reason." Barbie had to be found, Klarsfeld believes, to atone for the deaths of the children in the school at Izieu, and for the massacre of Jews at Bron and Saint-Genis-Laval. Both actions, he says, place Barbie in a distinct category, apart from most Gestapo officers assigned to France during the war.

Homes for Jewish children were raided only twice during the German occupation, he points out. One series of raids was carried out in 1944 by Alois Brunner, the SS Hauptsturmführer who was Eichmann's special envoy to France. Besides overseeing the infamous transit camp at Drancy, Brunner—whom Klarsfeld says is now living in Syria—scoured the country in search of Jews to deport to death camps in Eastern Europe. The other case of a Gestapo raid on a children's home is the one conducted at Izieu by Klaus Barbie.

"There are only two cases where the children were taken," says Klarsfeld. "It will be up to the trial to decide why in a certain number of cases the Gestapo did nothing, and why, in some cases, it acted. In my opinion, it has to do with the personality of those responsible. In other words, the most ruthless ones did it. In fact, the reason I undertook this search ten years ago was essentially for the children of Izieu."

Klarsfeld will be deeply involved in the Barbie trial, representing a number of the civil parties with claims against the accused Nazi. One of these is Itta Halaunbrenner; another is Simone Lagrange. The French judicial system provides for crime victims to enter their own complaints against the accused at the same time as the government prosecution. This is usually done to seek damages, but in the Barbie case the *parties civiles* will be there to assure that their evidence is presented. As a telling symbol, the Klarsfelds hope to locate relatives of the children taken from Izieu by Barbie's Einsatzkommando so that each of the youthful victims is represented at his trial.

"In the month of April 1944, Barbie had no one over his head to give him an order to arrest those children," Klarsfeld elaborates. "He was in charge of the Gestapo. There was no order from Paris. We have the records of the anti-Jewish section of the Gestapo. Paris didn't write to him, 'Kindly go arrest the children.' His free will came into play, and at that point he could have chosen to go take the children or he could have said, 'We've got other fish to fry, there's the Resistance, we're soldiers, we don't fight children.' But he chose to take the children."

Barbie made the same decision in ordering the Bron massacres, Klarsfeld believes. "There were only two massacres of Jews in France," he explains, "the one in Lyon and the one at Bourges, near Orléans, where 50 Jews were thrown alive down a well." In Bourges, the local Gestapo chief telephoned to the head of the Nazi Gestapo in Orléans, saying, 'We can't send any more Jews to Drancy. What should we do with them?' The reply was, "Liquidate them.'

"That didn't happen anywhere else in France—except in Lyon," explains Klarsfeld. "Obviously, it is a responsibility that has to do with the personality of the Gestapo of Lyon and the personality of Barbie. That is, if you can't transfer Jews, you liquidate them."

Defense attorney Vergès says he will wait until the trial opens to rebut the substantive charges against Barbie, but he has already laid out the general lines of his defense strategy. Referring back to the 1952 and 1954 trials in which Barbie was convicted *in absentia*, Vergès states that in those proceedings Barbie "became a generalization for crimes for which no one else could be found responsible." He adds: "Now they want to put together a case with acts that he was never accused of at the time."

The main government charge, Vergès explains, involves numerous acts directed against Jews, including their arrest, murder and deportation to the East through the Drancy transit camp. "Barbie's position," says Vergès, "is that he was responsible for action against the Resistance, but not for anti-Jewish questions. There was a subsection of the SS responsible for Jewish matters." According to documents, this subsection was led by Erich Bartelmus.

"Barbie says, 'You are right, I was the head of Section IV, and on the organizational chart Bartelmus was below me," Vergès continues. "But in reality, you are wrong. In reality, the Jewish question did not proceed in a hierarchical manner. It was directly controlled by Eichmann. And the orders were sent directly to Bartelmus from Eichmann."

This version of the operation of Lyon's Gestapo office will be contradicted by the testimony of victims such as Majerowicz, Halaunbrenner, Lagrange and other survivors. The prosecution will also present original SS documents bearing Barbie's name concerning the seizure of the children at Izieu and the raid on the UGIF office in the Rue St. Catherine. Some of these are telegrams that bear only the teletyped name of Obersturmführer Barbie, but others are letters personally signed by him, undoubtedly the most damaging evidence in the case. Vergès maintains, however, that these documents do not constitute proof that Barbie himself took a direct role. Barbie, he claims, merely signed these documents for other officials in their absence.

For Klarsfeld these documents are the most compelling evidence that Barbie had a direct hand in the persecution of the Lyonnais Jews. While it is not entirely certain that Barbie was actually at Izieu the day the children were arrested—there being only one eyewitness—the cable is conclusive proof of Barbie's involvement. "This document was read at Nuremberg," says Klarsfeld, "as part of the French accusation, in order to show what happened to the Jews in France."

As Barbie's defense attorney, Vergès will attempt to show that the crimes of which Barbie is accused are no worse than those committed on innumerable occasions in wars since 1945. Barbie himself has been offering this argument in his defense for years, ignoring the systematic method with which the Nazi state carried out a program of genocide against the Jews. "I don't recognize war crimes," Barbie said in 1972. "In war there is neither liberty nor humanity. Today, there would have to be thousands of trials, for the war in Korea, the war in Vietnam, in Algeria, and Truman would have been condemned for dropping the bomb on Hiroshima."

Ω

Barbie's defense promises to concentrate on the extremely sensitive point of French collaboration—that in his acts of violence the Gestapo chief was greatly aided in Lyon by many Frenchmen. It is a factor that disturbs even those in the Resistance whom Barbie arrested during the war. "He's going to tar everyone," says Dr. Frédéric Dugoujon, the physician in whose home Jean Moulin was captured, and who was taken and tortured by Barbie. "It smells already. It's going to be intolerable, giving a man like that the right to arbitrate our old quarrels—it would have been better if they had let the Germans take him."

But unless the judges of the Cour d'Assizes can tightly circumscribe the evidence and restrict testimony to that which bears directly upon the charges in the bill, Vergès is determined to make French collaboration with Barbie the centerpiece of his defense. "If the trial takes place," says Vergès, "Barbie will talk of the treason of French officials. In the end the accused will not be Barbie. He is not the traitor." Vergès has publicly stated that he fears Barbie will be murdered in prison to prevent his ever taking the witness stand. If Barbie's trial is televised, as some in France have suggested, this will place enormous power in his hands should he accuse prominent Frenchmen, living and dead, of being collaborators with the Gestapo.

Many in France are concerned about Barbie's testimony, but Resistance leader Raymond Aubrac does not believe this tactic will be effective. "I don't think so," he says. "I think that the problem of the collaborators was taken care of for the most part after the war." He adds, "It's not a question of judging the French. It is a question of judging a brutal, sadistic Gestapo chief."

Whether Barbie can name the collaborators and make his counter charges stick is debatable; no Frenchman is required to accept his accusations as truthful. For one thing, many of the postwar interviews he has given to the press have been transparently self-serving, laced with obvious distortions. In addition, forty years have passed since Barbie was a young Gestapo officer in Lyon. In his own defense he has already claimed lapses of memory in preliminary interviews with Judge Riss. The effect of age could similarly obscure much of what he might have known in 1944 about French collaboration.

In a 1972 interview with a Brazilian journalist Barbie was even unable to recall the name of his closest collaborator, Francis André, although he described him in considerable detail. "The leader of the French group of my commando was a man of great prestige, a celebrated rugby player... [who] had a large scar on his mouth due to an accident," Barbie said. "He was a very brave man. After the German defeat he surrendered himself to the authorities and was executed by the French. Unfortunately, I cannot remember his name today."

The issue of collaboration is very much alive in France today, despite the *épuration*, or purge, that engulfed the country after the Liberation. Some 4,500 people were summarily executed by the Resistance at the war's end and many of Barbie's French aides were among the 767 officially executed following the 125,000 collaboration trials held in the immediate postwar period. Some 38,000 collaborators received prison sentences, but a leading historian has noted that "the postwar trials and purges did not visit all sectors of the Vichy leadership with the same severity... Experts, businessmen and bureaucrats survived almost intact."

Even as Barbie awaits his trial, a number of cases of alleged prominent French collaborators are in preparation. One is against Jean Leguay, the former delegate of Vichy's secretary general for the national police to the Occupied Zone. Leguay, now 74, stands accused of playing a leading role in the deportation of thousands of Jews during the war.

He will be tried in 1984 by a Paris court for crimes against humanity, charges that arose from a complaint filed by Serge Klarsfeld in the name of six Jews whose relations were arrested in the Paris round-up of some 13,000 Jews in July 1942, a raid conducted with the help of French police. Leguay is accused of having played a major role in that action.

In a similar case, Maurice Papon, 72, formerly a minister in the government of President Valery Giscard d'Estaing, was indicted in January 1983, on the same charge of crimes against humanity. Secretary general of the prefecture of the Gironde region during the war, Papon allegedly signed documents requesting the local *gendarmerie* to provide the manpower necessary to send two convoys of Jewish prisoners to the Merignac detention camp near Bordeaux, a way station on the voyage first to Drancy, then to the Nazi death camps in the East.

A case more directly connected with Barbie involves Paul Touvier, a leader of the Lyon Milice during the war. Touvier, who disappeared after the war and has never been personally tried, was the beneficiary of a controversial pardon declared in 1971 by then-President Georges Pompidou. In any case, his crimes could not be prosecuted because of the statute of limitations, but the Pompidou action lifted sanctions which prevented Touvier from returning to Lyon and recovering properties seized after the war.

Numerous friends of Touvier interceded in his behalf, including Lyon Monsignor Duquaire, then secretary to Cardinal Gerlier, who began collecting attestations in Touvier's favor in 1962. One of those who provided a letter of recommendation was the noted philosopher Gabriel Marcel, who later expressed regret for having done so. Condemned to death *in absentia* in 1946 and 1947, Touvier is once again a hunted man. Civil parties filed suit against him in 1973 and obtained an indictment for crimes against humanity. In the Touvier case, as in that of Leguay, France's highest court found that passed in 1964, which legislation provided for prosecution of crimes against humanity could be applied retroactively to cover offenses dating from the war years. Touvier is believed to be hiding in a Catholic monastery in northern Italy or in the Savoie region of France.

Ω

The French will not be the only ones touched by the Barbie trial. The case has already refocused international attention on Nazi war crimes; and Barbie's trial will place additional pressure on West Germany to step up the prosecution of former Nazi officers and officials.

Nineteen eighty-three marked the fiftieth anniversary of Hitler's rise to power, a date observed more in press analyses of the political phenomenon than in soul-searching about the crimes of the Third Reich. The Germans displayed much the same attitude toward Nazism of fascination and repulsion to which Vergès referred. But the trial of one prominent Gestapo officer could be the catalyst that reactivates the guilt of those Germans who would prefer to leave the excesses of the Third Reich far behind.

Barbie's is not the only forthcoming trial of Nazi war criminals. Four other SS officers involved in the deportation of French Jews were scheduled to be tried in the autumn of 1983 in Bonn. Walter Naehrich, 74, Count Modest Korff, 74, Richard Freise, 74 and Rolf Bilharz, 73, are accused of having deported 1,700 Jews from France to the Auschwitz and Sobibor death camps in Poland. Serge Klarsfeld will be filing accompanying charges in those cases as well.

As of January 1983, nearly 1,671 cases involving war crimes were in progress in German courts or prosecuting offices. By February of that year there were eight jury hearings taking place in German cities, most concerning concentration camp offenses. In the 1980-81 period, West German prosecutors were pursuing 1,367 Nazi war crimes cases, and 17 jury trials resulted in 22 guilty verdicts among a total of 33 accused. Ten were acquitted and one case was dismissed.

The record of prosecution of Nazi war crimes indicates a less-than-obsessive desire to see justice done. Although these figures indicate that the question of Nazi war crimes is still open, most of those accused since World War II have never been convicted. Of nearly 88,000 war crimes cases opened by West German authorities between May 1945 and January 1983, only 6,456 persons received non-appealable sentences. Of these thousands, a mere 12 were sentenced to death and 158 were given life prison terms. Acquittals were obtained by 79,638—or over 90 percent—of the accused, for reasons ranging from the death of the person concerned to the fact that the person had already been judged in postwar Allied tribunals, or had escaped, or was found unfit for trial due to illness or old age. In many cases insufficient evidence forced acquittal.

The International Military Tribunal at Nuremberg began with some 5,000 war crimes cases but eventually tried only 210, including the 22 Nazi leaders whose cases were handled in the opening trial. Ten were executed and three were acquitted. Only one remains incarcerated; the aged Rudolph Hess is still being held in the Spandau Prison in Berlin.

American Military Tribunals handled another 184 cases; 12 death sentences were carried out, 20 persons were sentenced to life imprisonment and 98 received lesser terms. Other Allied tribunals led to 462 death sentences. However, by 1958 all prisoners convicted by these military courts had been released and were back in German society.

Ω

Where does Barbie fit into this often chaotic pattern of prosecution and leniency? That depends on the context in which one chooses to place his case. Even in France, a country traumatized by the Nazis, the handling of war crimes has relaxed with time. Although some German officers were executed in the immediate postwar period for their offenses, many served relatively short sentences and went home to Germany to resume normal lives.

A classic instance involves Carl Oberg and Helmut Knochen, the top SS officials in France during the occupation. They were condemned to death on October 9, 1954, after a trial that took ten years to prepare and served to outline the overall brutality of the Gestapo in France. They headed an organization that carried out 80,000 deportations, thousands of executions, and innumerable tortures and other criminal acts. But despite their record their death sentences were commuted in 1958 by French President René Coty, and they were freed in 1962 as part of an attempt to restore normal relations between France and West Germany. Knochen still lives in

Offenbach, West Germany, where he is a retired insurance salesman.

Other top SS officials who had escaped punishment were
brought to trial in Cologne in 1980, mainly through the efforts of
Serge Klarsfeld. Kurt Lischka, Herbert Hagen and Ernst Heinrichsohn received sentences ranging from six to 12 years for their
activities in France during the occupation. They were prosecuted
under the terms of a French-German treaty ratified in 1975 by the
West German parliament.

What is unique about the Barbie case is that it is the first trial
on French soil in decades involving a former SS officer. Moreover,
it is the trial of a major war criminal who has been sentenced to
death on two occasions but who has skillfully evaded justice for
nearly forty years.

Klaus Barbie cannot escape becoming a chapter in German,
French and American history. And as both his defenders and
accusers understand, he has become a symbol evoking the anguish
of French wartime experience. If France's honor and dignity are
besmirched during the trial, it will be incidental. Barbie's presence
in the dock will reaffirm the courage of the French Resistance,
acknowledge the suffering of his Jewish victims, and evoke the
memory of Germany's collective guilt. But in the end, it will be the
trial of one man, an individually responsible Nazi who by making
himself useful to various masters and by recruiting witting and
unwitting accomplices in his callous designs, demonstrated the
potency of evil in a frightened or complacent world. His prosecution will be a bitter victory, but a victory nonetheless.

Notes

CHAPTER I

Barbie in Cochabamba and La Paz: Interviews with Peter McFarren, other sources in La Paz and Cochabamba.
"*La guerra es la guerra.*": *Presencia*, March 13, 1983.
"What is there to regret?": Interview by Alfredo Serra, *Paris Match*, May 1973.
Barbie personal circumstances: Interviews with Peter McFarren, Merry Flores, other Bolivian sources.
Arrest of McFarren, Schumacher: Interview with Peter McFarren.
"It's a classic case...": Interview with Gustavo Sanchez.
"My great friend, Don Klaus.": Interview with La Paz journalist.
"He had direct control...": Interview with former Interior Ministry official in Hugo Banzer Suarez regime.
"Barbie always stayed in the shadows.": Interview with Gustavo Sanchez.
"Altmann Will Be the Next.": *Ultima Hora*, October 12, 1982.
Contraloria case: Interview with Bolivian Sub-contralor Jaime Urcullo.
Carrion advice to Barbie: *Figaro Magazine*, April 23, 1983.
Altmann-Flores relationship: Interview with Merry Flores.
Barbie expulsion and flight to France: Interview with Carlos Soria.

CHAPTER II

"It was startling...": Interview with Marcel Ruby.
Invasion of Lyon: Henri Amoretti, *Lyon Capitale* (Paris, Editions France-Empire, 1964), pp. 22-29.
Resistance attacks: Henri Amouroux, "La vie quotidienne a Lyon sous l'Occupation," *VSD*, February 10, 1983.
The Donar Mission: Marcel Ruby, *La Contre Resistance a Lyon 1940-1944* (Lyon, Editions L'Hermes, 1981), p. 19.
Arrest and torture of Mario Blardone: Interview with Mario Blardone.
Cries in the night: Interview with Dr. Sylvie Karlin.
Pineau Resistance activities: Interview with Christian Pineau.
"Do you know how the Nazi system of repression worked?": Interview with Raymond Aubrac.
Lyon SS hierarchy: Postwar depositions of Ernst Floreck and Francis Andre, Rhone dossier, Institut d'Histoire du Temps Present.
Knab accused of cowardice: SS file of Werner Knab, Berlin Document Center.
Paris SS structure: Marcel Hasquenoph, *La Gestapo En France* (Paris, Editions de Vecci, 1975), pp. 45-53.
"That big, somber city of conspiracy...": Albert Camus, *Resistance, Rebellion and Death* (New York, Vintage Books, 1974), p. 49.
Place Bellecour history: Bernard Hennequin, *A Lyon* (Paris, Hachette, 1982), p. 86.
Lyonnais traits: Bernard Aulas, *Vie et Mort des Lyonnais En Guerre* (Roanne, Editions Horvath, 1974), *passim*.
Development of French Resistance: Amoretti, *Lyon Capitale*, Chapter IV; Henri

Nogueres, *Histoire de la Resistance En France*, Volume I (New York, Laffont, 1967), *passim*; David Schoenbrun, *Soldiers of the Night* (New York, New American Library, 1980), Chapters 9 and 10; Henri Michel *Histoire de la Resistance En France* (Paris, Presses Universitaries de France, 1950), p. 23; Henri Frenay, *The Night Will End* (New York, McGraw-Hill, 1976); Marcel Ruby, *La Resistance a Lyon*, Volumes I and II (Lyon, Editions L'Hermes, 1979).

Lesevre Resistance activities: Interview with Lise Lesevre.

Aubrac on Resistance beginnings: Interview with Raymond Aubrac.

Petain at Montoire: Robert O. Paxton, *Vichy France, Old Guard and New Order 1940-1944* (New York, Columbia University Press, 1982), pp. 74-77.

Einsatzkommando operation: Interview with Barbie by Evaldo Dantas Ferreira, *O Estado de Sao Paulo*, May 1972.

Lesevre arrest, interrogation: Interview with Lise Lesevre.

"I spent my life in trains...": Interview with Anne Marie Bauer.

Support for Resistance: Interviews with Lise Lesevre, Raymond Aubrac.

History and description of Montluc Prison: Amoretti, *Lyon Capitale*, pp. 306-307; Interviews with Christian Pineau, Mario Blardone, Lise Lesevre, others.

"The vermin!": Ruby, *La Contre Resistance*, p. 139.

Jewish prisoners: Interview with Christian Pineau; Andre Frossard, *La Maison des Hotages* (Paris, Fayard, 1960).

Appelle sans baggages: Interviews with Mario Blardone, Zette Gomes.

CHAPTER III

Barbie as suborner: Interview with Lise Lesevre.

"Informers were to present themselves...": Floreck deposition.

"My office was just inside...": Gerard Chauvy, "Barbie, la Gestapo, les Autres," *Le Progres* supplement "Lyon, Les Annees Noires," February 1983.

Betrayal of Kaddouche family: Interview with Simone Lagrange.

Barbie offer to Blardone: Interview with Mario Blardone.

"Barbie was incredibly effective...": Hasquenoph, *La Gestapo*, p. 328.

"The main person responsible...": Raymond Aubrac.

Gestapo, French Gestapo, Milice: Hasquenoph, *La Gestapo*; Jacques Delarue, *Histoire de la Gestapo* (Paris, Fayard, 1962); Paxton, *Vichy*; Ruby, *La Contre Resistance*.

Vichy history: Paxton, *Vichy, passim*; Pascal Ory, *Les Collaborateurs* (Paris, Seuil, 1976), *passim*; Alfred Cobban, *A History of Modern France*, Volume 3 (Harmondsworth, Penguin, 1965), pp. 181-199.

"It is with honor...": Ory, *Les Collaborateurs*, p. 36.

"France needed someone...": Marcel Ruby, *La Resistance Chretienne a Lyon* (Lyon, CRDP, 1971), pp. 24-25.

Anti-Semitic legislation: Michael R. Marrus and Robert O. Paxton, *Vichy France and the Jews* (New York, Basic Books, 1981), p. 4.

"People continued to believe...": Interview with Raymond Aubrac.

"Public opinion was fooled by Vichy...": Interview with Anne Marie Bauer.

Development of Vichy paramilitary: Ruby, *La Contre Resistance*, pp. 53-89; Paxton, *Vichy*, pp. 228-298.

SOL and riot in Lyon: Francois Caviglioli, "Quand Barbie Etait le Maitre de Lyon," *Paris Match*, March 11, 1972.

"The Milice was raised...": Interview with Marcel Ruby.

Reynaudon letter to Darnand: Ruby, *La Contre Resistance*, p. 65-66.

Paul Touvier: Jacques Derogy, "*L'Express* a retrouve le bourreau de Lyon," *L'Express*, June 5, 1972; *Quotidien de Paris*, March 18, 1983; *Figaro*, March 13, 1974.

Parti Populaire Francais: Ruby, *La Contre Resistance*, pp. 67-77.

Francis Andre biography: Andre deposition.

Andre was "very brutal...": Floreck deposition.

"You ask the questions, I'll hit.": Interview with Lise Lesevre.
MNAT: Ruby, *La Contre Resistance*, pp. 73-75.

CHAPTER IV

Synagogue bombing: Interview with Jacob Kaplan; Pierre Pierrard, *Justice Pour la Foi Juive* (Paris, Le Centurion, 1977), pp. 78-80.
"There was a spiritual resistance...": Interview with Richard Wertenschlag.
Account of UGIF raid: Interview with Lea Rosen. (Real name withheld at her request.)
Weissman arrest, deportation: Interview with Dr. Sylvie Karlin.
Weissman correspondence: Courtesy Dr. Sylvie Karlin.
"Der Leiter des Einsatzkommandos...": Archives of the Centre de Documentation Juive Contemporaine, Paris, (XLVI-A).
Jewish community in Lyon: Interviews with Richard Wertenschlag, Robert Bloch, Rene Nodot.
Arrests of August, 1942: Amoretti, *Lyon Capitale*, pp. 150-151; Interview with Rene Nodot.
Cirange letter: CDJC Archives, (CCCLXXI-30).
Consistoire withdrew from Paris: Pierrard, *Justice*, p. 66.
"The Consistoire opened the doors...": Interview with Jacob Kaplan.
Kaplan and Gerlier: Ibid.
Gerlier pastoral letter: Amoretti, *Lyon Capitale*, p. 151.
Gerlier sheltered Grand Rabbi: Interview with Richard Wertenschlag.
Rescue of children: Interview with Jacob Kaplan; Pierrard, *Justice*, pp. 95-96.
Chambon-sur-Lignon: Marrus, *et al., Vichy and the Jews*, p. 207; interview with Rene Nodot.
Medal of the Just: *Le Progres*, October 8, 1974.
"No one recognizes more than I the evil the Jews have done to France...": Marrus et al., *Vichy and the Jews*, p.. 32.
Saliege statement: Ibid. pp.. 271-272.
Gerlier statement: Serge Klarsfeld, *Vichy-Auschwitz* (Paris, Fayard, 1983), p. 405.
"Gerlier reached all of France.": Interview with Rene Nodot.
Convoy stops in Lyon: Interview with Jacob Kaplan; Archives of CDJC (CCXIX-82).
Minkowsky family: Interview with Esther Majerowicz.
Halaunbrenner family: Interview with Itta and Alexander Halaunbrenner.
Vichy Jewish policy: Marrus et al., *Vichy and the Jews, passim*; Klarsfeld, *Vichy-Auschwitz, Passim*.
"Without any possible doubt...": Marrus et al., Vichy and the Jews, p. 7.
"It wasn't systematic...": Interview with Richard Wertenschlag.
"Every day there were arrests...": Interview with Jacob Kaplan.
Kaplan arrest: Interview with Jacob Kaplan.
Andre and PPF: Deposition by Francis Andre.
Arrest of Esther Minkowsky: Interview with Esther Majerowicz.
Arrest, interrogation of Simone Kaddouche: Interview with Simone Lagrange.
Arrest of Halaunbrenners: Interview with Itta and Alexander Halaunbrenner.
UGIF provided housing: ACDJC Archives (CCXIX-82)
200–400 francs a month: Statement by UGIF employee, *CDJC* Archives, (CCVIIIG-188)
"Pernicious work...": Zosa Szajkowski, "The UGIF organization in France during the Occupation," *Jewish Social Studies,* Vol. 9, No. 3. (Translation from French by author.)
"It's very difficult to sum up UGIF...": Interview with Serge Klarsfeld.
"Deported or shot...": Beate Klarsfeld, *Wherever They May Be* (New York, Vanguard, 1975), p. 241.

UFIG history: Szajkowski, *Jewish Social Studies*.
"A program of extermination...": Serge Klarsfeld, *Vichy-Auschwitz*, p. 360.
Jewish Resistance against UGIF: *CDJC Archives*, (CCXV-15).
Statement of UGIF employee: *CDJC Archives*, (CCVIIIG-188).
Tardy description of children: Interview with Gabrielle Tardy.
"I was walking back toward the village...": *Quotidien de Paris*, February 14, 1983.
Account of Izieu raid: *Humanite*, February 22, 1972; *Quotidien de Paris*, February 14, 1983; *Newsweek*, February 21, 1983; *France-Soir*, February 27, 1972.
"When I turned in the driveway...": *Humanite*, February 22, 1972.
"He even saved my life...": *Quotidien de Paris*, February 14, 1983.
"At the first turn...": *Humanite*, February 22, 1972.
"We had ended up by adopting those kids...": *Quotidien de Paris*, February 14, 1983.
Miron Zlatin executed: *France-Soir*, February 27, 1972.
Fate of Benguigi, Halaunbrenner children: Serge Klarsfeld *et al. Le memorial de la Deportation des Juifs de France* (Paris, Klarsfeld, 1978).
Gestapo telegram: CDJC Archives.

CHAPTER V

"The soul of the Gestapo...": Beate Klarsfeld, *Wherever*, p. 218.
Barbie early life, career in SS: Klaus Barbie SS file, Berlin Document Center.
"Modest gentility...": *Trierischer Volksfreund*, February 23, 1983.
Barbie student essay: Files of the Staatliches Friedrich Wilhelms-Gymnasium, Trier.
Background on Trier: Interview with Dr. Reinar Nolden, director of the Trier municipal archives.
"A very good comrade...": Interview with Konrad Jacobs.
History of Trier Nazis: Interview with Dr. Reinar Nolden, researcher Otmar Weiler.
Association with Karl Hormann: Alan A. Ryan, Jr., "Klaus Barbie and the U.S. Government; Exhibits to the Report to the Attorney General of the United States," August 1983, Tab 29.
History of SS: Heinz Hohne, *The Order of the Death's Head* (London, Pan Books, 1972), *passim*; Lucy Davidowicz, *The War Against the Jews 1933-45*. (Harmondsworth, Penguin Books, 1977), Chapter 4.
"I am a member of the SS...": Interview by Alfredo Serra, 1973.
Regina Willms: Barbie SS file.
Campaign against Dutch Jewry: Davidowicz, *The War*, pp. 437-440.
Barbie and Wieringermeer Jews: Interview with Dr. David Barnouw.
Barbie counterintelligence assignment: Interview by Dantas Ferreira, 1972.

CHAPTER VI

Except where otherwise indicated, material on Jean Moulin's life and Resistance activities has been drawn from personal interviews and from the following sources: Henri Calef, *Jean Moulin, Une Vie* (Paris, Plon, 1980); Laure Moulin, *Jean Moulin* (Paris, Presses de la Cite, 1982); Henri Michel, *Jean Moulin, l'Unificateur* (Paris, Hachette, 1971); Jean Moulin, *Premier Combat* (Paris, Editions de Minuit, 1947); Henri Frenay, *L'Enigme Jean Moulin* (Paris, Laffont, 1977); Charles de Gaulle, *The Call to Honour* (New York, Viking, 1955); Charles de Gaulle, *Unity* (New York, Simon and Schuster, 1959); Henri Nogueres, *Histoire de la Resistance en France*, Volume 3 (Paris, Laffont, 1972); David Schoenbrun, *Soldiers of the Night* (New York, New American Library, 1981); Henri Amoretti, *Lyon Capitale* (Paris, Editions France-Empire, 1964); Christian Pineau, *La Simple Verite* (Paris, Editions Phalanx, 1983); Henri Frenay, *The Night Will End* (New York, McGraw Hill, 1976).

Decoration of Moulin: Michel, p. 163-164.

Comments by de Gaulle: de Gaulle, *The Call*, pp. 269-273.

Moulin in Chartres: Jean Moulin, *Premier Combat, passim.*

"He was exactly what de Gaulle was looking for...": Interview with Christian Pineau.

"My first rendezvous with Moulin...": Interview with Raymond Aubrac.

"It was purely political...": Interview with Christian Pineau.

"I try to play their game...": Cited by prosecution in opening statement, April 1950 trial; quoted in Maurice Garcon's Plaidoyer pour Rene Hardy (Paris, Fayard), pp. 71, 78.

"I wanted to make my own investigation...": Rene Hardy, article in *France-Soir*, June 3, 1972.

"Contrary to the claims of Barbie...": Ibid., June 2.

"He asked me to take responsibility...": Interview with Raymond Aubrac.

"I had a long conversation with Jean Moulin...": *Le Matin*, February 3, 1983.

"Lassagne came over to my house...": Interview with Dr. Frederic Dugoujon.

"We all had the same reaction...": Noqueres, *History*, vol. III, p. 455.

"I was convinced as soon as we were arrested...": Interview with Raymond Aubrac.

"A note of apparent sincerity...": Andre Fontaine, *Le Monde*, April 27, 1950.

"If there remains the thousandth part of doubt...": Ibid., May 10, 1950.

"I have proven in two trials...": Reported in *Le Monde*, May 30, 1972.

"Barbie's return?": *Liberation*, February 8, 1983.

"In our conversations...": Interview with Dantas Ferreira, 1972.

"I heard a stamping noise upstairs...": Gottlieb Fuchs, *Renard*, pp. 148-154.

"On Wednesday they knew that Max...": Interview with Dr. Frederic Dugoujon.

"He was in very bad shape...": Interview with Raymond Aubrac.

Pineau shaving incident: Pineau, *La Simple Verite.*

Meiners testimony: *Le Monde*, February 13, 1983.

CHAPTER VII

Place Bellecour massacre: Amoretti, *Lyon Capitale*, pp. 310-311; Ruby, *La Contre Resistance*, pp. 195-198; Interview with Doninique D'Ermo.

Vercors attack: Schoenbron, *Soldiers*, pp. 383-388; Amoretti, *Lyon Capitale*, pp. 238-254; Interview with Dominique D'Ermo.

Maquis history: Nogueres, *History, passim*; Amoretti, *Lyon Capitale*, pp. 186-197; Schoenbrun, *Soldiers, passim.*

St. Claude: Interview with Maurice Emain.

German operation: Interview with Maurice Emain; *Le Courier de St. Claude,* April, 1945; Documentation of Association Nationale des Anciens Combattants de la Resistance du Jura.

Barbie presence, orders: Documents obtained by Beate Klarsfeld during 1971-2 investigation of Barbie case.

Chorier story: Interview with Rene Aime Chorier.

Kemmler interrogation: *Journal du Dimanche*, January 30, 1983.

German executions: Ruby, La Contre Resistance, pp. 179-189; Amoretti, *Lyon Capitale*, pp. 305-306.

Death of Leynaud: Camus, *Resistance*, pp. 46-47.

Gerlier protest: Amoretti, Lyon Capitale, p. 311

Huber massacre account: Ruby, La Contre Resistance, appendix, pp. 203-215

Saint-Genis-Laval massacre: Ibid., pp. 187-189.

Seta on Barbie role: Beate Klarsfeld documentation.

Andre testimony: Ibid.

Gerlier protest: Ruby, *La Resistance Chretienne*; Amoretti, *Lyon Capitale,* p. 312.

Montluc liberation: Amoretti, *Lyon Capitale*, pp. 311-316.

Retreat: Deposition of Francis Andre.
Barbie final combat: Interview by Dantas Ferreira, 1972.

CHAPTER VIII

Barbie in 239th place: Interview with Serge Klarsfeld.
"I took refuge...": Interview with Alfredo Serra, 1973.
The description of Barbie's activities in the SS underground of occupied Germany
    is based on information in the supporting documentation to the 1983
    Justice Department report by Allan A. Ryan, Jr., "Klaus Barbie and the U.S.
    Government." The main source of information is a series of reports on
    interrogations of Barbie conducted between December 1947 and May 1948
    in the European Command Intelligence Center, in Oberursel, West Ger-
    many. These comprise Tabs 22-29 of the "Exhibits to the Report to the
    Attorney General of the United States."
Kassel jewel theft: Ryan, "Exhibits," Tab 90.
Nazi underground movement: Ibid., Tab 1.
"Sinister figure...": Ibid., Tab 2.
Barbie escapes arrest: Ibid., Tabs 9, 29.
"Not unwilling to collaborate...": Ibid., Tab 9.
Merk connection: Ibid., Tab 29.
CIC background: Ryan, "Klaus Barbie," pp. 23-27.
"Prevent the reorganization...": Annual Narrative Report, 66th Counter
    Intelligence Corps Detachment, December 31, 1949.
"It would have been impossible...": Interview with Gene Bramel.
Buro Peterson: Ryan, "Exhibits," Tabs 24, 17.
Hajdu assessment: Ibid., Tabs 24, 17.
Arrest order: Ibid., Tab 15.
Browning background: Interview with Earl Browning.
"Our chief dislike...": Interview with James Ratliffe.
"There was no evident concern...": Ryan, "Exhibits," Tab 17.
"Preferential treatment...": Ibid. Browning order: Ibid.
Browning and communists: Interview with Earl Browning.
"A good doodly-damn...": Interview with Gene Bramel.
Troop survey: Interview with Earl Browning.
"Barbie was super-correct...": Interview with Gene Bramel.
Barbie glosses over war record: Ryan, "Exhibits," Tab 29.
CROWCASS: Ibid., Tab 19.
"Not advisable to intern him...": Ibid., Tab 29.
Merk wanted by French: Ibid., Tab 23.
"I remember this one outstandingly...": Interview with Erhard Dabringhaus.
Payment in commodities: Interview with Earl Browning.
"One of the most fruitful sources...": Ryan, "Exhibits," Tab 32.
"Ridiculous goddamn thing...": Interview with Earl Browning.
"They were incompetent...": Interview with James Ratliffe.
"Not very good military occupiers...": Interview with William Larned.
Lie detector problems: Annual Narrative Report, 66th Counter Intelligence Corps
    Detachment, December 31, 1949, p. 31.
"You tend to bend the rules.": Interview with William Larned.

CHAPTER IX

"Merk told me...": Interview with Erhard Dabringhaus.
French warrants: Serge Klarsfeld, "Quand les Etats-Unis refusaient de livrer leur
    'agent,' " *Le Monde*, February 16, 1983.
French interrogators: DST reports made public by Serge Klarsfeld, 1983.

"I got a call to pick him up...": Interview with John Willms.
"He taunted them...": Interview with John Willms.
Dabringhaus protects Barbie: Patrick E. Tyler, "U.S. Protected Nazi Hunted by the French," *Washington Post*, February 12, 1983.
War crimes not raised: Ryan, "Klaus Barbie,": pp. 67-68.
Whiteway overture: Ryan, "Exhibits," Tabs 57, 34.
"Barbie might be a war criminal...": Ibid., Tab 38.
"He's too skillful for that...": Interview with Eugene Kolb.
"I never knew the specifics...": Interview with Gene Bramel.
"His value was primarily against the left...": Interview with Eugene Kolb.
"Even the French authorities...": Ryan, "Klaus Barbie," p. 81.
Barbie dropped administratively: Ryan, "Exhibits," Tab 38.
CIC backs off: Ibid., Tab 39.
"What CIC headquarters is saying...": Ryan, "Klaus Barbie," p. 78.
"No one in OMGUS knew...": Ryan, "Klaus Barbie," p. 84-85.
Public Safety Branch queries: Ryan, "Exhibits," Tabs 42-44.
"Tell him how anxious the French government is...": Documentation provided by Serge Klarsfeld.
July 1947 Clay announcement: Ryan, "Exhibits," Tab 45.
"Our lists...increase every day...": Klarsfeld documentation.
"Bad faith...": Information brief, OMGUS, Legal Division, April 9, 1947.
State Department-OMGUS: Ryan, "Exhibits," Tab 47.
Poignet extradition request: Klarsfeld documentation.
Lebegue response: Ryan, "Exhibits," Tab 49.
Hardy trial: Ryan, "Exhibits," Tab 54.
EUCOM response: Ibid., Tab 55.
Vidal memos: Ibid., Tabs 56-57.
CIC resolves to protect Barbie: Ibid., Tab 57.
HICOG reactions: Ibid., Tabs 59-61.
McGraw reversal: Ibid., Tab 62.
HICOG-Paris Embassy: Ryan, "Exhibits," Tabs 65-66.
French outcry: Ibid., Tab 68.
"Something very embarrassing for us...": Ibid., Tab 72.
HICOG-CIC inaction: Ryan, "Klaus Barbie," pp. 115-116.
French reluctance: Ryan, "Exhibits," Tab 82.
HICOG-EUGOG meeting: Ibid., Tab 81.
"These representations...were false.": Ryan, p. 120.
Extradition proceedings: Ryan, "Exhibits," Tabs 86-87.
"Lying.": Ryan, "Klaus Barbie," p. 130.
"If worse came to worse...": *International Herald Tribune*, March 29, 1983.
"We didn't want to...": Interview with Gene Bramel.
Ratline background: Ryan, "Exhibits," Tabs 94-96.
Croatians: Ryan, "Klaus Barbie," pp. 136-137.
"Lt. John Hobbins...traveled...": Ryan, "Exhibits," Tab 96.
Travel documents: Ryan, "Klaus Barbie," pp. 150-156.
"This case is considered closed.": Ryan, "Exhibits," Tab 105.
"Justice delayed is justice denied.": Allan A Ryan, Jr., press conference, August 16, 1983.
"A grave misjudgement...": Ryan, "Klaus Barbie," p. 193.
"Responsible officials...interfered...": Ryan, "Klaus Barbie," p. 208.

CHAPTER X

Bolivian history: Drawn from numerous interviews and conversations with Bolivian journalists, politicians and historians, as well as the following sources: James Dunkerly, *Bolivia Coup d'Etat* (London, Latin American Bureau, 1980);

Herbert S. Klein, *Parties and Political Change in Bolivia 1880-1952* (Cambridge, Cambridge University Press, 1969); Mariano Baptista Gumucio, *Historia Contemporania de Bolivia* 1930-1976 (La Paz, Amigos del Libro, 1977); *Otra Historia de Bolivia* (La Paz, Amigos del Libro, 1982); Gregorio Selser, *Bolivia: El Cuartelazo de los Cocadolares* (Coyoacan, Mexico, Mex-Sur Editorial, 1982).

"He made friends with Kappauner...": German source in La Paz, name withheld by request.

Barbie and Rudel: Sources in La Paz, Cochabamba; Interview with Simon Wiesenthal.

Rudel and Kameradenwerk: Ladislas Farago, *Aftermath, Martin Bormann and the Third Reich* (New York, Simon and Schuster, 1974), p. 169; Interview with Simon Wiesenthal.

Transmaritima inauguration: Interview with Gaston Velasco.

Estenssoro-Ibanez: Selser, *El Cuartelazo*, p. 183.

Accion Maritima: Interview with Gaston Velasco.

"Barbie participated in various arms transactions...": Interview with Gustavo Sanchez.

Alexander bombing: E. T. Gil de Muro, *Alfredo Alexander Jordan, Biografia heroica de un periodista boliviano* (Madrid, 1977), pp. 213-214.

Heber deposition: Alexander family source.

Israeli arms deal: Heber deposition.

"He humiliated us...": Interview with Gaston Velasco.

Transmaritima collapse: Agence France Presse/UPI report in *Cronica* (Lima), January, 1972.

Transmaritima records in archives: La Paz government source.

Altmann-Schwend: Farago, *Aftermath*, p. 408; numerous Peruvian press accounts; Beate Klarsfeld, *Wherever*, p. 247.

"The new government is anti-communist...": Nicole Bonnet, *Le Figaro*, November 12, 1972.

Altmann-Schwend arms, intelligence schemes: *Le Figaro*. November 12, 1972; *La Republica* (Lima), October 24, 1982.

Schneider-Merk currency deal: *Le Figaro*, November 12, 1972.

L'Aurore story: Beate Klarsfeld, *Wherever*, p. 248.

"We were prisoners of war together...": *Ojo* (Lima), January 21, 1972.

"My legitimate name is Klaus Altmann Hansen...": Agence France Presse, January 21, 1972.

"If he is not Barbie, he is his brother.": Agence France Presse, January 22, 1972.

Klarsfelds' history: Charles Greenfield, "The Klarsfeld Saga," *International Herald Tribune*, March 5-6, 1983.

Barbie case: Interview with Beate Klarsfeld; Klarsfeld, *Wherever*, passim.

"We were afraid at the time...": Interview with Beate Klarsfeld.

"I arrived there all alone...": Interview with Beate Klarsfeld.

Official resistance: Ibid.

Debt charge: Interview with Jaime Urcullo.

Klarsfeld and Halaunbrenner: Klarsfeld, *Wherever*, pp. 264-272.

"I did it because it had to be done.": Interview with Beate Klarsfeld.

Diplomatic exchanges: *Le Monde*, March 6, 1972.

Hardy-Barbie encounter: *Le Progres* (Lyon), July 20, 1972.

Superior Court hearing: Court transcript, La Fiscalia Del Distrito En Lo Penal.

CHAPTER XI

Encounter in Cochabamba garage: Interview with Freddy Espinoza Teran.

Goldberg assassination plan: Interview with Michel Goldberg.

"That wasn't me...": Michel Goldberg, *Namesake* (New Haven, Yale University Press, 1982), p. 77.

"It appeared that Barbie was walking alone...": Interview with Gaston Velasco.
Barbie in Cochabamba: Sources in Cochabamba and La Paz.
"His role at that point...": Former official in regime of President Hugo Banzer Suarez.
Barbie and CIA: Interview with Peter McFarren.
Klarsfeld CIA allegations: Document from Direction de la Securite Militaire, French Ministry of Defense.
Ryan rebuts CIA claims: Ryan, "Klaus Barbie," pp. 165-168.
U.S. Army proposed "reactivation": Ibid., pp. 168-179.
"Urban guerrillas were still raging...": Interview with Eudoro Galindo.
"He was supposed to be a counselor...": Interview with La Paz source.
Sanchez on torture allegations: Interview with Gustavo Sanchez.
Austrian tanks: Interview with Simon Wiesenthal.
Altmann business interests: Interview with Peter McFarren, other La Paz and Cochabamba sources.
Stier confrontation: Interview with Gustavo Stier.
Post-Banzer and coup history: Dunkerly, *Bolivia Coup d'Etat*, pp. 51-83.
"We took the picture just as a joke.": Interview with Jacques Leclerc.
Novios: Interview with Peter McFarren; Carlo Rosella, "Un uomo in vendita," *Panorama* (Rome), September 27, 1982.
"Barbie was a friend of Arce Gomez...": Interview with Gustavo Sanchez.
Barbie movement: Interview with former official of Garcia Meza regime.
"People in the east had the problem...": La Paz diplomatic source.
"One day we were visited by Klaus Altmann...": Rosella, *Panorama*.

CHAPTER XII

Barbie in Saint-Joseph: Associated Press, June 1, 1983.
Bill of particulars: *Le Monde*, February 25, 1983.
Statute of limitations: Interview with Judge Christian Riss.
Jury: Interview with Jacques Verges.
"Klaus Barbie Will Be Judged at Lyon for Memory": *Liberation*, February 7, 1983.
Mauroy, Defferre comments: Ibid.
"Barbie: The Demons Exhumed": *Le Figaro*, February 8, 1983.
"Behind Barbie...": *Liberation*, February 8, 1983.
"At heart...": Interview with Philippe Viannay.
"What I hope is...": *Le Nouvel Observateur*, February, 1983.
"A mirror that I will hold up...": Interview with Jacques Verges.
Verges defense: Ibid.
"He is a prototype of the Gestapo agent...": Interview with Serge Klarsfeld.
"I don't recognize war crimes...": Interview by Dantas Ferreira.
"He's going to tar everyone...": Interview with Dr. Frederic Dugoujon.
"I don't think so...": Interview with Raymond Aubrac.
"The leader of the French group of my commando...": Interview by Dantas Ferreira.
Figures on postwar purge: Paxton, *Vichy*, p. 329.
"Bureaucrats survived almost intact...": p. 333.
Leguay case: *Le Matin*, March 12, 1979.
Papon case: *Le Monde*, January 19, 1983.
Touvier case: *L'Express*, June 5, 1972; *Le Progres*, February 1983; *Quotidien de Paris*, March 18, 1983.
Cologne Nazi trial: Reuters, *International Herald Tribune*, March 29, 1983.
Figures on war-crimes prosecutions: Michael May, "Nazi War Criminals: the Search and the Legal Process Continue," Research Report of the Institute of Jewish Affairs, in association with the World Jewish Congress; May, "Trials of Nazi War Criminals: Has Justice Been Done?" August 1981.

Oberg and Knochen: *Le Monde*, February 20-21, 1983.
Lischka, Hagen, Heinrichsohn: Ibid.; Interview with Serge Klarsfeld.

PHOTO CREDITS

Klaus Barbie in uniform: Courtesy of Beate and Serge Klarsfeld
Fort Montluc, Lyon: Keystone Press Agency
Jean Moulin: Keystone Press Agency
Rene Hardy: Keystone Press Agency
Charles de Gaulle on radio: Keystone Press Agency
Heinz Hollert: Berlin Document Center
Erich Bartlemus: Berlin Document Center
Barbie in civilian clothes: Berlin Document Center
Place Bellecour, Lyon: Photo Boyer, Collection Andre Gamet
Pierre Laval: Wide World Photos
Pierre Cardinal Gerlier: Wide World Photos
Rabbi Jacob Kaplan: Wide World Photos
Great Synagogue of Lyon: Courtesy of Rabbi Jacob Kaplan
Jewish childern: Courtesy of Beate and Serge Klarsfeld
Halaunbrenner family: Courtesy of Beate and Serge Klarsfeld
Barbie's telegram: Archive du Centre de Documentation Juive Contemporaine
De Gaulle and General Giraud: Wide World Photos
Massacre victims: Photo A. Klavel/Collection Andre Gamet
Carl Albrecht Oberg: Wide World Photos
Josef Merk: Courtesy of Beate and Serge Klarsfeld
Erhard Drabinghaus: Goldberg/Sygma
Barbie's passport: Courtesy of Beate and Serge Klarsfeld
Barbie and bodyguard: Wide World Photos
Hans Ulrich Rudel: Wide World Photos
Beate and Serge Klarsfeld: Pavlovsky/Sygma
Anthropometric diagram: Keystone Press Agency
Barbie in jail: Wide World Photos
Barbie taken out of Bolivia: Wide World Photos
Barbie arrives at Fort Montluc: Wide World Photos
Back cover photo: Courtesy of Beate and Serge Klarsfeld

Index